MR. MIYAGI AND ME

James H. Lilley

First Printing

Cover design by Lien Duong

Dedication

To Mr. Takeshi Miyagi, my teacher, friend, and a man who exemplifies the very essence of humility, honesty and integrity. He is a great role model who taught me so much more than the art of karate.

To Len Neidert, brother Marine and true friend, who shared the lumps, bumps and bruises as we dared to take the road no other American before us had the courage to travel.

Jim Lilley, Takeshi Miyagi and Len Neidert (left to right) July 1964.

Acknowledgements

I want to thank everyone who contributed to the writing of this book: Mr. Takeshi Miyagi for the time he gave to provide information relevant to he and his family. Doctors Benjamin S. Carson and Moody D. Wharam of the Johns Hopkins Hospital for their input regarding Andrew Miecznikoski, and Nancy Trimble-Oliver, mother of Andrew and Michael Miecznikoski, for her contributions relating to her sons. To Dan Simons, Bruce Charity, Will Adams, Richard Kelley, Lee Cunningham and Bob Lucido, long time friends and fellow martial artists for taking time to offer their thoughts for this work.

A special note of thanks goes to my computer wizards, Lien Duong and Dean Clark, for the help they provided along the way, and a thank you to Al Hafner for his assistance with photo work.

As always, to my lovely wife, Jody, I don't believe I can ever find the words to thank you enough for your love and support along the way. Not only were you there for me while I was writing this book, but also standing beside me every step of the way in my battle with cancer.

Introduction

It is important for everyone reading this book to keep in mind that what is written here pertains to Miyagi Sensei's Dojo, and what he passed on to his students. Some of the katas taught in his dojo are not the same katas taught in other Shorin Ryu Dojos and that applies to katas with as well as without weapons. In fact, there are katas, which are taught exclusively in his dojo because they are his katas. Again, that holds true for katas with and without weapons. Miyagi Sensei chose for his dojo what best suited his character and what he believed best to represent the art of karate.

Names of Martial Arts Masters, included in the lineage chart given to me by Mr. Miyagi, will be found in not only the Shorin Ryu System, but also other systems. The teachings of the great masters impacted more than one style, and certainly more than a handful of future masters. Many of those who would pass on their Martial Arts knowledge to future generations sought out more than one teacher to advance their skills. Thus, the reason for certain of the great masters to have connections to more than a single system.

Miyagi Sensei also adhered to a particularly strict code of ethics. There was no free ride in his dojo and, I can assure you, there was no contract guaranteeing anyone a black belt. There was only one promise he ever made to me. "If you want to learn, and learn the right way, come back and I will teach you." Although he did guarantee me the night we met that I would never be anything but a white belt, because Americans found him too strict and quit after only a few classes. I returned the following night and began a journey that has continued for over 50 years.

Make no mistake, the rules I came to know were indeed very rigid, but I learned they were also stern for a reason. Miyagi Sensei told me time and again, "It takes a humble man to be a black belt," and he had so many subtle ways of making a man feel humble. He said attaining the rank of First Degree Black Belt is not the ultimate pinnacle of learning karate, or any martial art. It is merely the very beginning of a man's journey on the road to greater knowledge.

Okinawa

My initial interest in the martial arts was just a momentary thought as a teen in high school. The idea was gone almost as fast as it materialized. Then, not long after high school, I enlisted in the Marine Corps and, after recruit training at Parris Island, my interest returned. My first duty station, after boot camp, was Camp Lejune, and there I met a few other Marines who practiced various forms of martial arts from judo to karate. As my curiosity began to grow, I considered asking for an assignment to some of the duty stations in the Far East. I was thinking about an opening that was available in the Philippines, but I was about to go home on a ten-day leave. So, the idea of the transfer to the sunny Philippines would have to wait until I returned from home.

When my leave ended, I walked back into my barrack at 1st Battalion, 8th Marines, to a chorus of laughter and shouts. "Hey, man, you've been transferred to the Rock." I knew immediately that I'd been reassigned to Okinawa, which was "lovingly" called the Rock by most Marines who'd been stationed there. But, unlike so many that had gone before me, I wasn't upset by the thought of going to Okinawa—not in the least. I'd heard from dozens of other

Marines that Okinawa was the best place in the world for martial arts training, especially karate. So, my dream of learning karate could now come true and in a land rumored to have the world's greatest masters.

I learned that a few of my friends from 1-8 were also being sent to the Far East. In a matter of weeks, Lou Caruso, Armand Sargen, newfound friend Conrad Giacalone and I were aboard a ship crossing the vast expanse of the Pacific Ocean. But, Lou wouldn't be going to Okinawa. He had been reassigned to a post in Japan. We made a stop in Hawaii and then headed to Japan to off-load a number of Marines and enjoy a day of liberty.

We docked in Yokohama on November 22, 1963 and soon proceeded to take in the sights, sounds and tastes of the Far East. Not one of us walking the streets of Japan, laughing, sampling our first Sake and foods of the Orient expected that we'd soon hear news of an unthinkable and positively unimaginable tragedy. Yet, when we awoke on the morning of November 23rd word was spreading through our ranks, and around the ship, like wildfire, that President John F. Kennedy had been assassinated. At first, I don't think any of us believed that President Kennedy had been killed by an assassin's bullet. Most of us were certain that the news was wrong. Somebody in the media was making up a story—a story that would far surpass the shock of Japan's attack on Pearl Harbor. Surely nobody would kill President Kennedy. He was respected—loved by everyone. Then as the morning wore on, and with ears glued to any available radio, we began to realize the sad truth. The President of the United States had been assassinated. Numbness turned to anger, and many Marines, then and there, wanted a war with anybody. Vengeance and spilling blood was the only topic for hours on end. Anger, and thoughts of revenge, at last gave way to a strange empty feeling, and I saw a lot of men with tears in their eyes. Now, as I think back to that day so many years ago, I wonder if the anger was because we were Marines and Sailors over 2,000 strong aboard a ship, and could do nothing about what had happened in Texas.

The trip from Japan to Okinawa seemed very long, and it was difficult to focus on one topic for any length of time. But, in due time we arrived, and life would somehow find a way to return to the day-to-day routines of the Marine Corps.

Within hours of my arrival I was settling in, and putting my uniforms away when I met Len Neidert. I still remember the big smile on his face as he extended his hand to me, and within a matter of minutes it seemed like we'd been best friends for years. To say Len was an outgoing personality would indeed be an understatement and, in fact, I think boisterous personality would be better. He could laugh at just about anything, and had a way of making his presence known. At a shade over six feet tall and knocking at the door of 220 pounds, it was as though his character fit his size.

Before the night was over we got around to the topic of martial arts. Len said he'd looked at a few nearby dojos, but hadn't been impressed. We agreed that we'd look together, and not give up until we found just the right school. Of course, we wondered how we'd find that just right school and I casually said, "Let's ask a cab driver." With that out of the way, we went to the Chesty Club for a beer, and talked about the murder of our President and our future.

A day or two later we were standing outside the gates of Camp Sukiran, in a pouring rain, waiting for a taxi. When one finally came along, we got in, and both of us said, "Take us to the best karate dojo you know of." A moment later we were headed in the direction of Naha, the capital city of Okinawa, with absolutely no idea of where we'd end up, or what we'd find. We drove for what seemed like an eternity before the driver made a left turn, and we were traveling down a dirt road. A few moments later he stopped the cab and pointed to his left. "Back there. That's the dojo you want."

We made our way along a narrow sidewalk, between two buildings, and found ourselves looking at what was obviously an outdoor training area. We knocked on the door we guessed was connected to the dojo, and suddenly found ourselves face to face with a stunningly beautiful woman. When we could finally speak, we asked to talk with the karate sensei. In an instant we discovered that this most beautiful woman couldn't speak a word of English, but we did manage to understand that the teacher wasn't home, and would return in about two hours.

Len and I figured we shouldn't waste time. So, we hailed another cab and took off for Naha to purchase a gi. We thought it was better to be prepared to start classes as soon as possible, and having a uniform was a step in the right direction. It wasn't long before we had a gi, and were on our way back to the village of Gusukuma.

When we knocked on the door our knock was answered by a man whose very appearance alone held our attention. He wasn't big by any means, standing at best 5' 6" in height and maybe tipping the scales at about 145 pounds. In spite of his stature, he looked strong with thick, muscular forearms and broad shoulders. A quick look into his eyes said he wasn't a man to be taken lightly. When we asked about joining his class, he directed us to a side door, and we were instantly relieved that he could speak English.

A minute later we were seated across from him in his living room while his wife, (the stunningly beautiful woman we'd met earlier), hurried to fix a pot of tea. Len and I introduced ourselves, and learned that the man sitting opposite us was Takeshi Miyagi. He sat up very straight and was quiet for a moment or two, and it was evident that he was studying us very carefully. Finally he gave a nod and said, "Why do you want to join my class?"

Naturally the standard answer from anyone back then was "to learn to fight" or "so we can defend ourselves." I mean, what other reason was there for taking up the practice of any martial art but to kick somebody's ass? So, Len and I gave him the very answer he expected.

His facial expression didn't change when he leaned back and said, "Learning karate is a life-long practice. It can't be learned in a day, a few weeks or few months."

His wife came back with a pot of tea, filled three cups, and put a small tray of cookies on the table. Miyagi took a sip of his tea and went on. "If you come to my class you will probably not stay. No American stays in my class. My class is much too strict—too hard for Americans, and they always quit." He paused and looked at us, as if he already knew we were no different than all the other Americans who had knocked on his door over the years. He was certain we too would be quitters—if we decided to come to his class at all.

Another sip of tea and he continued. "No American has ever stayed in my class for three months. I am too tough for them."

We decided to avoid his topic and go straight to another question. "How long will it take for us to get promoted? Maybe to brown belt, or even black belt?"

He laughed, and shook his head. "If you come to my class you will never be promoted. You will always be a white belt. You will never be promoted to brown belt, and a black belt for you is impossible. Too much work, too much discipline." He went on for another 15 or 20 minutes telling us how Americans were too soft, and how they wanted everything the easy way. Yet, with each new damnation of Americans, or us in general, we could see his eyes always searching, always looking, almost as if he was waiting for us to leave or argue with him. We did neither.

There was another pause while he finished his tea, and then he looked at us once again with that stern gaze. He stood up. "If you are sincere, and you really want to learn karate, and learn the right way, you come back and I'll teach you."

We assured him we wanted to learn and he said, "Come back tomorrow night. Classes begin at seven o'clock."

When we left his house, and went back out into the rain, we were quiet for most of the walk to the end of the street. We hailed a cab, and on the ride back to Camp Sukiran we discussed what we'd been told by Mr. Miyagi. He gave us dozens of reasons to avoid his dojo. He didn't make any promises of promotions to any rank. He sounded as though he didn't really want Americans coming to his dojo, because they were much too soft, and unable to endure his disciplined training regimen. And believe me, the look in his eyes said he was an uncompromising teacher that ruled his class with an iron hand. But, he did say if we wanted to learn and learn the right way, to come back and he'd teach us. Yet, in the end there was one point that stood out about him like no other, and for that reason and that reason alone, we knew we'd found the right school. Mr. Miyagi was honest.

The next day was filled with anxious anticipation, and Len and I weren't going to be late for our first class. We were there a full hour ahead of the starting time, but lessons began before our first awkward steps in the dojo.

Miyagi Sensei's dojo wasn't inside. Classes were conducted

on the hard dirt outside the back door of his house. Before each session, the lowest ranking member, or members of the class were required to take a broom and sweep that hard dirt surface to ensure it was free of the tiny pebbles that seemed to collect daily. I guess the only description I could give of that broom is that it resembled every depiction I'd ever seen of a witch's broom. Thick, long bristles held securely to the bottom of the pole by a cord that had been tightly wrapped round and round and then tied.

So, our education in humility came before anything else, and we each took turns stirring our very first batch of humble pie. Of course, we soon learned the lesson didn't end there.

Part two required lowering a bucket into the well beside the house and bringing up water for our fellow classmates to drink. That segment of the lesson also told us there was no running water in the homes around us, and anyone wanting a nice warm bath had to bring water up from the well, heat it on the stove, and pour it into the tub. Anyway, Len pulled up the bucket and poured the water into the metal teapot Mr. Miyagi had given to me.

And so we found, that sweeping the dirt floor, and filling the water pot was to be the very first thing we did each and every day before class.

When others began arriving, and stepping inside the small room to change into their gis, we noticed that each arrival cast a questioning glance our way before closing the door. When they came outside, they didn't say a word to us. They simply began limbering up, and ignored us, even though we greeted them. They talked amongst themselves, every now and then casting curious looks our way, but that was it.

It wasn't long before we understood that Miyagi's students didn't trust us. We were gaijin, (foreigners) trespassing on their sacred grounds, and surely like the few Americans before us, we too would dishonor their teacher and their art. Suddenly, Len and I knew the journey that was ahead would be far more difficult than we'd anticipated. And, I guess for the very first time we were facing prejudice, simply because we were Americans. This was something new to us, but it wasn't going to chase us away.

A few minutes before the starting hour, the door opened and

a sudden hush fell over the group. Miyagi Sensei stood in the doorway, and looked around the classroom, but didn't say a word. He remained there for a few seconds before saying something Len and I didn't understand, but whatever it was it sent everyone hurrying to a spot where they stood at attention facing him.

Miyagi looked at us, and pointed to a place between two students, one a black belt, the other a brown belt. The black belt to my immediate right gave a command and everyone bowed to Mr. Miyagi, and again words were spoken that we didn't understand. At that very moment I knew I was in a place like no other I'd ever been before.

Soon Miyagi was giving commands, and everybody around us was stepping and snapping off crisp, sharp punches. Len and I looked at each other and tried to follow the routine, but we made that proverbial "bull in a china shop" look pretty damned graceful. And, the night didn't get any better. Just about the time we thought we were catching on to what was happening around us, there'd be something new. The student body turned to the right and Len and I went left, backward, straight ahead, or tripped over our own feet. Of course, nobody was offering to lend a hand, and point us in the right direction, or give even the smallest of hints as to what we should do.

Then again, I'm sure they would have gladly pointed us to the street, and told us never to return.

I was completely lost. I couldn't grasp even a remote idea of what was going on around me, or what I supposed to be doing. Hell, I'd played football, baseball, basketball, and ran track in high school, so I wasn't a complete klutz—at least until now. And, Len wasn't doing any better. Our frustration only grew as the night wore on, and it seemed like the two-hour class had certainly gone far beyond that. Miyagi would step up and roughly put us into a position, or a stance now and then, but that was about it. There was no instruction that went with the positioning, and I wondered how many of the student body were enjoying our embarrassment. And, I could only imagine how comical we must have looked, stumbling, and falling around the classroom.

At last the night ended when the black belt that must have been Miyagi's senior student gave a command, and everybody lined up and faced the front of the class. There were a few breathing exercises, and then we bowed to Mr. Miyagi. After bowing, Mr. Miyagi told Len and I to join the others inside where we changed clothes.

Soon we were dressed in our street clothes, but no one was leaving. I wondered if they were about to tell us to get out and stay out. But, Mr. Miyagi directed us to sit on the floor around a small table that someone had put in the middle of the room.

A few moments later, Mrs. Miyagi put a pot of tea, a plate of cookies, and a tray of cups on the table. Everyone ate cookies, drank tea and talked. However, Len and I were not deeply involved in the conversation.

Finally Miyagi looked at us and said, "Okay. See you next class."

That was it. We'd been thoroughly humiliated, dismissed with a few words, and sent on our way. But, I'm sure the instant the door closed behind us everyone laughed and said, "That's the last time we'll see those two."

In spite of the humiliation, and feeling like clumsy jackasses, Len and I didn't even mention the word "quit." We agreed though, that the road to learning in the world of karate was paved with rocks, broken bottles, and probably a hidden minefield or two somewhere around the next bend in the street.

I'm sure everybody was quite shocked when they returned for the next class and found the dirt floor swept clean, and water pot filled and waiting. Even more surprising to them, had to be finding Len and I waiting patiently to be embarrassed once again.

Class started as it had before, except tonight Miyagi Sensei introduced me to Yutaka Nakanishi, a second-degree black belt, and certainly Mr. Miyagi's right hand man. Then, he introduced Len to Meiyu Takara, a brown belt who was soon to become a black belt. Nakanishi was a slender young man who stood about 5'7" tall, but like Miyagi gave the impression that he wasn't a man to tangle with. Takara was powerfully built for an Okinawan, with broad shoulders, and a weight lifter's chest. Later, we learned that he was a shot-put champion on the island.

We stumbled along in our second class, but tonight at least Miyagi gave us some verbal instruction as to what we should be doing—or attempting to do. When time began to wind down, Miyagi gave a command, and a second later I was standing face to face with Nakanishi, and Len the same with Takara. Tonight, in addition to the humiliation, we'd begin our lessons on the painful side of learning. Len and I were introduced to a training drill, (named ticado) to strengthen the wrists and forearms. The drill consisted of cracking the top portion (bone side up) of your partner's arm with the bottom portion of your arm (bone side down). The resounding crack was followed by immediate pain, but that didn't mean the drill was over. It ended when your mentor, which Takara and Nakanishi turned out to be, said it was time to stop. I don't recall how many whacks I received or administered that night, but the following day my forearms were bruised from wrist to elbow, top and bottom.

At the conclusion of our second class, we once again sat around the small table in the changing room. We sipped green tea, and ate a cookie while everyone else carried on a conversation, which surely had to be about the two clumsy American Marines. Again, I'm sure they believed this would be our last night, because after the beating we took from Nakanishi and Takara, we'd run and hide. I vividly recall Len and I hurrying back to our 12th Marine barrack, and heading straight for the shower room. We stood with our arms extended into icy cold water for as long as we could take the chill, but it did take away some of the terrible pain we were experiencing.

Much to the dismay of Mr. Miyagi, and his students, Len and I returned for a third class. And, once again, they were surprised to find the dirt floor swept clean of pebbles, and the water pot filled and waiting. A few quick glances said that some of them were beginning to wonder what we were made of, or they could've been questioning our state of mind.

The third class was much like the others, with us being the recipients of dose after dose of humble pie, and a thorough bruising at the end of class. In spite of the torture being heaped upon us, we shocked everyone and survived two full weeks. That's when Mr. Miyagi told us that the following Saturday they would hold a dojo party, and he expected Len and I to attend. He then asked us to purchase the alcoholic beverages for the party, as we could buy it much cheaper on the base. We agreed, and he gave us the money he'd collected from everyone, but we were surprised when he told us to buy whatever we wanted. Apparently no one had a preference in beverages, as long as it was alcohol, and 80 proof or better.

We made it through another week of classes, and we were actually beginning to learn how to walk again—in the karate sense.

Each class brought something new, whether it was a kata, self-defense move, or the ever-pleasant bone battering and evening ending, conditioning drills. We were assured that eventually the bruises would go away and our arms wouldn't ache as much because we'd get stronger. That assurance always came with a nod and a smile.

The day of the party, Len and I arrived early with several bottles of Jim Beam Kentucky Bourbon. And, as it turned out, this would be another day of learning for us.

First, there was food, and lots of it, prepared by Mrs. Miyagi, but we were about to discover there were no knives and forks in the Miyagi household. Suddenly, our number one priority was learning to eat with chopsticks, because neither of us wanted to miss out on the dishes of beef, chicken, rice and vegetables. I think we surprised ourselves at how quickly we adapted to using chopsticks, but it was learn fast, or go hungry.

Second, and to me the most important lesson, was to always make sure you didn't run out of the alcoholic beverages you picked up for the party. Although we learned that Miyagi and his students didn't party often, when they did, they took their parties as seriously as their karate classes.

As the night wore on, and some of the students loosened up and tried to communicate with us, the booze flowed faster. Then the bourbon was gone. Not to worry. Mr. Miyagi told one of his students to go to the corner liquor store and pick up more. Can you believe the corner liquor store didn't have Jim Beam Kentucky Bourbon? They didn't have anything American on their shelves, which meant the party beverage switched from bourbon to Sake.

Oh, God, why did I drink that? Because Mr. Miyagi poured a glass, handed it to me, and said, "Jimmy, you drink."

Well, I drank it—slowly, very slowly, because the taste was quite different than the Sake I'd sampled in Japan. This had a rather distinct taste—something along the lines of a mixture of gasoline and Panther Piss. And, rather quickly, I was beginning to feel as if I'd been hit by a freight train. Though I had no idea how large that train was going to become over the next hour or so. I was doing fine sipping bourbon, because I'd eaten plenty of food, especially the rice and beef. Full stomach or not, Sake and bourbon don't mix well with the overall scheme, and chemistry of the human body. I hurtled right on by feeling good, tipsy, and slightly intoxicated to positively blind drunk.

I recall that, sometime during the party, Len and I asked if anyone knew the story of Japanese Karate Master, Mas Oyama's having killed a bull with his hands. Of course, we wanted to know if this was true, or just one of those legends that came about because someone spun a yarn over a few beers. Almost immediately, Gibo, a friend of Mr. Miyagi, and one of his black belts, said he could do the same thing.

Naturally, this was after he'd downed a rather substantial amount of alcohol. His boast opened the door for a round of sharp verbal jabs and challenges, which only made him more resolute in his claim. Soon, he was insisting that Len and I accompany him in search of a bull and, after locating the animal, he'd prove once and for all that he could indeed slay the beast with his hands. In the end, cooler heads prevailed and the great bull massacre of Okinawa was soon forgotten. But, Len and I never did have our question answered.

It was sometime after midnight when Len and I finally left the party. And, Gibo, who'd driven to the party in his 1955 Chevy, offered to drive us back to Camp Sukiran. Hell, he could barely walk, and he wanted to drive. Somehow Len ended up driving, although to this day I don't know how, and actually drove to Camp Sukiran without running over anything, or anybody. He drove straight to our barrack, made a left, drove up over the curb, down the sidewalk, and stopped at the front steps of the building. We said goodnight to Gibo, got out of his car, and went inside.

A minute later, I was making my first offering of the night to the porcelain god. Suddenly, I understood the infamous saying, "I was so sick, I'd have to get well to die." I know for certain that I had a hangover that lasted three days, but I'm not too sure that I wasn't still drunk for that same time period. Len wasn't doing much better, but I think his hangover lasted only two days. And, to make matters worse, we were headed into the boonies bright and early Monday morning for training. I vowed that night, that never again would I drink Sake.

We missed one class because of being in the field, but were there all the earlier for the next one. We received our conditioning treatment from Nakanishi and Takara before class concluded, and we went inside for what had become our after class ritual.

We sat around the table expecting to be left out as usual, but tonight Mr. Miyagi wanted to know if we enjoyed the party. After Len and I described our condition, which Miyagi eagerly translated with a bigger than ever grin, everyone laughed. While they laughed, Len and I tried our best to explain how miserable we were, which only made them laugh even more. In turn we laughed, and soon the room was shaking from the laughter. That's when we realized they were laughing with us, not at us. So, the initial crack in the door to acceptance had opened, although it took a hangover half the size of the Pacific Ocean to break a small opening in the first barrier.

A second crack in the door appeared after the following class. Len and I were having difficulty keeping up with the proper names of Miyagi's students, and decided nicknames might be appropriate. Sitting around the table again, we pointed to one of the students, and called him Smiley. His nickname was easy to come by—we never saw this kid without a smile, a smile that looked as if it had been glued permanently to his face at birth. He nodded, and Miyagi called him Smiley, so that made it okay. By the end of the night we had an English nickname for almost everyone in the room: George (Nakanishi), Sampson (Takara) and Shorty (Funakoshi) who was only 4' 9" tall, and Lucky (Uchima) were just a few named that night. But, out of respect, we didn't brand Miyagi Sensei with a nickname. Yet, in a matter of a few days, even he referred to them by the nicknames we'd given them.

By the beginning of our third month, Miyagi and his students were growing accustomed to our presence in class. Still, that didn't mean they were certain of our sincerity, and willingness to stick with the tough regimen. But, we surprised them when we learned that Nakanishi worked the night shift at a bakery, and told him he could share our cab when we were leaving for the base. He would arrive at work quicker, and it wouldn't cost him bus, or cab fare. Miyagi translated our message, Nakanishi accepted, and now a new door was opening, one of friendship. I know that very first ride he took with us was awkward, but there was no question that he was grateful. And, as time passed, that ride was as routine to him as coming to class.

Soon we were in our fourth month of classes, and it was at that time Miyagi said, "Well, I think you two are serious. So, now we get down to business."

I looked over at Len, and I know we were thinking the same thing. Get down to business? What the hell have we been doing all this time, playing? If the previous classes were merely playtime, or preparation for the real thing, God help us.

Though we didn't think it was possible, the intensity of our training increased. Kata repetition was endless, the self-defense practice faster, and various new reflex drills were added. And, newer katas always meant Mr. Miyagi had additional ways to test us. He pounded our legs to guarantee our stances were correct, or he slammed a powerful forearm against ours when we executed a block. He'd say nothing as he did this. He'd simply nod and move on, or strike us again. After classes now we'd find new bruises—those of handprints on our legs. And in spite of our awkward first steps, and those hundreds of clumsy missteps, we were learning. Our balance was improving, we were getting stronger, and many of those never ending kata repetitions were beginning to make sense. Still, there was a long, long way to go.

***

Len and I found that taking karate classes made us targets of opportunity for our fellow Marines who were taking classes at other dojos. With so many styles to choose from, we had a mixture of just about every system on the island represented in our barrack. And that meant the eternal digs of "my style's better than your style" or "our teacher's the best" and so on.

Len and I tried to avoid these discussions, but Len wasn't the type of man to stay out of any argument for too long. One Marine, who'd already earned a black belt from a very different style, knew he was pushing Len's buttons, and made it a point to go out of his way daily to fire a few verbal volleys. Finally he threw down the gauntlet and said he could take Miyagi's best black belt, and destroy him in a matter of seconds.

That did it. Len was going to stand up for Miyagi, Nakanishi and the entire Shorin Ryu Karate Do Association, and set a time and place for a no holds barred brawl with anybody who was willing to show up. He was that legendary mad bull, snorting and charging around looking for someone to gore, and come hell's fire or typhoon winds, he was going to smack the piss out of somebody.

We couldn't get to the next class fast enough. Len was sure he could convince Miyagi, and every member of the student body, to charge over to the other dojo and defend our honor. Surely, Miyagi Sensei wouldn't tolerate an insult to himself, his dojo, and his entire association. He would be willing to go along, and throw the first punch to get things going. Then this argument would be settled once and for all. And, what the hell, I wasn't going to allow Len to get into this brawl without me.

Well, much to Len's dismay, Miyagi only laughed when he was told about the challenge. Of course, Len was breathing fire while he related everything that had been said, but it only seemed to cause Miyagi to laugh more. When he translated the message to everyone else, they too laughed, and quite loudly.

I must admit, that I was very surprised by their reaction. I thought they would've been upset, and angry over what was said about us. But, it was certainly obvious they didn't take these insults as seriously as we did.

Miyagi knew Len and I were willing to go fight, and I'm not sure how he felt about that. He just sat back with a big smile on his face. "Don't worry about beating someone else. Only worry about beating yourself."

Naturally we looked at him, and I said, "What do you mean?"

"If you can beat yourself, there's no need to worry about someone else," he said, while looking me right in the eyes.

"I don't understand."

Again he smiled. "In time you will. One day you will become a wise man, and then you will understand."

Len wasn't going to give up easily. He said we had been insulted, and he was sure there'd be much more trash talking (in those days it was referred to as meat mouthing) when we went back to the barrack.

There was that Miyagi laugh again. "Anybody can talk. Talk means nothing. If you don't like what the person is saying, don't listen."

The discussion stopped abruptly when Miyagi raised a hand, and signaled that it was time for class to begin. I think a great of deal of anger over the taunts was left on the dojo floor, and we had settled down by the time class ended. It was time for tea, cookies, and our tableside chat.

While we sat around the table, Mr. Miyagi seemed rather quiet, as though he was deep in thought. Finally he looked over at Len and I and said, "To conquer another person is sometimes very easy. To conquer yourself is sometimes very difficult. But, you must learn to conquer yourself." He nodded, picked up his tea and we knew that our evening philosophy lesson had ended. And we had no idea how much more wisdom he'd divulge along the way.

It wasn't long before Len was scheduled to leave for the rifle range, and his annual qualification. So, I'd be headed to class alone for the next week or so, and I laughed when I told Len I'd miss his nightly entertainment on the ride to and from classes. And believe me, Len was truly a master of amusement. We would no sooner get into a cab, and he'd start telling the cab driver how to make time with the women on the island. It didn't make any difference if the driver spoke English or not, Len definitely wasn't going to pass up an opportunity to share his expertise on thrilling the ladies. Every now and then we'd get a driver who spoke, and understood the English language very well. For Len, this was the same as throwing a hungry shark into a swimming pool. He had a captive audience, and the lessons in love flowed fast, furious, sometimes comical, and they were free of charge. We often wondered how many followed his advice, or ended up divorced because they took it.

Len left for his two-week stint at the rifle range, and I went on to the dojo. It was probably the second night of making the trip alone and, after class Nakanishi left with me for his ride to work. We were walking along the dirt road, Nakanishi on my right, and we had traveled only about 30 yards or so, when a motorcycle came toward us. Certainly it wasn't unusual to see a motorcycle on the street, but this one swerved and came straight at us. We moved a few steps to our right to let it pass, but a few seconds later the rider cut directly across our path. The motorcycle stopped, and the two Americans, neither of whom I recognized got off and stared at us. I knew they were GIs, but I didn't think they were Marines. Finally the operator said to me, "What're you doing back here?" His tone was less than friendly.

Not wanting to say I was taking karate lessons, I said, "Coming from a friend's house."

He sneered. "Oh, you have friends in this country?"

"Yes," I said, while wondering what Nakanishi was thinking, and if he understood this wasn't exactly a cordial chat I was having.

It was the passenger who half growled. "And just what is it you do at your friends house?"

I didn't know what to say, and the only answer I could come up with was, "I go to school there." Still, I wasn't saying anything about karate, because I was sure this would only cause them to want to test me. And, I sure as hell didn't want to put Nakanishi in an awkward position.

"Is this one of your friends?" the passenger said jabbing a finger at Nakanishi.

"Yes," I answered as I saw Nakanishi calmly put his lunch down on the road and push up his sleeves. That's when I realized that even though he couldn't understand, or speak English that well, he understood something was wrong. I admit, that suddenly I felt very good about the situation, because I was positively certain that if trouble started, I had a surprise coming out of my corner. Then I wondered if the shit hit the fan, if I'd even get a punch in before Nakanishi flattened both of the idiots.

The operator of the bike took off his helmet, put it on the seat and said, "And just what's this guy do at that school you go to?"

"He's a teacher." And, with that, the light bulb must've clicked on very brightly.

The guy standing directly in front of me muttered, "Oh," blinked, and reached for his helmet. Within a matter of seconds, the motorcycle was speeding away from us, and soon was out of sight.

Nakanishi pulled his sleeves down, picked up his lunch, and we went on our way. He didn't bother to try and ask about what had just happened, but after the following class I found that he was anxious to find out.

He spoke with Mr. Miyagi while we were having tea, and Miyagi turned to me and asked what happened. When I explained, he said Nakanishi could feel that the two Americans were not really friendly, and possibly wanted to fight.

I told him they probably wanted to fight, but then I couldn't help but laugh when I said, "I don't think a fight would've lasted too long. I believe George would've beaten both of them before I even had a chance to throw a punch."

Mr. Miyagi relayed my comments to Nakanishi, and they laughed. They talked for a few more moments and Miyagi turned back to me. "George was prepared."

I felt good, knowing that Nakanishi was willing to jump into a fight with me if it had been necessary. It spoke volumes about his character, but more than that, it said he wouldn't have left me alone. This was also the time that I found that Mr. Miyagi was very good at springing surprises. He informed me on a Thursday evening that he wanted me to participate in a karate demonstration, with members of his dojo, on Sunday afternoon. I was honored, but I must admit, I was a little apprehensive about exhibiting my very limited skills in front of a group of strangers. He told me not to worry, because he was certain that I'd do just fine.

Late on a Sunday afternoon, in front of several hundred Okinawans, I took part in my very first karate demonstration. It wasn't as bad as I thought, and I performed a kata (Naihanchi San Dan) in front of all those people without fainting, or making a mistake. Though one or two in the crowd, who had obviously guzzled a good deal of the free Sake, yelled loudly at my every move. Of course, a number of other participants were greeted with the same enthusiasm.

I believe it was around this time that I learned that it isn't always a good idea to attend class when you're not at the top of your game. It was just one of those days when my body was telling me that all wasn't well, but I was determined to go to class anyway. I had recently learned the kata Seisan, which required a great deal of tensing—certainly isometric in nature, during the movements of the kata. The tenth count put me in a position with both feet planted flat and firmly on the dojo floor. Both arms were locked with the elbows pointed downward, insides of the forearms turned inward, and my fists squarely under my eyes. But, I was not feeling on top of the world, and my arms weren't as tense as they should have been.

Naturally, Miyagi Sensei chose this time to test my strength. He turned quickly and slammed the palms of his hands against my arms.

An instant later my knuckles cracked soundly into my face just under my eyes. I don't know if it hurt more than embarrassed me or not, but it was certainly a shock when my knuckles crashed into my face. Every class for the next month it seemed Mr. Miyagi was waiting for that tenth count, because he was standing right there, poised to test me. But, never again did he catch me with anything less than a 110 percent effort.

Len returned from the rifle range, and we became regular fixtures in Miyagi's class. Two other Marines, Terry Rock and Michael Needham, joined and stuck it out with us.

After a Saturday evening class, Len and I were headed to the Oyama Restaurant, which had been a regular hangout for us for almost two months. We liked the Oyama restaurant for several reasons, two of which were Susie and Yoshiko. In time Len was hooked up with Yoshiko and I with Susie.

The building housing the Oyama Restaurant was three stories, with the first floor being a clothing store and tailor shop. The second floor housed a rather formal dining area, with each party being seated in a separate, enclosed room. But, the top floor was our home, and you had to climb a rather narrow concrete stairway to reach it. There was a small bar area with only three booths, four stools at the bar, a jukebox in the corner, and a small restroom. Then there was the outside area where, during good weather, which was most of the time, you could dine and drink at one of the half-dozen tables.

As we finished our tea, and on the spur of the moment, we decided to ask Mr. Miyagi if he'd like to go for a beer. To our surprise, he accepted the invitation, and the three of us enjoyed a sandwich, several cold beers and a very good conversation. And, Mr. Miyagi's English had gotten better with each karate class we attended. He told us he was happy we stayed in class, because it gave him the opportunity to practice his English.

Armed Forces Week was celebrated by hosting an Open House on each base. The celebration was to last a week, and we were encouraged to invite Okinawan citizens to visit the various bases, see the displays, and enjoy the hospitality. All military clubs were open to visitors and we were encouraged to bring Okinawan guests to the clubs.

Len and I invited Mr. Miyagi to visit Camp Sukiran with us, and have a meal at one of the clubs. He welcomed the opportunity, and after a tour of our barrack, we took him to the U. S. Army club, which was only about two blocks from our quarters.

The first thing we were asked when we entered the club was "Who is the senior man?" I raised my hand, and was told I'd have to register our guest, and as the Senior NCO, I was responsible for Mr. Miyagi while we were in the club.

After the formality of entering his name in the club logbook, and signing the log, we walked into the restaurant. The U. S. Army club at Camp Sukiran was one of the better military clubs, probably a close second to the club on the U. S. Air Base at Kadena. The dining room was spacious, and the food excellent.

We spotted a table, and Len started leading the way, with Miyagi directly behind him, and me following. We'd taken only about a dozen steps when a GI started toward us, passed Len, and purposely stuck his shoulder into Mr. Miyagi.

Mr. Miyagi took a step back, bowed and said, "Excuse me please." With that, the GI stuck his shoulder into him again. Miyagi stepped back, bowed and said, "Excuse me please." But, the GI took a quick step, and shouldered him again. Once more, Miyagi Sensei stepped back, bowed and said, "Excuse me please."

Before the GI could test his shoulder strength again I said, "Stupid, you're gonna get your ass killed." He looked at me, then at Mr. Miyagi, and made a hasty exit from the club without uttering a word.

As we took the last steps to our table, I knew it was probably better that I was following instead of Len. If Len had been behind Mr. Miyagi when the GI purposely shouldered him, we would've had a riot in the club for sure. But, within a few moments, Len and I would be taught another lesson.

After we ordered our first round of beer and our meal, I began talking about what had happened. Of course, I thought we'd need a collar and leash for Len, but he finally settled down and listened. We wanted to know why Mr. Miyagi hadn't knocked the guy on his ass. There was a quick smile that appeared on his face and he said, "It wasn't necessary. He just had too much to drink."

Hey, that wasn't good enough for us. There had to be more, and naturally we had to ask. This time there was a nod when he looked at me. "I understood what was said to you when we came in. They made you sign the book, saying you are responsible for me. If I hit the GI, then you get into trouble. I don't want to be the cause of trouble for you because you are my friend." Then he laughed and said, "Besides I didn't want to get beat up."

Now we laughed along with him, and understood that he knew it would've been a very quick, very one-sided fight had the GI persisted. He was quiet for a few seconds before he looked at us. "It's not necessary to fight all the time."

We raised our glasses in a salute to him, and another valuable lesson in humility.

***

It was different being stationed in Okinawa because, unlike the USA, we were required to be on base and in our barrack by midnight. So, the term Cinderella Liberty was attached to the grounding hour. I don't know how many Marines strictly adhered to the rule, but in order to stay out beyond the "bewitching hour" required a special leave pass to accompany your everyday Liberty Card. The special leave passes were like gold, and issued only on certain occasions, and you can bet you weren't going to get one every weekend. But, I had a very special talent back in those days, a talent I found by accident while stationed at Camp Lejune, North Carolina. I could forge just about every signature of every officer simply after studying it for a few moments. In fact, at Camp Lejune I was so good with my art that Lieutenant Dennis M. Naughton often wondered if he'd signed a document, or if I'd forged his signature.

I used it often when we were aboard ship with the meal pass system. Naturally, only so many could get into the mess hall at one time, and color-coded cards were issued to each Marine. When the color code was announced, that's when you ate, and the midday meal could sometimes take over two and half-hours to complete. It was the same for breakfast and dinner. Now, there was something that kicked my appetite into high gear when we were out to sea. I couldn't get enough to eat—and didn't gain an ounce. Well, the moment we boarded ship, I set about searching for the location of the meal passes, and I never failed to find them. Pretty soon I had a signed card for every color code, and would eat at least two of each meal. There were times, of course, when the Marine assigned to check passes at the Mess Hall entrance gave me a strange look. Still, he couldn't challenge me by saying, "You look like a guy who was here earlier, with close cropped hair and wearing Olive Drab BDUs."

That was the description of almost every Marine on the ship. So, my stomach was content, and my talent for forgery would come in handy later in Okinawa.

Saturdays were the only times Len and I really cared about going out after class and unwinding. But, with classes ending at 9:00 PM, and then not leaving the dojo until sometimes close to 10:00 PM it didn't leave much time for fun. The first thing any Marine did when he arrived in Okinawa was suddenly "lose" his everyday Liberty Card, and apply for a duplicate. The duplicate was never checked out of the card box when going on liberty, because the one that you'd "lost" was tucked safely away in your wallet. That way, things didn't get complicated on those nights you didn't come back to the barrack. You guessed it. Len and I lost our Liberty Cards. I already knew I could sign any name from the Regimental Commander, to each and every lieutenant assigned as Officer of the Day. So, it was just a matter of getting our hands on those special liberty passes.

Only a day or two had gone by when I saw one of our clerks running off copies of the passes. Within a minute or less he was getting a message that the First Sergeant wanted to see him right away. And sure enough, he left an entire stack of passes on the desk. The instant he left the room, I scooped up enough passes to cover Len and I for three years. Greedy I know, but I didn't want to take any chances, because opportunity might not open its arms like that again. So, every Saturday we left for class with a special liberty pass signed and stuffed in our pockets. But, the pass would be checked only if you were crazy enough to attract the attention of the Military Police. We were never that foolish.

Naturally, our Saturday nights out didn't go unnoticed. Mr. Miyagi had worked on a Marine Corps Base, and he was familiar with leave and liberty procedures. He thought it was unusual that we were able to stay out beyond the midnight hour so often, but never questioned our "good fortune."

Our workouts seemed to increase in intensity and, as Mr. Miyagi had promised, we were coming to class and learning. A half-dozen or more Marines from our barrack asked to come along and join, but most of them didn't last. As Mr. Miyagi had predicted most quit before three months had passed.

As the weather warmed, we began to gather an audience for our classes, with a group of young children showing up to watch our nightly workouts. Some would stay for only a few minutes, some longer, but there was one who often stayed and watched the entire class. And it seemed like he had some mysterious way of knowing when I'd arrive early for class. I'd step out the door in my gi and he'd appear, smile and take his usual place on the bench by the wall. At the time it never occurred to me that 30 plus years into the future I'd once again meet this young boy, who had almost become my constant shadow.

I don't recall if he stayed around for the entire class on the evening when disaster struck. I'm sure everybody is familiar with days when absolutely nothing goes right. Well, Len's and mine arrived on the first Saturday of June, and it was so bad we wished we'd decided to skip the whole thing and have a beer—actually several beers. Len and I felt like crawling under a rock, or finding a nearby cliff and jumping off. We were that bad. We were turning right instead of left, fumbling and stumbling around like we'd gone back to our very first night. In fact, we were certain this hot, humid Saturday was far worse than our first night.

To make matters worse, Mr. Miyagi thought it would be a good night to call us up in front of the class to perform a kata for everyone. It was an unbelievable performance. But, our abilities as executioners were indeed outstanding. Len and I butchered the entire Shorin Ryu System in only a matter of a few minutes. And, believe me, after we took our places back in line, the night couldn't end fast enough. We simply wanted to run and hide.

Still, there was no leaving without our nightly formality of green tea and cookies after class. So, we sat on the floor, completely humiliated, and drank our tea. But, there was something going on. Mr. Miyagi was talking with Nakanishi and Takara, and Len and I were mentioned often. We guessed that they were probably trying to come up with some way to put together a firing squad and have us shot.

After a few minutes Miyagi turned to us. "Okay, tonight you both get brown belt."

I'm not certain whether Len or I spoke first after we looked at each other and tried to understand what he'd just said. I was sure I'd heard him say we were getting brown belts, but then again that couldn't be right. After all, he'd told us the night we met that we'd never be anything but white belts. Len and I had resolved ourselves to that fact and, in spite of the promise that we would never be promoted, we came anyway. We were there because Mr. Miyagi was honest with us and, up to this point he'd kept his word. Now, just imagine somebody in the United States being told they'd never be promoted, and that they'd be nothing more than a white belt for as long as they came to class. I don't think you'd finish the sentence before the door slammed.

I know that at some point I said, "You mean we're being promoted?"

Miyagi smiled. "Yes."

I admit I was confused. Len and I had just made total asses of ourselves in front of the entire class, and now Miyagi wanted to promote us to brown belt. It didn't make sense. I felt as though I not only embarrassed myself in front of the class, but also Miyagi Sensei. After a little stammering I said, "I don't deserve a brown belt."

He just smiled. "That's okay. I think so."

What he was saying was having a difficult time sinking in, so I said, "You mean when we come to our next class we wear a brown belt."

Again he smiled. "Yes."

"Well, I don't think I deserve the belt, and I don't want to wear it," I said, hoping he'd see my point.

He only laughed. "Good. You wear it anyway. That means you work that much harder to prove I'm not a fool."

Right about that time I realized I was engaged in an argument that was actually very one sided. I was stating my objection to the man who'd already declared himself the winner of our debate. He won in a landslide. After all, he made the rules.

We left the dojo that evening with a promotion and another lesson in humility.

Mr. Miyagi had purposely chosen our worst night to promote us and remind us of the message he was always sending. "It takes a very humble man to be a black belt." And, it seemed a brown belt as well. After the lesson we'd just been taught it was very unlikely that we'd be strutting around like peacocks when we returned to class.

It was a strange feeling stepping out of the dressing room on to the dojo floor, the very first time, wearing a brown belt. But, there were chores to be done. Len went to fill the water pot while I swept the floor. I had only been sweeping for a few seconds when a newer Okinawan student walked in. He nearly passed out when he saw me pushing the pebbles to the side. He dropped his bag, hurried over and reached for the broom saying, "No sweep. No sweep." I tried to explain that it was okay because it was my job, but he shook his head vigorously as he pulled on the broom and said, "You brown belt. No sweep. You no sweep. I sweep." I reluctantly gave up the broom and stood by while he swept the floor.

Len was shaking his head when he walked over to me. "I guess that's not our job anymore."

Well, maybe not, but it didn't make me feel any better about standing there and watching this young man perform a task that Len or I had done night after night for months. I guess it was another way of learning humility.

We survived our initial class as novice brown belts, but the promotion didn't mean the intensity of the workouts dropped off. As a matter of fact, with the new belts more was expected of us. And, as always, Mr. Miyagi didn't waste time preparing us for additional tasks. He merely opened the door and tossed us into the lion's den. Before we knew it, he directed us to teach two Okinawan students who had only recently begun classes. Later when we asked why he'd trusted us with a teaching assignment he took a sip of his tea and smiled.

"When you teach, you also learn," he said. "Many things you didn't understand in the past, you will see. Teaching opens many new doors to learning, and in time you will achieve much wisdom."

That was the first time that he'd indicated that he wanted us to teach when we left Okinawa and returned to the United States. But, our education for the evening wasn't over. He went on. "And as you teach always remember that you can learn from your students.

One day as I've taught you, you will teach me."

We were baffled. How could we possibly teach him? In our eyes he was the master. He was already a 5th Degree Black Belt, and hadn't reached his 30th birthday. "In time you will see and understand the things that are in front of you. But now you don't see and understand." And that was our philosophy lesson for the night.

***

When I think back now, I often smile over some of the unintentional teaching Len and I did with a few of our nightly quip sessions. After we'd broken down some of the barriers between the other students and us, Len and I would sometimes fire a few verbal shots back and forth at each other. The others didn't miss this, even though they acted as if they didn't know, or understand what was going on. And, we later discovered they were learning a lot by their somewhat subtle eavesdropping.

One evening after class we jokingly said to Nakanishi, "Hey, George, we hear you're getting married next week."

"Bullshit," he shot back, without so much as a blink. His comeback even brought a laugh from Miyagi.

Some weeks later, Uchima (Lucky) was a minute or so late for class, and was hurrying to get into the dressing room to change. The ground was still somewhat wet near the entrance from a recent rainfall. Lucky hit one of those spots near the door, slipped and blurted, "son-of-a-bitch."

I don't know how we didn't fall apart in the middle of our kata, but Len and I somehow managed to keep our composure. Still, out of the corner of our eye, we saw the faint smile flash across Mr. Miyagi's face.

Obviously, we'd been doing more teaching than we were aware of. Though it was amazing that Nakanishi and Uchima chose the appropriate comment, with the proper voice inflection, for their use of a newly learned language.

With the promotion to brown belt, Len and I earned a greater degree of trust and acceptance from everyone. This was very clear the night we asked Mr. Miyagi about his family. Until now we'd never really felt comfortable venturing into his personal life, and accepted whatever family stories he offered.

One of the questions we asked was about his father. We'd met his mother, and actually saw her quite often because she lived next door, but he'd never talked about his father. Mr. Miyagi began by telling us that he and his family had been forced, by the Japanese to leave Okinawa, and go to Japan during World War II. They were put aboard ships, and a convoy headed north toward Japan. His father, however, was ordered to remain on the island, along with most of the adult male population of Okinawa. A U. S. Submarine attacked the convoy, and the ship in front of the one he and his family were aboard was sunk.

When U. S. Forces began the invasion of Okinawa, Miyagi's father along with many other Okinawan men where forced to face U. S. Marines as they landed. These men were literally used as human shields for the Japanese soldiers. U. S. Marines subsequently killed Mr. Miyagi's father during the fighting.

Len and I were stunned by this revelation and couldn't help but ask if he felt any hostility toward us, because Marines had killed his father. He said, "It wasn't our war. We didn't start it. It was the Japanese who started the war. There is no reason for me to feel hate for you because of what happened. And there is no reason why we should not be friends."

Miyagi continued to amaze us with his thinking, and the way he approached life. Each time we talked with him, our respect and admiration for him grew. He proved time and again that he was a man of honor and great courage. And, in this conversation there was another lesson learned. He pointed out that he is not Japanese, but Okinawan and even today the older generation Okinawans are quick to point out that fact. He told us Chinese and Polynesian traders, who traveled the waters of the Pacific Ocean and South China Sea, visited the island of Okinawa often. As years passed, the marriages of Chinese and Polynesians gave birth to the Okinawan people. But many, unfamiliar with the culture of the island, still mistakenly refer to the lifelong inhabitants of Okinawa as Japanese.

It wasn't long before we found yet another door opening for us. Mr. Miyagi told us we'd been invited to visit the dojo of Mr.

Katsuya Miyahira, an 8th Degree Black Belt at that time, and the man who would, in just a few short years, become the Grand Master of the Shorin Ryu Karate Do Association.

We left early on the night of our visit, and soon after being introduced to Mr. Miyahira, he invited us in for tea. It was evident that he was very pleased that Len and I had been the first Americans to persevere, and not falter in the face of Miyagi Sensei's training regimen. After talking with Mr. Miyahira for about 20 minutes, we went into his dojo to watch his class.

As we sat on the floor waiting for the class to begin, Miyagi Sensei pointed out one of Mr. Miyahira's black belts, saying he was a Third Degree Black Belt, and one of Mr. Miyahira's best students. He hinted that we should watch him very closely during the evening workout.

When the class began Len and I made the student Miyagi had pointed out our focal point of the session. He was impressive. He was very fast, agile, and it was evident that he had a great deal of power in his punches and kicks. His movements in the katas were crisps and his self-defense techniques effective.

After biding Mr. Miyahira goodnight, we started back to Gusukuma to drop off Mr. Miyagi before continuing on to the base. It wasn't long before Miyagi asked what we thought of Miyahira's student. We agreed that he was as good as Miyagi had said, but both of us didn't hesitate to say, "George is better."

A week later Nakanishi was promoted to San Dan, and Len and I often wondered if what we'd said that night had any influence whatsoever on Miyagi's decision. Though we never asked.

Soon it was party time again. Mr. Miyagi announced the upcoming event during one of our after class tea and cookie sessions. Of course, we were once again expected to pick up the alcoholic beverages for the party, and when I muttered to Len that this time we weren't going to run out of bourbon, Miyagi began laughing. So, he hadn't forgotten my giant hangover from last time.

This party turned out to be far more than we'd anticipated. By now, Len and I had erased just about all doubts regarding our sincerity. While our very first party was somewhat subdued, this one warmed up to a let your hair down (what little Len and I had) and enjoy yourself to the fullest, celebration.

Still, before things got wild and crazy, Mr. Miyagi offered us another history lesson. He talked of the Okinawan dances, and said they held many similarities to karate katas. He even demonstrated some of the dance moves to show us how close they resembled those in the katas we practiced. There was time for a lot of picture taking before things got too out of hand, and those photos still provide a lot of fond memories. Yet, some of the photos taken after things reached a rather frenzied pitch bring back more than just a flood of fond memories. There's a recollection of laughter and friendship, shared far from our homes in America, with newfound friends in a land that had come to mean so much to us.

Our second party ended on a much different note than the first. Len and I had our share to drink, but this time we made sure the bourbon did not run out. We partied well beyond the midnight hour, but there was no head pounding, gut-wrenching hangover when we awoke later on Sunday morning. We gave ourselves what we thought was a well deserved pat on the back for having learned a very valuable lesson.

With the party behind us, classes resumed and again the intensity of our training seemed to rise to yet another level. Our punches and kicks were much faster now, and as I stood beside Nakanishi night after night I tried my best to match his speed, even if for only a single punch. His fist was almost a blur as it snapped out time after time, and I could hear the sharp pop of his gi jacket. Then it just happened. Mr. Miyagi counted, and I fired the fastest punch I could muster and we were dead even in our timing. Fists flashed and gi jackets popped as we arrived at the finish line at the same instant. There was no time to gloat in my moment of glory. Another count and I was right on his heels again. I left class that night feeling like I'd finally reached another plateau in my training.

Len and I were still regulars at the Oyama Restaurant, and we were there on a Saturday evening after class while somebody was having a Sayonora Party downstairs. We had just finished our first cold beer, and were about to order a sandwich, when somebody from the party wandered into the bar upstairs. He was ahead of us by several cold ones, and for some reason he wanted us to know that the party was in his honor, and he was going home. We were unaware that the party was for an American, but we congratulated him on completing his tour of duty in Okinawa and wished him luck. We turned back to the waitress to order our sandwiches, but he slapped his hand on the bar and informed us that he'd also been promoted to black belt.

Instantly I thought *well, here we go*. But, being in the middle of trying to complete our order, we didn't immediately acknowledge his promotion. All of a sudden, he hurried to the door, shouted a string of obscenities at us, and ran to the stairs. While running down the stairs, he was screaming something we couldn't understand, but by the time we made it outside his friends had poured out of the restaurant to meet him.

Len and I stopped, and stood at the top of the stairs trying to figure out what the guy's problem was. That's when he started to go into what we recognized as a sanchin stance from another style, and he proceeded to go into a very exaggerated breathing exercise. He was hissing, and trying his best to growl, while performing various tense arm and flexing movements. Naturally, that brought out the "Mad Bull" in Len.

"Uechi Ryu," he spat. "I'm gonna kill this guy." And, with that, he started down the steps to meet him.

I grabbed him by the shoulder and told him to wait. After all, we had the high ground, and running down to the landing below wasn't in our best interest. The stairs were steep and narrow, and there was no way the hissing drunk and his friends were going to charge up and get us. Len and I couldn't even stand side by side on the steps, and the advantage for us was to stay right where we were. While the drunk went on with his hissing and snorting, I ran inside and grabbed an armful of beer mugs. What the hell, there were at least 16 of them and only two of us, so a little heavy artillery might balance the odds a fraction.

I hurried back and lined the beer mugs along the flat concrete barrier at the top of the stairs. It was right about the same time when someone wearing an Army uniform appeared in the group, and was trying his best to get the drunk to calm down. He called up to us that he was a Chaplain, and asked us to be patient while he tried to get the drunken black belt to leave.

That's when Len and I realized that it wasn't only the Chaplain who was trying to get the guy to leave, but most of his friends as well. It looked like he was the only one in the group that wanted to fight. We were more than a little surprised by this, because it usually only takes one drunk to incite the rest to join in and start a brawl. In the end, it was the cooler heads that prevailed, and they hauled the drunk, still hissing and snorting, down the stairs to a waiting taxi.

We went back into the bar, and the only thing I had to worry about was getting Len "The Mad Bull" Neidert to settle down. Well, another cold beer, and he was on his way back to earth and, by the time round three was on the bar, he was calm enough to order that sandwich he'd wanted.

The following day we had a few good laughs over the whole thing, but naturally we couldn't help but wonder what would've happened if the crowd followed the drunk's lead and charged up the stairs.

Len saw only one outcome. "Hell, we would've kicked their asses," he laughed. And given our position, and the circumstances, maybe he was right.

As we continued our karate training, Mr. Miyagi took every opportunity to bring up the subject of teaching when we returned to the States. At times during classes he would casually say, "You will see this when you teach." But, it was after class, and over tea that he often spent time reinforcing his philosophy of how much we'd learn when we taught others. And, there were the constant reminders to be smart enough to learn from your students as you teach. He painted a picture of a martial arts world filled with endless opportunities to learn something new, if we had the wisdom to look at what was offered to us. And, in all of his messages, there were so many other subtle hints of what a good karate teacher and practitioner should be. The words patience and humility were never forgotten in our after class discussions, and went hand in hand with being that very good teacher he spoke of.

Our next half dozen or so trips to the Oyama Restaurant were uneventful, but it seemed that the restaurant had another surprise in store for us. It was probably getting close to three in the morning when we left, and for some unknown reason, we turned to our right and went down a narrow street. I don't know if it was just a notion for a change of pace or what, but we'd never walked down this street before. We always turned left and waited for a cab, or sometimes we walked to Susie's house where we'd meet her and Yoshiko.

It was very dark, but as we got closer to the bottom of the hill, we noticed something lying in the middle of the road. A few seconds later, we found that something was an Okinawan man lying in the intersection. He was face up, no shoes or socks on his feet, and wearing only a pair of light color pants, and a shirt that was open down the front.

We couldn't just walk by and pretend he wasn't there, so we stopped to check on him. He was cold to the touch, and we couldn't find a heartbeat. I think we both said, "Oh, shit" at the same time.

While Len was leaning over him checking for a carotid pulse, I looked over my shoulder and saw a few men walking toward us. My first thought was where in the hell did they come from at this hour? But, in no time at all, they were standing around staring at us. Len was talking to the man lying in the street, but the he didn't move a muscle. And, now it looked like people were coming from every direction, and Len and I were the only Americans in the crowd. I thought *Jesus Christ! Was everybody awake and just waiting for us to come by?*

Len glanced up at me and shook his head. "Christ, Jimmy, I think this guy's dead."

"We'd better hope to God he's not," I said, glancing back at the crowd. "These people think we're the ones who hurt this guy."

"But there's not a mark on him," Len said, while he kept trying to find some sign of life. "There's not a bruise, or a cut anywhere that I can see."

I looked around once more, and I swear there were close to 75 or 80 people there, standing around and staring at us. Nobody said a word, they just stared. I tried to ask if anyone knew the guy, or where he lived, but luck sure as hell wasn't on our side. Either nobody spoke English, or they were ignoring me. And, it wasn't long before things started to take another slide downhill. Someone in the crowd said something, and a few others joined in. The chatter wasn't that loud, but it certainly didn't ring with a friendly tone, and the circle around us was closing tighter and tighter.

Things were looking bad, and we didn't really have many options open to us. We probably couldn't break through the crowd and run and, unlike the confrontation with the "hissing black belt," there was nothing at all favoring us in a street fight with this group.

Soon our situation was desperate. The attitude of the crowd was growing very nasty, and out of the corner of my eye I saw a man holding a wooden club. Len's efforts to find some sign of life had failed, and another man appeared, clutching a large beer bottle in his hand.

Len was starting to stand up and as he did, his hand ran over the man's stomach. We were sure we saw him twitch. Len quickly put his hands on the man's sides and began tickling him. His feet jumped and he gave a faint laugh.

"Christ, he's shit-faced," I said.

Len continued tickling his sides for a few seconds, and then went to his feet. The instant he touched the bottoms of the man's feet, he began jerking from side to side and laughing. Len yelled, "Stink-o. Stink-o," a term the Okinawans understood, and kept tickling the man's feet. And now, almost everybody in the crowd was laughing.

We helped the man to a sitting position, and finally a few of his friends in the crowd came to help. We managed to get him on his feet, but it was obvious that he wouldn't be walking home. With a little effort, some of them picked him up and started to carry him down the street.

Len and I said goodnight, and a few people from the crowd came out and shook our hands as we started to walk away. We went back up the hill, knowing the bar was still open, and we were sure as hell going back for another cold beer. I don't mind telling you, at that moment that was probably the best beer I'd ever tasted. After downing about half of it, I turned to Len and said, "What made you tickle the guy?"

"Damned if I know." He hoisted his mug and said, "There was nothing else I could think of."

"Well, it sure saved us from an ass kicking, or worse."

Yet, it seemed that the Oyama Restaurant just couldn't let us go without one more confrontation. The fight gods must've been testing us because when we arrived for our next class it began to rain, and rain hard. Mr. Miyagi cancelled class, and we were more than a little disappointed when we left. But, we could stop by for a cold one on our way back to the barrack.

On this particular night, Terry Rock was with us when we went to the Restaurant. We took our usual seats at the small bar and ordered a big mug of Orion Beer. Our beers had just been put on the bar, when an Okinawan gentleman we recognized sat down on the only remaining barstool. We'd seen him there quite frequently, and although he didn't speak a work of English, we'd exchanged a cordial greeting each time. He was always very polite and quite soft-spoken, but Len and I had suspected that he was a lot more than he appeared to be. He dropped the small bag he usually had with him at the foot of his barstool, and ordered a beer.

Maybe it was the rain that brought them in, but before we'd even finished our first beer, eight or nine Okinawan men came in and sat down in the booths that lined the wall on the opposite side of the room. Two of the men were rather big for Okinawans, and one of them stood almost defiantly beside the booth and eyed the four of us seated at the bar. Almost immediately they were yelling to the waitresses to bring beer. I looked at Len, and he just shook his head.

When their beers were served the men wasted no time at all guzzling them down and yelling for more. Soon, there was no doubt that these guys were trouble, and looking for a place to raise hell. After round three, the biggest, and clearly the leader of the group got up and walked into the restroom. When he came out, he stood by the Jukebox and stared at us for a few seconds before saying something to his companions. Someone from behind us answered, and we assumed they were talking about us. He went back to his table, but didn't sit down.

I decided it was time to stand up. As soon as I got off the barstool, the entire party in the booths was up and coming toward us. But, it was the Okinawan gentleman seated at the end of the bar that they went to. The big guy snatched his bag off the floor, and tried to open it, but the man grabbed the bag, and said something to him. By now Len and Terry were standing, and the three of us were clutching empty beer mugs. Maybe we didn't really know the man, but we weren't going to stand by and let him deal with these thugs on his own.

The big thug continued to pull on the bag, but the gentleman seemed very calm about what was going on. The tough guy and his friends were starting to say things to the man, but he still looked very much composed. At one point, Len and I nodded to him hoping he understood we were going to step in and help him if things became physical. The big thug pulled again, and this time ripped the zipper open on the bag. A gi jacket and black belt fell out, and all of a sudden it was as though a hand grenade had fallen out of the bag.

The entire group backed up and began bowing to the man, and what they were uttering as they backed away was surely an apology. And, it was the big thug who dropped to the floor, picked up the jacket and belt, and put them back into the bag. He went back to his table, but they didn't stay long. They paid their bill, bowed to the man again and left.

When the last one disappeared down the stairs, the gentleman said something to Susie. A few moments later she turned to us and said, "He wants to thank you. He knows you were going to help him, and is very grateful. He would like to buy you a beer."

We tried to tell him it wasn't necessary, but he insisted, and we knew that by the custom of the Okinawan people, it would have been an insult to refuse his kind gesture. We accepted his offer that night, but the very next time we saw him, we bought the first round. Language difference or not, we still found a new friend.

Time suddenly seemed to be moving ahead much faster than we wanted, and it was getting close to Len's date of departure to return home to the U. S. The days were filled with all those last minute things—picking up gifts for the family, and making sure he had everything he wanted. And there were classes to attend, but before we knew it we were sitting around the table after class with tea and saying goodbye. Still, it wouldn't have been a complete farewell without a final stop at the Oyama Restaurant. Though the mood, as we drank our beer, that night was certainly rather subdued. A day later, Len was on a truck headed for Naha, and the ship that would take him home.

It felt odd attending class without Len, but I had to be sure and keep up our side of the promise we'd made when we started. We were going to stick it out to the very last day. There was one more kata I needed to learn to complete everything practiced in Mr. Miyagi's dojo. Oh, there were others, but these weren't part of the daily routine. When the time came to learn Gojushiho, it didn't take long at all. I'd been studying it carefully for over two months, and had already learned most of it by the time Nakanishi called me aside to teach me. With the completion of Gojushiho I reached the level required for black belt, though I didn't expect a promotion to that grade before I departed. There were still other tests I'd have to pass before Mr. Miyagi would write that certificate. Most of all, I think he wanted to be certain I'd continue practicing when I finally went home, and that I'd keep another promise—become a teacher.

Like Len, I found the final weeks went by much quicker than I'd anticipated. All of a sudden, there was only a week left on my tour, and I admit, that I felt sad knowing I'd be leaving something that had become such an intricate part of my life. I mean, not that I wouldn't continue practicing when I got home, it would just take some time to become accustomed to being on my own, and going through those routines. Then I'd also be leaving behind a group of very special friends, and I guess I was wondering if I'd ever see them again.

Before I knew it I was boarding a ship, and looking back over my shoulder. Then I was standing on deck, watching Okinawa slowly vanish, as if the ocean had swallowed the entire island.

Home in the U.S.A.

The moment Okinawa disappeared from sight, panic set in. I was sure I'd forget everything I'd learned before I reached the United States. There was no place to practice in private, and I certainly had no desire to be a showboat and go through katas in front of hundreds of other Marines, almost all of whom I didn't know.

The ship couldn't reach San Diego fast enough to suit me, but it finally arrived. Since I had less then four months remaining on my enlistment, (actually around 96 days) I was sent to a barrack to await final processing. It took five days, and on a Friday morning I was released from active duty. When I arrived at the airport, I soon learned the only direct flight to Baltimore wouldn't be leaving until around 10:00 PM. There were about a dozen of us waiting for flights out to various parts of the country, and we had time to kill. We sat and talked for a while, and then ended up in a restaurant sitting around a table over lunch and a beer. By five o'clock, there were only four of us left, and by 7:45 I was the last man nursing a beer and waiting.

I flew from San Diego to LA, and soon was on my way back to the East Coast. I couldn't sleep on the flight to BWI, (It was still Friendship Airport then) so I sat and talked with the stewardesses in the back of the plane. It was certainly a rude awakening when I stepped off the plane in Baltimore. The air temperature was a very beautiful five below zero, compared to the balmy 75 degrees I'd left behind in San Diego. To make matters even worse, I hadn't been in temperatures like this in almost three years. I was ready to take the next plane to any location with a warmer climate.

I enjoyed a good breakfast at home with my family, but I was too fired up to sleep. We talked for an hour or so, and I knew it was time for me to find out if I'd really forgotten everything I'd learned with Mr. Miyagi in Okinawa. I pulled my gi out of my duffel bag, put it on, and went down into the basement.

God, what a strange feeling it was limbering up alone, and trying to get myself in a frame of mind to workout in a place that suddenly seemed very unfamiliar. Although I'd been in this room hundreds, maybe thousands of times growing up, it just felt odd. The bottoms of my feet were thickly callused from the months of moving them over the dirt floor of Miyagi's dojo and, now, standing on the tile floor in my own home I felt out of place. But, I finally took a deep breath and began with what I'd learned my very first night with Mr. Miyagi. It took only a minute or two to push aside everything else that clouded my mind, and get into a rhythm that was now a part of me. The punches, kicks and blocks flowed as they should, and when I reached the last step of Gojushiho I found that old familiar satisfaction that I'd known at the conclusion of the classes in Okinawa. The ancient art I'd brought back, from what I considered my second homeland, was with me. For the moment at least, I relaxed a little. And yet, I knew I'd never be satisfied until I began keeping my word I'd given to Mr. Miyagi. I had to teach. I couldn't break my promise and destroy his faith in me.

I was ready to go upstairs and take a shower when I suddenly felt a very strange emptiness. For the first time in many months I wasn't going to sit down with my teacher, and friends after class for tea and cookies. I stood alone in the basement for a few minutes, recalling those nights, and how Len and I felt so out of place in the beginning. At first, we were the not so welcome gaijin, but in time we became a part of something that truly was very special. Mr. Miyagi had so often said that the class was a family and we became members of that family. Night after night, sitting around the small table and sipping green tea, we learned that karate was the bond that made us brothers. The bond was forged with aches, pains, a lot of sweat, a few drops of blood and "I'll be damned if I'll ever quit" determination. And now, pacing slowly around on a chilly tile floor half a world away, I realized just how much I missed my family in Okinawa.

***

I thought finding a few students would be easy. After all, I had written to some old friends and classmates telling them about my karate classes in Okinawa and my desire to open a small dojo when I returned home. Their responses to my letters had all been positive, and I was sure I'd have half a dozen eager students in no time at all. But, I quickly discovered that most of them had excuses, and so many other things to do. The one person who showed up wanted to learn everything in a single lesson, and we didn't get beyond the basics of punching. Needless to say, my first effort to start classes was a failure.

I kept asking neighbors and friends, and at last found two high school aged boys who wanted to begin karate classes. At least these two students were putting forth an effort to learn, and almost immediately I was seeing some of those doors open that Mr. Miyagi told me about. It was very different being completely in the teacher's role, but it certainly wasn't something that was unfamiliar, because I'd been put there already in Miyagi's class. Although I didn't know it at the time, I was actually preparing myself for the months and years ahead. I was learning a great deal about the role of the teacher, and what it would take to help my students become better.

In less then three months I was teaching only one student, but this young man, Charles "Chuck" Chaney seemed to have a stick with it attitude. He paid attention, was eager to learn and missed class only when high school studies demanded more of his time. A few others came and went, but Chuck proved to be "Mr. Reliable."

Of course, I'd been in touch with Len by telephone, and we were anxious to get together. In April 1966 I went to Rochester, New York to see Len. He'd just completed his academy training for the Rochester New York Sheriff's Department and, just like the last time I saw him, he was wearing a uniform. We went to his house, and suddenly it was like old times again, laughing and telling our "war stories" to his family while we sipped Jim Beam Kentucky Bourbon. Naturally, there'd be no parting ways without putting on our gis and working out. We went through our katas, and I taught him Gojushiho, the kata he didn't learn before leaving Okinawa, and then we spent time pounding away at each other in self-defense drills. It was good to spend time with my friend again, and for a few days it was almost like being back in Okinawa.

***

I was keeping in touch with Mr. Miyagi by writing regularly, and giving him progress reports on my "class." He was pleased that I was teaching and his advice was still coming with his letters. One afternoon I received a package from him and was surprised, and humbled when I opened it. It contained a black belt and a certificate, officially promoting me to Shodan (First Degree Black Belt). He informed me that my time requirements had been met for that rank and he expected that I would continue to practice and teach. Yet, I'm sure it was a lot more than a time requirement that had been met. I kept my word and became a teacher.

At the same time, I learned that a First Degree Black Belt was not a license that authorized me to promote anyone to any rank whatsoever. This was, and still is a rule adhered to by the Okinawa Shorin Ryu Karate Do Association. I would have to reach a grade of Yondan, (Fourth Degree Black Belt) and be grated permission by my sensei to promote. Any member of my class who met eligibility requirements for promotion could only receive a promotion through Mr. Miyagi after my recommendation. That also meant that I would be holding my students to a very rigid standard, because I certainly wasn't going to ask Miyagi to write a certificate for anyone who was not highly qualified. Somehow I think he knew this.

Chuck was promoted to brown belt, and shortly thereafter I was promoted to Nidan (Second Degree Black Belt). By now a few others had joined class, upping my student count to four. Chuck was teaching as well, and now it was his turn to see those hidden doors swing open. I sometimes wondered how Miyagi Sensei could have foreseen the events he predicted, but I only had to remind myself that he too had been through the same things. I couldn't help but ask myself, from time to time, what secrets the future still held.

Soon I had another new student, Richard "Rick" Lubinski and almost immediately he reminded me of Nakanishi. He was very strong, with powerful punches and kicks, and I knew that if he persevered he'd be an exceptional student. And, he didn't let me down.

Before long we moved the classes to the basement of Rick's house because he had more room there. Within our first days of working out in Rick's basement, we had a few others ask to join class and, I guess it was bound to happen. The first "bad ass" arrived.

We'd been working out for about an hour, and took a quick break to get a drink of water. While Rick was getting his drink, I was talking with another student. That's when I was grabbed by the shoulders and the man was saying, "I wanna see just how much you know." He wasn't exactly a little guy, and he probably outweighed me by 75-85 pounds. He tried to put me in a bear hug, but I was a little faster than he anticipated, and he was unable to trap my arms. I strongly suggested that it would be a good idea if he let go, but he only laughed and said, "You're supposed to be such a bad ass, you get out of it."

A few seconds later he was on the floor with tears welling up in his eyes. I helped him to his feet, showed him the door, and told him not to bother coming back. When Rick learned what happened, I had to stop him from going outside and taking the guy apart. He said, "Nobody comes in here and starts a fight with my teacher. If they wanna fight, they start with me." And, I have absolutely no doubt whatsoever that Rick would've shown far less mercy than I did.

Our class reached about eight members at just around the time I was accepted to the police academy. I was hired by the Howard County Police Department in July 1967 and was assigned to work in the communications section while waiting for the police academy classes to begin. Within just a few days of my hiring, I met Robert "Sweet Bobby" Moore, and like Len Neidert, Bob and I became instant friends. Bob had begun his martial arts training in Japan in the art of Judo, and was a Fifth Degree Black Belt when we met. You wanted Bob on your side when there was trouble, and he was the kind of man that if you truly wanted to hurt him, you'd have to hit him with a truck. And, it would probably take a very large truck hitting him at about 80 miles per hour, and then you might want to consider trying to hit him while he was looking the other way. If not, he just might rip your truck in half.

When I entered the academy, I still managed to keep up with my karate training and my required studies for classes. I had set a personal goal for myself when I entered the academy—I wanted to graduate at the top of my class.

While hitting the books and studying criminal law, motor vehicle law, constitutional law, and first aid I discovered something new. I found a new discipline in my study habits. My mind didn't wander like it seemed to do in high school. I could concentrate and maintain a focus on the material, and I was able to see things clearer than ever before. At first, I wondered why, and then I just smiled when I remembered what Mr. Miyagi had so often said. "Karate training will become a part of your everyday life. Things will be different now. You have more discipline." Once again, the words of my personal prophet were coming true and on graduation day they rang louder than ever. I achieved my goal.

At about the same time, Chuck was preparing for college and before I graduated from the police academy it was down to just Rick and I. It remained that way for several months, and then we started to get the next wave of new students at about the same time I was promoted to Sandan (Third Degree Black Belt, January 1968).

A long time friend of Rick's, Charlie Murray, joined class and after we gave a demonstration at the Holiday Health Spa, (now Bally's) we picked up three additional students. Among those new arrivals was Howard Zachmann, who would win the title of Mr. Maryland the following year. Needless to say he wasn't lacking in strength or size, sporting about a 54-inch chest and close to 19-inch arms. Rick and I just had to convince him not to worry about his power, but to work constantly on flexibility and speed. It took time, but Zack or "Z" as I called him then, and still do, began to see the results of the stretching. He improved his speed working on his own time at home with a boxer's speed bag. And, as Mr. Miyagi had predicted, more and more doors were opening for me. The more I taught the more I learned.

When "Z" joined the class, two young brothers, Frank and Vince, also joined. They were complete opposites, with Frank being very athletic and a quick study. Vince, on the other hand, seemed to have very little athletic ability, and had great difficulty in learning. At the end of their first class, their father informed me that Vince was a slow learner, and was also having problems with his studies in school.

By now we'd moved our classes to Mt. Hebron High School in Ellicott City, after working out the arrangements with James R. McCrumb, the Principal. With the school, and its main and auxiliary gymnasiums at our disposal three days a week, we were able to accept more students. We reached a peak of about 15 students and that number held for some time.

Everybody was doing well, and learning as expected, but Vince was struggling and lagging far behind. Still, that didn't mean that we were about to give up on him. Zack started working with him at the end of each class, trying to help him with pushups and sit-ups. And, it was a tremendous effort for Vince to perform even one pushup or sit-up. Yet, he never complained, he just kept trying, and it seemed as though he was beginning to look forward to his after class workouts. "Z" wasn't a heartless taskmaster by any definition, but he certainly knew how to motivate and inspire others around him. He was a special education teacher in Prince George's County, and that always shocked people when they learned his profession. They couldn't picture a man of his stature working in classes with special needs children. But, he became Vince's personal physical training mentor, and week after week they'd spend time working together.

Vince began to show progress all around. He was learning

his katas, and finding that working with "Z" was paying off. He finally reached five push-ups and sit-ups, and his father was pleased with his improvement. In class, he never complained about others who joined long after him and soon passed him by, or those who were promoted ahead of him. He didn't ask if he was going to be promoted, or when he'd get a belt that was any color other than white. He just kept working harder and trying to improve. There was another noted improvement as well—his elementary school studies. His father told me that his teachers were seeing a new attitude in his approach to his schoolwork. His grades and attention span were steadily improving. And the words of Miyagi Sensei were ringing in my ears once more. "Karate will become a part of everything you do."

After our Sunday morning classes, Rick, Charlie Murray, Zack, Frank and a few others began playing a few minutes of basketball. It wasn't a game, but more a time for them to test their skills at getting the ball through the net. Vince, at first, stood on the sidelines and watched, until one of them tossed the ball to him and told him to take a shot. His initial effort proved that, like karate, his basketball needed a lot of work. The ball travelled but a few feet before falling to the floor, but Charlie tossed it back and told him to shoot again. His second effort wasn't much better than the first. Still, every now and then, somebody would toss the ball to him and encourage him to try again.

"Z" kept working with Vince on his push-ups and sit-ups and, after a time, there was a good deal of progress noted in his performance. Vince reached eight and finally 10 of each. But, Zack wasn't through with him. He kept after him to do better and before long Vince was heading for 15 and up. Zack also took time to work with him on his self-defense and sparring, which Vince also looked forward to. Of course, he especially liked the fact that "Z" would let him land his punches and kicks, absorbing the blows on his back, shoulders and stomach. And, it seemed to go a very long way as a confidence builder.

Vince worked hard enough to earn a green belt, and he was promoted according to his efforts and his progress. His rules for promotion were the same as those for anyone else, and his endeavors were rewarded accordingly. He was advanced through his katas at a much slower pace than everyone else, but it was a pace that enabled him to learn and retain the routines. I can't explain how or why I knew this when he first began classes, but I realized that pushing him along just to try and keep him up with the others wasn't the right way. In fact, he probably wouldn't have learned, and soon would have become discouraged and quit. Maybe it was as Mr. Miyagi had said. "As you teach, you'll also gain much wisdom."

As I've said before, I held everyone to a very high standard, but their advancement was based solely on what they accomplished individually. No student was, or is, judged on the merits of another's abilities. It wouldn't have been fair to hold any student to Rick's level of overall excellence, or Zack's strength, in order for them to advance. If that were the case I'd still have only two black belts.

The Sunday basketball "games" had become a weekly event, and Vince was there on the sidelines waiting for his cue to join in. After a few minutes somebody would pass the ball to him and he'd try to loft it toward the basket. As always, it sailed a few feet and hit the floor, but never once did he seem discouraged. Rick, Charlie or Zack would toss the ball back to him again, and encourage him to take another shot.

I spent most of those Sunday's watching the game along with Vince's father. I liked watching, because there was so much more going on out there on the court. It wasn't a world-class event, with top athletes competing for a spot on a team, or to bolster their egos. There was a group of men out on the floor, playing a game for their own enjoyment, who were also doing something that maybe they didn't even realize. They were helping Vince gain more confidence in himself. He wasn't told to go away and leave them alone because he was a poor player who was taking up their time. He was urged to come out and join them and, week after week, he was given dozens of chances to take a shot at the basket.

Those weeks on the basketball court led up to months, and I couldn't tell you how many shots Vince had taken and never come close to hitting the backboard, let alone making a basket. He was just thrilled to have the opportunity to play with the "big guys" and take a few shots. As the months went by, I'm sure he'd taken hundreds of shots and missed, but nobody was going to deny him a part in the game. It was becoming obvious that the push-ups and sit-ups were working, because he was definitely getting stronger, and his shots going a little higher, but he was no closer to the backboard or basket.

His father was happier though because of his schoolwork. Vince was showing even more progress in his studies and his grades steadily improved. Rick, Charlie, Zack and I also found that Vince was doing his push-ups and sit-ups at home. At first, he was only doing them when he was in the dojo, but his father said he'd been taking a few minutes almost every day to workout.

During the next couple of Sunday games we could also see Vince's coordination on the court was improving. He was becoming more a part of the game, "guarding" and "blocking" his opponent and slapping at the ball. Because of this, the tempo of the game started to pick up a little, and it was beginning to look a little more competitive. That didn't mean Vince was being denied opportunities to shoot. It was quite the contrary. It looked like he was being give more chances to take shots.

It was during one of those Sunday games that Charlie Murray spun and tossed the ball to Vince. He was about a step or two behind the foul line and everybody began yelling, "Shoot, Vince, shoot." He calmly launched the ball toward the basket, and the instant it left his hands, everyone in the gym froze in their tracks. The ball was spinning up and toward the basket while everyone stood frozen to the floor and watched its path. When it started its downward arc, I think every last one of us held our breath and prayed. A second later the ball hit the back of the rim and dropped through the net. For the next 15 or 20 seconds it was as if Vince had just beaten the buzzer to win the NCAA title. But, it wasn't Vince doing the screaming and yelling it was his "teammates" cheering for him.

Vince looked more like he'd been taking the winning shot every day of his life, and he was as calm as I had ever seen anyone when he walked over to his father. Then a big smile lit up his face when he said, "Hey, dad, I made a basket." His father could barely whisper, "I know," and he certainly couldn't hide his tears.

That Sunday every one of us was given a lesson in what

having heart can do for a person. And, there were so many more lessons that belonged to the "game." Nobody had given up on Vince, but more importantly, Vince hadn't given up on himself. Nobody told him he couldn't play basketball, or that he'd never make a shot. And, it didn't matter that he'd probably missed hundreds of shots, the only thing that mattered was the basket he made. Everybody kept giving him the ball and telling him to do it, and I have a feeling that in spite of the misses, he never doubted for one minute that one day he'd hit the bucket. When I left the building that day I couldn't help but wonder if Mr. Miyagi might be smiling in Okinawa and saying, "See, I told you, you can learn from your students." Of course he was right, but I think all of us learned a lot from each other about caring and encouraging our students. And everybody who had spent time with Vince indeed learned something from him about heart.

In the coming months, however, I was still going to learn another very valuable lesson from Vince. Once again, it seemed as though Sunday was the designated day for being educated. We had completed our kata practice and broken down into smaller groups to concentrate on newer katas or defensive tactics. I had given Vince the task of observing one student perform the Naihanchi katas, and was occupied with Zack and a few others in sparring practice. I'm not sure how long I'd been keeping an eye on the fighting drills, but I noticed Vince standing a few feet away, and I walked over to him.

I asked him what was wrong, and he said, "Nothing. He's got the katas down pretty good. Do you want me to teach him Seisan?"

I was shocked. I'd never asked, or for that matter, thought about asking Vince to teach. He'd had so many problems over the years learning, that I guess it never occurred to me that he could teach. He'd been a green belt for a long time, and by now had reached the minimum requirements for brown belt.

"Do you think you can teach him the kata?" I said.

"Sure," he answered, without hesitation.

"I'll make you a deal, Vince," I said, wondering if he could really teach the kata. "You teach him the kata—and you know it

47

doesn't hafta be perfect the first time they learn it, and I'll promote you to brown belt."

He didn't even blink. He just said, "Okay," turned, went back and started to teach the kata.

Normally, I'd have anyone who wasn't paying attention to what they were told to do in the corner doing push-ups. But, this was no ordinary day. Everybody there that Sunday had spent a lot of time working with Vince, and I know they were asking themselves the same question I was asking myself. "Can he really do it?" And, even knowing the consequences for not doing as they were told, they were watching Vince. On this particular Sunday I wasn't going to stop, or punish them.

There we were, once again, seeing first hand what heart and perseverance could do. Step by step he took his student through the kata and, even though not a word was uttered by a soul, I could hear everyone one of them saying, "Come on, Vince, do it. You can do it." And right there, with almost 30 witnesses, he never missed a beat, or made a mistake while teaching the kata. At the end of class I announced his promotion, and he was treated to a well-deserved ovation.

As always, I was the last to leave the building that day, and it was time to think about lessons learned. Again, a student had taught me something. Never underestimate anyone's courage, their heart, and belief in themselves. At that point, I realized that I should've known that, and probably better than anyone else. After all, I'd been told time and again that I couldn't do various things, but I managed to beat the odds and do them, including earning a black belt. Of course, I thought about Mr. Miyagi, the prophet, and I think I just shook my head. I had written to him about Vince, and now I had another chapter come true that he could add to his list of prophecies.

I had kept him informed about a lot of things in my life, my karate class, the students and their progress, and especially my job. I still valued his opinions and certainly his teaching, and more than logical concepts had a tremendous impact on my life. He didn't believe in fighting, except as a means to defend yourself, loved ones or friends from harm. When I wrote and told him of my first fight on the job, his reply was simple and to the point. "It was necessary to defend yourself. You did what was right." At the same time, I couldn't help but recall the story he told Len and I of his fending off an attacker who had chased his wife home.

His wife, Atsuko, had been out, and was returning home when a drunken American soldier started following her. As she began walking down the darkened street to their home, he attempted to grab her, but she broke away and fled. He chased her down the street and right to the house. As she ran into the house, he attempted to follow, but Mr. Miyagi heard the commotion and hurried to see what was wrong. He stepped between the soldier and his wife, pushed the man back and said, "Please go away." The man rushed at him, but again was pushed back out the door as Miyagi said, "Please go away." This time the man picked up a piece of wood that was lying on the ground and tried to strike Miyagi. Miyagi parried the blow, struck the man with a powerful back-fist, knocking him unconscious and opening a gash that ran from just above his lip to a point under his left eye. Although he had every right to defend his wife and home, he said to us, "I couldn't sleep for almost three days because of what I did." After he finished the story, Len and I tried to tell him he would've been justified if he'd killed the man because of what the drunk intended to do to his wife. But, Mr. Miyagi said he still felt guilty over what he'd done.

When teaching I often spoke of Mr. Miyagi, and told students of the things he'd said to me. I tried to pass along his philosophy, and add a few of my own thoughts as well. I began telling my students that anything was possible, as long as they believed in themselves and put forth their best efforts when striving for a goal. As time went by, I insisted that the words "I can't do it" would no longer be a part of their vocabulary. And, with the younger children I told them to leave "I can't do it" outside the dojo.

I also found Mr. Miyagi's philosophy and teachings were becoming even more a part of me, and it was my turn to smile when one of my students finally asked about testing for belts. I told him exactly what Mr. Miyagi had said to me. "Every day is a test. One day is not sufficient to test for a belt. So, every day in my class is a test." And, that certainly held a great deal of logic. If I have to test a student after they've spent months, or years in my class to determine their qualifications for promotion, I certainly haven't done my job as a teacher. They learn as I teach and if I can't see their skills, strength and desire improving with each class, as a teacher I'm a failure

I did have a test, but it wasn't for the purpose of determining a student's skill, or qualification for a rank. The main purpose of the test was to find how well they could handle pressure, and everyone deals with stress in different ways. But, let's face it, when the time comes and you find yourself cornered, and you have no choice but to fight, the stress level might be off the scale. I figured that a person who could handle the pressure of being called up in front of their peers to perform, would fare well if they had to defend themselves. It's often easier to speak, or demonstrate a task in front of total strangers, than to stand before even a dozen people who know you well.

I had only one student who failed miserably the first time he stepped up in front of his peers. He couldn't perform a kata, or execute even a basic self-defense technique. It was as if the fear of being called upon to do things he'd done for months on end with the class were erased from his memory when he stood separate from them. Yet, he'd also led the class in katas and taught other students. And, this same person often performed musical solos in front of hundreds of people. For weeks, I made him come out in front of the class and lead everyone through the katas. I'd also have him perform a kata, demonstrate self-defense techniques, and spar while everyone watched. Eventually he overcame his fears and went on to earn a brown belt.

***

Rick Lubinski was a strong force as a teacher and a student. He indeed possessed many of Nakanishi's qualities, and was an inspiration to so many in the class. It was a shock to all of us when we learned that Rick would be leaving to take a job in Ohio. His absence would certainly have a big impact on the class, and leave a void that would be very difficult to fill. Before he left for Ohio he too was promoted to San Dan, and the class presented him with a trophy for his contributions to them and his devotion to the true spirit of the martial arts.

In January 1971 I was promoted to the rank of Yondan (4th Degree Black Belt), and at the same time Mr. Miyagi informed me that I would be allowed to award promotions without having to recommend them through him. He said I had permission to write up certificates of promotion, which would also be recognized by him and the Okinawa Shorin Ryu Karate Do Association.

In the spring of that year Daniel Simons joined the class, with Bruce Charity and Will Adams following in January and March of 1972, and took the first steps that marked the start of a long journey. Much like me, I don't think they realized in those early days just how long they would continue to come to classes, but it was obvious that a strong bond of friendship was forming. More than any time since I began teaching, I was finding that family atmosphere around the class.

Will and Bruce became friends quickly, and I think the fact that they both drove Chevrolet products helped open the door to their friendship. Bruce owned a Camaro and Will had his prized Corvette. Of course, Will would take every available opportunity to point out to Bruce, that his Vette had a beer rack. Actually, it was a luggage rack, but Will insisted that he'd never transported anything on it other than a case of beer. Within no time at all they were seen driving along U. S. Route 40, top down, and a case of Tuborg Gold strapped to the rack. Of course, in those days it wasn't against the law to sip a beverage while driving, and one or the other would reach back and pluck a bottle or can from the case. Will always said the only reason they drove together in his Vette was because of his beer rack.

Within a few months they found another reason to fire the verbal barbs at each other. If they drove somewhere to meet for a beer, they would park their cars side by side. The very first time they met at a pub, and later returned to get their cars, Bruce's Camaro was gone. Somebody had helped themselves to his deep red, prized possession. It was found with little harm done, and soon they met again for a beer, but at a different bar. The end results though were the same. Bruce's Camaro was stolen, but this time it was recovered stripped and, of all places, in Will's neighborhood. It was put back together, but it was certainly jinxed. It was hit by a deer and finally caught fire, but only after Bruce cancelled the Comprehensive Section of his insurance policy because of college costs. He gave in and bought a green Corvette and, of course, with a beer rack. After all, why should Will be the only one to boast of such a luxury?

Dan Simons also had problems holding on to his new Chevy Camaro and would often leave his college dormitory, or one of his weekly musical gigs and find his car gone. And it does seem strange that Will stopped by to listen to Danny's band one evening, parked next to Danny's Camaro, and it was stolen. But, it was definitely beginning to look like car thieves followed Will, and stole whatever car he parked beside. Danny wouldn't let go of his love for the Camaro, and his son Kyle now drives one. Although I don't think Kyle is having it stolen on a weekly basis. But, back in those early days the car thefts always gave Danny, Bruce and Will something to joke about over a cold beer.

Some time when joking about their cars being stolen, they usually ended up talking about another class member who'd fallen victim to car thieves. Rick Lubinski had purchased a brand new Chevy Camaro in 1968, the year of their debut.

Rick and Charlie Murray drove downtown for their classes at the University of Baltimore, and certainly were looked at with many envious eyes as they drove by. One evening they were walking on to the parking lot after class, when they saw Rick's Camaro going by them into the evening breeze never to be seen again. Of course, everyone always said they only wished Rick and Charlie could've arrived about a minute sooner. They were certain the Baltimore City Police would have been more than pleased with the bloody jigsaw puzzle that Rick and Charlie would've probably made of the thieves. And, I would agree that Rick was certainly more than capable of dismantling a car thief one-body part at a time.

In Okinawa it had been green tea and cookies after class, but here we began to go out to the Pizza Hut for cold beer and pizza. The first couple of times there were only three or four who made the trip, but as time passed the numbers sometimes soared as high as twenty. The Pizza Hut never complained about our group, especially Stephanie, who became our regular waitress. She was certain that Tuesday and Thursday evenings would bring her cheerful greetings and a very generous tip. When a brand new manager was hired and objected to our laughing and joking on his first night, Stephanie rather quickly put him in his place. The manager might have been more than a little uptight about our fun group, but Stephanie wasn't going to lose her best customers. We went to the same Pizza Hut so often that we said we'd bought and paid for every table and brick in the building.

Every now and then we would alter our routine and go to a nearby Pappy's Restaurant in Ellicott City just for a change of pace. This particular restaurant had had some problems with a number of the locals coming in and starting fights after a few beers. It reached the point where the manager decided he would only serve beer by the mug instead of by the pitcher.

One evening after class, about 16 of us went there and had just ordered our first round of beer, pizza and sandwiches when at least 10 of the troublemakers came in. They went immediately to the table where the manager was seated, surrounded him, and began yelling at him. At first we just watched and listened to what was going on, but it soon looked as if things were about to turn physical. Without anyone ever saying a word, or giving a signal, 16 chairs slid back simultaneously from the tables, and all of us stood up. There were at least five police officers in our group, but when we moved toward the troublemakers, everybody went. It was apparent that the young men didn't see us when they came in, because a number of us had arrested some of them at one time or another. We escorted them outside without incident and instructed the manager to call the police station and tell them there was a problem at the restaurant. Outside only one of them refused to leave the restaurant grounds before on duty officers arrived. And, he should've left when he was given the opportunity, because a few obscenities later he found himself in the back of Officer Bruce Harrison's squad car and headed to the station.

It was right around this time as well that Kung Fu began its television run. With the airing of Kung Fu, I found new students flocking to our class by the dozens. There were evenings when, as many as 15 or more people would arrive, saying they wanted to join and learn. Our Sunday morning classes at Mt. Hebron High School were conducted in the main gymnasium. In the first weeks of Kung Fu, we had three rows of students lining the entire length of the basketball court. Enthusiasm and expectations were very high in their early days, but when it became obvious that many months and years of hard work were required to be a better than average student, class size dropped dramatically. A few hung on, hoping to be the one who could become a "master" quicker than most, but soon they too fell by the wayside.

One evening, eight students from another karate school came by and said they'd heard about my class and wanted to join. They said they'd heard I had a reputation for being very strict, but also for teaching so much more than was available elsewhere. At the end of the first hour seven of them left. The remaining student told me the class was far too disciplined for their liking, but he wasn't leaving. He lasted for the evening, and that was the last I saw of him.

Early one evening a young man stopped by and asked for the teacher. One of the students pointed him in my direction and he beat a very fast pace to where I was standing. He immediately said, "I don't have a lotta time to waste coming to classes. Just teach me a few kill moves and I'll be on my way."

After I stopped laughing, I tried to explain that what he was looking for wasn't something he was going to learn in a matter of minutes. I told him it required a great deal of practice, time and patience to become a skilled martial artist. But, that was not a satisfactory answer and he practically ran out the door to search for another dojo.

I had learned from Miyagi Sensei not to be disappointed, because students quit, and some do so quickly. He was absolutely right when he said some are not meant to practice karate, because of the strict discipline and its demands. Learning is more than mere repetition of movements. There is a joining and maturing of the body, mind and spirit, and it takes the combined elements of all three to be a true practitioner of the art. The skills and discipline are much more than physical exercise. One can exercise by weight lifting or running. Yet, even to do those things correctly and regularly requires discipline and spirit. Learning karate, or any martial art, requires a commitment of complete focus to master even the basics, because the basics are the building blocks for what must be accomplished on the road ahead.

I think many of those Kung Fu idealist became disillusioned when they found they weren't going to be sparring, and learning how to use various weapons during their first days and weeks of class. They didn't understand the "crawl before you walk and run" concept also applied to the learning of martial arts. I've repeatedly told my students you have to learn to punch, kick and block correctly before you do anything else. And, I've always believed "you should never build up an opponents confidence by blocking his punches with your face." Still, some couldn't seem to grasp the reality of that concept.

***

I often took time to reflect on my days in Okinawa, and how Mr. Miyagi and his teaching had changed my life. I had begun college classes and, like the police academy, I found a very strong discipline in my study habits, which certainly helped me to attain excellent grades. Then too, there was the knowledge that what I'd learned from Mr. Miyagi, and my continued practice and teaching, had given me the edge in a number of situations.

My very first fight, as a police officer, was a test in more than one way. I was sent to a home on St. Paul Street in Ellicott City for a domestic argument, and I was already well aware of the man's reputation as a police fighter. Indeed, it was a call that would require a back-up officer, but on this night there were none available due to a fatal car collision, and other serious calls in the county. So, going into the house and facing the man would be my responsibility, and mine alone. Prior to my arrival at the residence, the dispatcher informed me that the man had assaulted his wife, and his two sons and daughter were also home. Both sons already had criminal records and I wasn't sure whom they were siding with, but often times even the victims turn on the police in these cases.

The moment I went into the house I knew I was going to have to fight the man. He'd had a few beers, and his attitude and body language said "Rookie, I'm gonna kick your ass." And, this being our very first face-to-face meeting, I could see that he felt he had a decided advantage. The instant I told him he was under arrest for assaulting his wife, he grabbed a claw hammer from the table and started to raise it. Much to his surprise, and that of everyone else in the room, the hammer was just as quickly sailing through the open door. He calmed down for a few moments, but then he was showing me a razor. In hindsight I probably should've just shot him and today, believe me I would, but I shocked him once more, took the razor away and tossed it out the door. His wife, both sons and his daughter backed out of the room and closed the door. The man sat down, and again I told him he was under arrest. This time he said the only way he was going was if I took him out, and a second later he sprang out of the chair. His daughter opened the door just as the first kick slammed into his groin. She screamed as the second kick caught him in the chest, and both sons fled when I struck him in the back of the neck with a hammer fist. Just as I finished handcuffing him, a back-up officer arrived and said, "What happened?"

Before I could answer his wife said, "My husband just got his ass kicked that's what happened."

It was much later that I realized going against a man with an edged weapon wasn't the best, or smartest thing to do. Even with the training I'd had, I was running a great risk of very serious injury or death by disarming him, but at the time shooting him didn't even cross my mind. Maybe it was just as I've often said over the years since. "I was young and foolish then."

In two other instances only months apart I'd disarmed two men, one who was armed with a pistol, and the other with a double-barrelled shotgun. In both cases there was no time to think about what was happening. What I did was a matter of instinctive reflex, and there was absolutely no time whatsoever to draw my weapon and either shoot, or hope for a standoff that would eventually end peacefully. In reality, in both cases it would have been impossible to draw my weapon and fire. It was the countless months, and years of repetition that had trained me to react without having to think about what needed to be done, or how to do it. And, I've said it thousands of times. "If you have to think about what to do before you react, you've already lost."

The first instance occurred on a cold December night, and several days before Christmas. It was a Saturday evening, and calls being dispatched were steady early in the shift. I was working in the Criminal Investigations Division by then, and still relatively new in the division, having been assigned there in late August as a member of the recently formed drug team. I was in the Columbia area of the county when a call crackled over the radio, reporting a suicide off of

Sebring Drive. I didn't rush to the scene, presuming that it wasn't necessary because all indications were that a man had taken his own life with a firearm.

I was one of the last to arrive at the location, and the first thing I noticed was the police officers and fire and rescue members standing around talking. Next, I saw a man lying on the ground face down, with his arms slightly above his head. I quickly noted that the man was about 6' 3" and probably weighed somewhere in the area of 235 pounds or better. And, it was obvious he'd spent a good deal of his spare time in the gym. Lying only inches from his right hand was a semi-automatic pistol. I was surprised that the weapon hadn't been picked up and safely secured in one of the police cars, but I wasn't the officer in the charge.

I was turning to walk away when I saw the man raise his head and reach for the pistol. Suddenly, everyone stopped talking and stared at him, but no one moved to stop him from grabbing the weapon. Although everyone was much closer to him than I was, I darted by them and dove to the ground beside him, pressing my left shoulder against his right shoulder, pinning him down. I grasped his right arm above the wrist with my left hand, grabbed the pistol with my right and, with a quick twist, snatched it from his hand. I was on my feet and moving away from him, with the weapon, when the others finally rushed to control him. A few minutes later I handed the pistol to another detective and left.

There were a number of careless errors made in that instance, but the primary mistakes were not securing the weapon and checking for signs of life. The combination of the two could have been fatal to police or fire and rescue personnel.

The second incident took place on a Sunday evening and only about two months after the first. Jim Robey and I were on Shepherds Lane when a call was dispatched reporting a shooting at a residence only a half-mile from our location. We were the first to arrive, and a man, who was standing outside and near the back door of the house, greeted us. We immediately asked if he was okay and where the victim was. He said there was nothing wrong, and that someone must have made a crank call. We talked with him for a few more minutes, because he was very evasive in some of his answers.

Yet, he continued to insist that nothing was wrong, but when we asked to go inside, he refused to give us permission.

It was at about that time that a car pulled into the driveway and a woman got out of the car, asked us who we were, and why we were there. When we explained the reason for our presence, she asked if her husband was okay. Of course, the man who had first met us said he was alone in the house. A few quick questions of the woman and we learned that her husband had been threatening to commit suicide for the past month or so. She asked us to go inside and check on the condition of her husband.

We went into the house and immediately began searching for the woman's husband. Jim Robey walked into another room, after passing threw a heavy beaded curtain. Within a matter of seconds he was yelling, "Jim! Jim, get in here."

I pushed through the curtains and, it seemed that out of nowhere, both barrels of a .12 gauge shotgun were only inches from my face. I caught the shotgun by the barrel and stuffed it under the man's chin as I grabbed for the stock. I took a few hurried steps back from him, rotating the gun and twisting it out of his hands. A few moments later I opened the weapon and found two live shells in the chambers.

Some time later, and again, on a Saturday evening, I had an encounter with an armed man. By this time I had been promoted to Corporal and was a Squad Leader on the 4th Platoon. It was a very warm evening in mid June and we were busy from the start. It was around 6:00 PM when the dispatcher called me and said a man had just tried to shoot his wife at a home on Triadelphia Mill Road. The wife had fled the residence and was currently at a neighbor's house, but the husband had remained in their home.

I ordered other officers to meet me while I talked to the wife. She told me her husband had had a few drinks and they soon began arguing, at which time he shot at her with, what she described as a small pistol. When officers arrived, she described the house and told us there was another home, a barn and several other buildings around it. We asked if he had other guns in the house and she said, "No." She was asked the same question again, because it was difficult to believe that anyone residing in a farmhouse in rural Howard County had only one small handgun. She insisted that was the only weapon in the house.

We tried to call him several times, hoping we could talk him out of the house, but he wouldn't answer the telephone. Using the driveway to approach the area around the house and other buildings would leave us at his mercy. So, I decided we would move in on foot and try to talk him out of the house.

Officers Owen Smith, Larry Horn, Bill Seifert, Scott Buck and I began walking toward the home, using trees and tall grass to conceal our approach. When we entered the boundaries of the property, the home the woman described was immediately in front of us. Larry Horn and Bill Seifert moved to the right to try and get positions at the side and rear of the house. Within seconds there was a commotion and Owen Smith and Larry Horn were yelling that the man was on our left with a gun.

I looked to my left and the man was standing on the porch of the house—the house where he was not supposed to be. He was also aiming either a rifle or shotgun at me—a gun he wasn't supposed to have. Fortunately, I only had to take one step to get behind a very large, and certainly welcome, Oak tree.

Now, seeing that he was armed with more than just a small handgun, it was time to reassess the situation. And certainly the big question was "How many other weapons does he have?" As for us, we were armed only with .38 caliber revolvers, which clearly put us at a tactical disadvantage. I had enough officers to maintain a safe perimeter and keep the situation contained and decided to ask for the SWAT (Tactical) Team to respond.

I immediately discovered one major problem was radio communication, or lack thereof. Our radio system at the time was very antiquated and my first request for the Tactical Team to the dispatcher received a response of "10-9" or unable to copy. Repeat your message. I keyed the mic and said, "The subject has a rifle pointed at us. Requesting the Tactical Team at our location."

Again there was a response of "10-9." I repeated my radio transmission over and over, until I finally lost patience with the entire process. I took a deep breath, keyed the mic again and yelled, "He's got a goddamn rifle pointed at us."

There was a long pause before the dispatcher said, "10-4 on the subject pointing a rifle at you."

Now that that issue was out of the way, I turned my attention back to man on the porch holding the weapon. I ordered him to put the weapon down. He refused, but he was no longer aiming the weapon in my direction. He had lowered it to a point where it was trained on the ground several feet in front of him.

I told him again to put the weapon down and he yelled back, "You put your gun down." I almost laughed, but suddenly I called back to him. "I won't put it on the ground, but I'll put it in the holster if you'll lean your gun against the porch rail." A few seconds later he took a step to his left and leaned the gun against the railing.

Although he moved away from the gun, he was still close enough to grab it. I was about to ask him to step off the porch when he said, "I wanna talk to you. Come up here and I'll talk to you."

That wasn't my first choice, but he said he wanted to talk to me. If I ignored his request, it could have sent him into a rage and had him opening fire on us. So, I decided to take a chance and do as he asked. I holstered my revolver and told Larry Horn to circle around and try to move closer to the house from the man's left. As soon as Larry started to move, I stepped out from behind the tree and began walking very slowly toward the front porch. While keeping an eye on the man and talking with him, I was also asking Owen Smith, Bill Seifert and Scott Buck if they had clear lines of fire if he reached for the gun. While each called back, telling me they had direct shots, I was still carrying on a conversation with the suspect. At that point, I told Owen, Bill and Scott that if the man reached for the gun, I was going to drop to the ground to give them clearer shots. Still today, I don't know how it was possible to talk with the suspect and communicate my intentions to the officers behind me. I guess under the circumstances, anything was possible.

As I neared the steps to the porch, I saw Larry Horn sprint to the side of the house. A few seconds later I was standing at the steps, looking up at the suspect. Suddenly he smiled. "I like you," he said.

"You've got balls and I wanna shake your hand."

He leaned forward and extended his hand toward me. That's when I knew I had him. I reached up, brushed the palm of his hand with mine and an instant later grabbed him by the wrist. With a quick turn to my right and a snap downward with my hand, I pulled him from the porch. He hit the ground with both feet in front of me as I continued turning to my right. I struck him in the back of the head with my left elbow and drove him to the ground. By that time Larry Horn was leaping over the porch railing and a moment later we had the man in handcuffs.

Owen Smith unloaded the gun, which was leaning against the porch rail, telling us it was a .12 gauge shotgun. Through an open window, he noticed another weapon. We went into the house and found several shotguns and high-powered rifles, all of which were loaded and placed by open windows on the first floor. There was also extra ammo at the ready for each weapon.

The realization hit home rather quickly and bluntly, that had he started shooting instead of choosing to challenge us verbally, there could have been a blood bath. And the blood being spilled would have certainly been ours. He clearly held the edge in superior firepower and the element of surprise had he chosen to shoot and not talk.

His wife misled us, though probably not intentionally, at the very beginning, but the responsibility for the approach and outcome rested squarely on my shoulders. Our good fortune rested in the fact that we trained together for tactical situations, often training on our own time, and we had complete confidence in each other. It was those hours of training that kept eyes continually scanning for the out of the ordinary during our approach. That's why Owen Smith and Larry Horn saw the suspect at the moment he stepped out to challenge us.

We located the pistol his wife had described, a .25 caliber semi-automatic along with six spent shell casings. Her husband had no problem telling Larry Horn that he had shot at her. Next, he boasted that he initially intended to open fire on us the moment he saw us, but changed his mind and came out to order us off the property.

When I arrived for work on Monday, I was summoned to the office of Colonel Robert O. Mathews, Howard County's Chief of Police. He wasted no time getting to his point. "Why didn't you shoot that man?"

"It wasn't necessary," I said.

"Why?"

"As long as he was talking, I don't believe he was going to shoot. When I asked him to put the gun down, he did." I paused for a second or two and then said, "Colonel, if the day comes when I shoot a man, you can positively believe I had no other choice."

There was no further discussion.

***

I teach disarming tactics as part of my classes, however, my students will also tell you I often sound like a broken record. I preach that taking a weapon away from anyone can be your final act if you aren't fully prepared to fight to the death. Once you commit to disarming someone, you've crossed the point of no return, and that's especially true when you go after a firearm. You might be able to turn and run from a man with a knife, but it's impossible to outrun a bullet. The moment you react to take a gun away, there's no calling time out, or turning back. If you begin your tactic and falter, or flinch, you'll probably get shot. Once wounded, there's the possibility that you'll be shot again, and your failed attempt might have angered the assailant to the point where he will stand over you and execute you. That's the cold, hard truth.

Then too, if you stand and think for a few seconds or more about whether or not you should attempt to disarm an assailant, you could fail. In all likelihood, while thinking about your situation, you will start to tense your muscles. Tensing your muscles will slow your reaction time considerably, and lessen your chances of success, and certainly increase your probability of being shot. That's just another harsh fact in the real world.

There were encounters that even offered a bit of comic relief afterwards, and those that built a larger than life reputation.

I was the only officer in the Howard County, Maryland,

Police Department, and probably in the state, authorized by the Chief of Police to carry the nunchaku in lieu of the standard issue police baton. At that particular time, almost everyone was unfamiliar with the Okinawan weapon, and it wasn't until the surge of Bruce Lee movies that the nunchaku became easily recognized. Early on, there were a few people who thought it was some type of new police weapon that was thrown to stop a fleeing suspect.

Ellicott City held certain notoriety for being a rowdy town, where the street fight or poolroom brawl was commonplace. And, Main Street was the focal point for nearly all of these showdowns. Indeed, tales from the days of World War II, the Korean War and into the middle and late 60s told of blood spilled early and often in those battles. And, in truth, many of those legendary altercations were far more fact than fiction.

My very first fight with a suspect was only one block off the main thoroughfare on St. Paul Street. Over the years that followed, I had several other clashes on or around Main Street. One of those encounters occurred on a Friday night, after dozens of complaints about fighting, vandalism, and people blocking the street, refusing to allow cars to pass. A number of officers were assigned to quell the problems and the order from the top was "No tolerance" for even minor infractions of the law.

I was a member of the Criminal Investigations Division at the time, but was told I'd be part of the detail, and working in plain clothes. Recruit Officer Harry Monroe, who was in the police academy at the time, asked if he could come along as an observer and was assigned to ride with me. Of course, I informed him at the outset to be prepared for a boring night of sitting and watching people cross the street.

The first three or four hours went by as most nights of surveillance go, anxious anticipation in the first 30 minutes or so, and then never ending thoughts of "God when will this night be over?" When boredom hit its peak, Officer Terry Chaney called that there was a problem outside a restaurant. In only seconds, I was there and out of the car as Terry tried to disperse a small crowd. There were a few who were getting quite loud, and he finally gave them one minute to clear the street or be arrested. They crossed the street to their cars, but were still yelling and causing a disturbance. Before I realized what was happening, Terry was running toward the group calling out to one of them. "That's it. You're going."

I followed him across the street and he placed one man under arrest with no problem at all. The second, however, was a different story, and he tried to pull away when Terry attempted to put him in handcuffs. I grabbed one of his arms, and that's when he turned on me and started screaming. "If you didn't have them funny sticks in your hand, I'd kick your ass.

I passed the nunchaku to Harry Monroe and said, "Here, Harry, hold these." Then I turned to the man. "Never let it be said that the funny sticks got in your way."

With that, Officer Don Bathgate very calmly announced to the crowd, which had now swelled to nearly one hundred people, "Okay, let's make a circle. We're gonna have a fight."

The guy made a production of taking off his jacket and leaning over to put it on the street. I saw his sucker punch coming long before he dropped his coat and, sure enough, the instant he let go of the jacket, he tried to bring a haymaker up from the ground. He hadn't reached the half way mark with his punch when he let out a loud groan, doubled over, and fell face first against the trunk of a car. I heard a lot of those in the crowd muttering. "What happened? What happened to him?" Nobody saw the foot catch him square between the legs, and actually lift him off the pavement. Nobody that is, except Lieutenant Michael Kradz, who was driving by when everything started. A few days later he called me into his office and said, "That was a damn nice shot you gave that guy." And that was all he said.

Still, Terry Chaney made one of the better comments just after the guy's face hit the trunk of the car, and he landed in the street. He calmly said, "Jim, you wanna nail this guy again before I put the cuffs on him?"

I just smiled. "No, I think one shot was enough."

On the other hand, the guy who took the shot wasn't that happy. Even though he was in a lot of pain, he wanted to have the last word with me from his cell. He said, "I would've whipped your ass if you hadn't kicked me in the balls."

I smiled, and nodded. "Well, in a street fight there're two kinds of people, winners and losers. You're a loser."

Later that night I told Officer Chaney, "TC, you need a new watch. Yours runs a minute off in around 10 seconds."

He chuckled. "Yeah, I guess that was a damn quick minute wasn't it?"

With the flood of Bruce Lee movies, the nunchaku became a "toy" for everybody and a problem for police. Before martial arts supply stores, or local martial arts schools could order abundant supplies to meet the huge demands, people were cutting up broom, mop, rake, and shovel handles to make their very own "Bruce Lee Sticks."

They were called "numchucks" and "chako sticks" because nobody knew or understood the term nunchaku. Regardless of what they were called, hospital emergency rooms were being swamped, because of injuries caused by the weapon. People were quickly finding that, unlike the Bruce Lee movies, those struck by the weapon didn't jump right up and continue with the battle. Most were down for the count. Research had shown that someone who knew how to use the nunchaku could deliver a blow with 1,600 pounds, or more, of pressure at the point of impact. Naturally, it didn't take the state of Maryland long to pass a law banning the carrying, displaying, or use of the nunchaku by anyone other than a law enforcement officer, or someone traveling to or from a valid martial arts class. As you might imagine, there were hundreds of people upset with this decision, but it cut down on the number of assaults and injuries to those "playing" with a deadly weapon.

I first used the nunchaku to subdue an assailant on Main Street, Ellicott City on a very warm April evening while off duty, and returning home from classes at Catonsville Community College. I saw an unusually large crowd of people lining the sidewalks and standing in the street and, at first, I couldn't see what seemed to be holding them almost spellbound. A few seconds later, I saw a police officer lying in the street being kicked, and beaten by a number of men, and a Sheriff's Constable trying to fight them off. A second later I was out of the car, nunchaku in hand, and running to help the officer.

As it turned out, the nearest guy to me also happened to be the biggest. I think I was still running when I swung at him, but an instant later there was a loud, almost sickening crack, and he fell like a broken rag doll right at my feet. His eyes rolled back and he didn't move. I hesitated for a moment thinking maybe I'd killed him, but then went after the others who were still attacking the officer. I hit two more people and that quickly the fight was over. About a dozen from the fringes of the crowd ran off, and for a few seconds there was an odd silence from those that remained.

By the time I arrived at work, around 1:00 PM, the following day the rumors were running wild. Stories were circulating through the police department, the courthouse, and up and down Main Street that, single handed, I'd beaten anywhere from 10 to 20 people, depending on who happened to be telling the tale at the time, to a bloody pulp. There were "eyewitness" statements from some that had been in the crowd the night before, swearing that they saw first hand what I did, and that the numbers were "accurate." I went to talk with a few of the "eyewitnesses" to set the record straight, and they looked me right in the eye and swore they saw me "wipe out 10 or 12 guys easy." When I denied that I "wiped out 10 or 12 guys easy" they laughed and said, "Man, we saw you do it." And it seemed the more I denied it, the bigger the tale became. So, in the end, I gave up and let them spin their yarns. Even years later when I'd run across some of those "eyewitnesses" they'd bring up the April night on Main Street, and begin telling a few strangers of an historic brawl they bore witness to. And, suddenly the legend grew ever larger.

The next time the nunchaku came into play was after Police Officer Richard Middleton walked into a Crap Game, while making a routine bar check at Bluebeard's Hideaway in Mt. Airy. Dick encountered a group of men shooting dice, and when he told them to break up the game they attacked him. He was able to get on his radio long enough to call a Signal 13 (Officer needs help), and that was about it.

This wasn't the first time an officer had been attacked while checking this bar, and every officer responding to Dick's call for help knew there'd be even more trouble when they arrived. It was a very warm Saturday afternoon, and it was a certainty that the bar and parking lot would be packed, and nobody was going to side with the police. Maryland State Troopers, and officers from surrounding counties, were also responding to help, and Officer Bruce Harrison drove to the scene in his late 60s Corvette Stingray.

By the time I arrived, there was complete mayhem inside and outside the bar. I saw Dick, and asked him to point out those he wanted arrested. We stepped inside, and Dick attempted to take a man into custody and was immediately punched in the face.

As a Howard County Officer and a Maryland State Trooper rushed toward the man, I swung the nunchaku. Oh shit! I forgot that I was inside, and the lead stick struck the florescent ceiling lights, causing them to explode and shower everyone with glass and the fine white powder from the bulbs. The force of the swing, and follow through, brought the lead stick down on top of the bar, and now it was shattering beer bottles and glasses as it travelled along the bar. But, that didn't stop me from trying again. I continued the swing around and in a low arc, just above my head, and launched another shot at the man. The lead stick went between Police Officer Dave Richards and Trooper Ober just as they grabbed for the man, and he fell like a sack to the floor. They stopped and stared at each other for a second, and then looked down at the man who lay unconscious and bleeding between them.

Before it was over, we'd arrested 23 people and sent a half-dozen of those to the hospital. I decided to end any further problems by taking the bar's liquor license, and telling the owner he couldn't serve alcoholic beverages until the liquor board returned his license.

As we were about to drive away with carloads of prisoners, Maryland State Trooper Neiman Brown walked over to me with a big smile on his face. "I don't recall your name, but I remember the sticks."

Monday, I was called on the carpet for taking the license, and essentially shutting off the bar's profits from beer and liquor sales for the remainder of the weekend. When I was asked to explain my actions I calmly said, "It was for the safety of the citizens of Howard

County residing in and around the area of the bar, and the safety of the officers under my command." And, with that any arguments to the contrary fell apart. The next question was, "And who punched that woman and knocked her unconscious?" I nodded. "I did. She was kicking, scratching and slapping every police officer that tried to arrest her, but I think they hesitated to do anything because she was a woman. I figured if she wanted to act like a man, then she should be treated like one, so I decked her." There were no more questions.

Diane Schulte, from the Howard County Office of Law, who was present at the meeting, later called me aside. She flashed a big smile and said, "Jimmy, you gave the perfect answer for seizing the license. There was nothing anybody could say after that." There was another big smile. "And, there was perfect logic in your reason for hitting the woman."

Each time I was involved in confrontations that ended with violent conclusions, I found time later, usually when alone, to think about what had happened. Each and every time my thoughts went back to Okinawa, and the days in Miyagi Sensei's class. I often wondered what the outcome of those altercations would have been without the training I'd received while in Miyagi's dojo. I could never envision the outcome of those fights with the same successful results if I'd failed to continue my practice while in Okinawa, or after returning home. My training, continued practice and teaching kept my reflexes honed to a much sharper edge, and I was certainly able to see and feel things quicker than others, like the sucker punch that was intended to catch me unaware.

Still, there were times when things didn't work as I thought they would. The first, and certainly the most memorable, took place when I was off duty, and stopped by the police station to drop off some paperwork.

At just about noon on a Saturday, I walked in the back door of our old station on Fells Lane in Ellicott City, into what was our briefing room and report writing area. The last thing I expected to find was about a half dozen police officers fighting with a very powerfully built man, who was taking everything they could throw at him, and still standing.

I threw the papers on the floor and hurried toward the battle, and most of the officers stepped aside. The man was facing me directly, and I launched a front kick that caught him squarely between the legs, and hard enough to lift him off the floor. He didn't blink, flinch, or fall to the floor as everyone, including me, expected he would. He stood there snarling like some kind of crazed animal, so I launched another kick and once again lifted him off the floor. Again, he didn't blink, flinch or show any signs that he was even close to falling down, or surrendering. That's when I knew it was time for another course of action, because this guy didn't feel a thing, and it would be a very long afternoon if we didn't find a way to subdue him. I moved in close, and managed to spin him around, and apply a chokehold. I knew I had applied the hold correctly, but he had a neck like a bull, and he wasn't going out easily. At last, the chokehold started to work, and he stopped struggling and went limp. But, I quickly found that I couldn't release the hold entirely. As soon as he could begin to breath, and the blood flow started back to normal, he began fighting. I had to keep the chokehold on him while the officers handcuffed him, and picked him up to carry him to a holding cell.

Everybody thought he'd calm down once he was placed in the cell, and someone removed the handcuffs before they closed the door. That was a big mistake. As soon as the cuffs were off the guy attacked again. I knew hitting him was useless, and somehow got by the mass of humanity that was blocking the cell door, and applied the chokehold again. This time when he went out the cuffs were left on him, but that didn't mean he'd lost his desire to fight when he regained consciousness. He kicked at the cell door, and screamed that he'd kill all of us as soon as he could get free.

I figured since he was confined and unable to carry out his threat, I could drop off my paperwork and leave. Well, that's where the saying "fat chance" came into play. I was ordered to remain at the station because, "You're the only one who can control this guy, and we don't know what we're going to do with him."

In the meantime, I learned that he had been arrested for shoplifting at a nearby store and became combative immediately after being taken into custody. But, it wasn't until they arrived at the station, and removed the handcuffs that he went completely out of control. A woman, who'd been arrested with him, told one of the officers that he'd been using PCP and snorting cocaine. Well, that certainly explained why he was out of control, and impervious to pain.

The encounter with this man was my first, but certainly not my last, with someone under the influence of drugs. I learned a very valuable lesson from my battle with him, and at times it seemed almost priceless in future skirmishes, not only with those under the influence of drugs, but also a few suffering extreme mental distress.

A few days later I had the opportunity to talk with the man before he stood trial on an array of charges, including assault and battery, resisting arrest and shoplifting. He gave me credit for all of the injuries he'd sustained in the fight, and nothing I said would convince him that he was battling half a dozen officers when I happened to walk in. For reasons I can't explain, I was the only one he really remembered from the incident, saying I'd given him the "worst ass kickin' I've ever had." Maybe I stood out in his mind, because I was only one in plain clothes.

There was a very strange twist in our meeting though, when he offered me a job as his right hand man in a street gang. He told me he controlled an entire area of Baltimore City, and wanted me to come on board as his second in command. I couldn't help but smile over the offer, and I actually thanked him for it, but said I was going to stick with my career in law enforcement.

Some years later, I was a Squad Leader in Columbia and just beginning a tour of duty on the evening shift. Almost immediately Officers Susan Goldman and Eric Harne were dispatched to call for a domestic quarrel where the wife had fled the home because her husband had become violent.

A fine way to start the shift, I thought and began driving toward the address. I hated the domestic calls more than any other, because there was always an uncertainty as to their outcome. So many times officers are told, "there are no weapons" involved or available, which is completely false. There are weapons everywhere from kitchen knives, to lamps, chairs, or just about anything a person can pick up and utilize as a weapon. In this instance the dispatcher had mentioned the possibility of a butcher knife being in play.

Officers Harne and Goldman arrived, but when dispatchers

began to call and ask if they were okay, there was no response. I stepped up my pace and arrived at the home, wondering what I'd find. I hurried into the house, and when I went inside, I found Goldman and Harne on the floor, engaged in a struggle with a man and a butcher knife on the floor close by. The man was very stocky and putting up a battle.

I moved toward them and saw that I had only one opening that would allow me to do anything to subdue the man. I dropped to one knee and gave the man a very quick, knife hand chop to the throat. The blow stunned him and he immediately stopped fighting.

At the police station I went to the cellblock to make sure everything was going smoothly and that there were no other problems. The man appeared very calm as Harne and Goldman wrote up the arrest report and prepared to process him.

I walked over and asked if he was okay, and he nodded, saying he was fine. A few seconds later he said, "Hey, man, no hard feelings. You did what you had to do."

***

Time was passing and, in August 1974, I received a letter from Miyagi Sensei, telling me he wanted to promote me to Godan (Fifth Degree Black Belt). I was more than a bit overwhelmed by his desire to promote me to Godan, and actually I felt embarrassed to even think about holding that rank. After all, Mr. Miyagi held that rank when I first met him, and I certainly didn't believe I belonged on a level such as that. I wrote to him and, very respectfully declined his wish to promote me. He responded saying he would honor my refusal, but one year later he didn't give me advance notice of his intentions and August 1975 marked my promotion to Fifth Degree. I still remember opening the package, removing the certificate of promotion, and for a long time staring at it. I felt deeply honored that Mr. Miyagi would even think that I deserved to hold the rank of Godan. Then I couldn't help but smile as I recalled a certain part of what he'd said when he promoted me to brown belt. "That means you'll work that much harder to prove I'm not a fool." Now with the higher rank, I figured that meant the job on the road ahead was an even greater challenge. Indeed, I found that sometimes those tasks come in different ways.

One of those challenges came when I was assigned as the physical training and defensive tactics instructor for the police academy. There I'd have to be teacher, and disciplinarian, or a combination of Mr. Miyagi and Marine Drill Instructor. I had 22 weeks to work with 18 recruits, who possessed varying degrees of fitness, and little to no skills in self-defense. I had a good plan in place, but the question in everyone's mind was, "Will it work?"

I had already taught one recruit class very early in my career, along with teaching experienced officers periodically over the years during in-service training. I had taken the skills Mr. Miyagi gave me, and put together a relatively simple self-defense program and, for police purposes, the simpler the better. Complicated tactics might look most impressive to the very inexperienced, or on the movie screen, but those schemes aren't worth much in a street fight. A confrontation should be ended as quickly as possible. It lessens the chances of injury to the police officers and reduces the possibility of brutality complaints.

The fitness portion of the program was designed to bring everyone up to a level of maximum strength and endurance. To ensure there'd be no crying and groaning about the toughness of the curriculum I, along with my assistant, Police Officer Clarke Ahlers, did everything we required of the recruits. There was a fitness test on Friday in their initial week of training, which almost all of them failed miserably, and a test every three weeks thereafter. Test results were posted in the main classroom so they could see them first thing every morning when they arrived. Officer Ahlers and I took the same test and announced our results hoping it would help motivate them.

The first weeks weren't exactly a cakewalk for us, because of the condition of some of the class members, but in time they began to show marked improvement. Each and every day Clarke and I preached to them about believing in themselves and continued to push them through endless repetitions.

Well, it worked, and suddenly our jobs became much easier. When they saw the results of their aches, pains, sweat and hard work, they began challenging themselves to do better, and their final test showed some shocking numbers.

Officer Thomas Guercio pumped off an astounding 156 push-ups in 2 minutes. In another segment of the training he completed two consecutive circuits of pull-ups, finishing with 27 in each set. Another recruit, who managed only nine push-ups on his first test, completed 112 on his last. Yet, the final challenge was met on the very last day of training when the entire class completed a nine-mile run. That run had nothing at all to do with their final test, it was something they wanted to do, and we made it together. Still, there was one recruit who showed he had a lot of heart when his legs began to cramp. A marked police car had followed us on the entire route, and when the recruit's legs began to cramp I told Sergeant Wayne Ridgely to put him in the car. The recruit refused saying, "I'm gonna finish this run if it takes me 'til midnight. I won't be the one to embarrass my class." I think it would be safe to say it was simply a matter of pride.

There were a number of lessons learned during their academy training that were not in the scheduled routine. From the beginning, I told the recruits they would often find that a person who "ranted, threatened," or made belittling remarks, noises or nasty gestures was usually more "wind" than action. And, a day came when it was time to prove that the philosophy also applied to groups of individuals.

In the early stages of their physical training, I kept the running phase confined to the Howard Community College Campus. As the weeks passed, and their conditioning improved, I began to lead them off campus and around some of the neighborhoods. One particular day I took them down Hickory Ridge Road toward Cedar Lane where we passed by an office building under construction. As we ran by in formation we were greeted with "jeers, catcalls" and some "colorful" obscene remarks.

I continued with the run until we were out of sight of the building and then called the formation to a halt. I turned to the recruits and told them we were turning around, going back to the construction site and that we were going to run up the ramp into the building, down the hallway and out the back door. I told them the reason for this was to establish who was in charge of the situation. I said if we walked away and pretended nothing happened, each day the insults and jeering would get worse, and they would also find this held true in day-to-day police activities. I warned them that the workers could say anything they wanted when we entered the site, but if anyone reached out and put a hand on them, it was open season. Needless to say, this was like a shot of adrenaline for the recruits and they were more than ready and willing to test their wings.

We began our run once again, turned around and went back to Hickory Ridge Road. When we reached the entrance to the site, I turned left with 18 recruits, in a column of twos, wearing their dark blue academy PT shirts and sweatpants running behind me. I hit the ramp and, at the top, said, "Good afternoon" to a man I assumed to be the foreman of the job. He said nothing. He stared blankly at me, and the recruits running close behind me. By the time we reached the back door, I noted that, except for our footsteps, there was a very strange silence in the air. Not a single jeer, catcall, whistle, or other comment had been directed our way since we entered the site. And, not a single worker dared to reach out and put a hand on anyone in the formation. We exited the back door, circled the site and finished our run without further incident.

In the days that followed, I made it a point to run by that construction site from time to time. Not a word or sound was uttered and it was safe to say that the recruits had gained a great deal of respect by "standing their ground" and demonstrating that they would not be intimidated.

I often believed that the recruits were disappointed that someone didn't reach out and put a hand on one of them the day we ran into the construction site. But, it was important they learned that not every confrontation had to be settled with physical force. Simply holding your ground and not being intimidated was often enough to defuse a situation.

As the final days of their academy training was approaching, another of the many issues I preached about unfolded in a very unexpected way. I had often talked of the brash behavior of people and that some would be so brazen as to commit a criminal act in their presence.

I began bringing my own heavy bag to the class, because sometimes it was very difficult borrowing the equipment from the college. On a Friday afternoon everyone headed to the weight room at the conclusion of the defensive tactics portion of the class. As was our custom, the heavy bag was brought along and placed against a wall just inside the door.

About 15 minutes into the session, a young man walked into the room and very casually leaned against the wall beside the bag. Soon he was resting his arm on top of the bag and, before long, was giving it a more than an aimless going over. He ran his hands over the bag, patting it now and then, while seeming to ignore the name "Lilley" very clearly written on the bag in bold letters. And he was also overlooking, or perhaps he was blind to, the large police logo on the shirts worn by the men in the weight room.

His actions had not gone unnoticed by the recruit class and one by one they began paying more attention to him. While they were watching him, they would cast a glance my way as if asking, "Is he really going to try and walk out with the bag with all of us standing here?"

He started tapping his hand on top of the bag and looking over his shoulder and out the door. By now many of the recruits were beginning to smile and every now and then a faint chuckle would slip out. Suddenly, and directly in front of 18 police recruits and their academy instructor, the young man leaned over, hoisted the bag over his shoulder and walked out the door.

I waited only a few seconds while the recruits stared at me, wondering what to do next. I laughed and said, "Would a few of you gentlemen chase that young lad down and bring him back here?" I guess I should have pointed out one or two of the recruits to chase him down, because their definition of a few turned out to be the entire class.

A few moments later they returned with the young man in tow along with the heavy bag. I asked him why he took the bag. He nervously said, "I thought it was abandoned property and I was taking it for safekeeping."

"With 19 people here in this room, and a name written on it, you thought it was abandoned property?"

He shrugged his shoulders. "Uh… Yes."

I smiled. "I find that hard to believe, but I'll give you a break." Besides, after being run down and surrounded by 18 men, he probably needed to hurry home, shower and change clothes. I nodded to the recruits. "Gentlemen, escort this young lad outside and show him the way off campus."

When the time came for the recruits to leave the classroom and go into the field for their final training phase, I'm certain they took with them many valuable lessons learned over the 22 weeks we had spent together

As for me, no matter what the job, whether it was teaching in the police academy, my daily assignment as a Squad Leader, or the karate class, the discipline and learning from Mr. Miyagi's class was a part of everything I did.

***

I continued a regular correspondence with Mr. Miyagi, and in his letters he often made other predictions for the future. He knew of every physical confrontation I'd had since leaving Okinawa, and in one of his letters he made another philosophic prediction. He said, "There will be times when it will not be necessary to fight."

Naturally, I didn't understand what he meant, and when I asked, I received his usual answer. "Don't worry. In time you will see." Miyagi proved, as always, that he could foretell the future.

There were times when it wasn't necessary to physically subdue a man in a fight. But, one time in particular stands out because it had an almost comical side to it. I knew two officers had taken a prisoner into the cellblock at the police station, and it wasn't uncommon for someone to stop by and look in on them. I was nearby, and drove to the station to make a routine check on their safety. When I walked into the cellblock, they were rolling around on the floor with the man, and it looked to me like he was holding the upper hand in spite of two to one odds.

Far too often in a situation like this, other officers just pile on and create a greater problem. I'd always thought it was better to find an opening, and end the struggle quickly, and with as little force as possible. Besides, in a pile of humanity, you can't tell whom you're striking when you throw a punch. So, instead of jumping into the fray and adding a fourth body to the heap, I moved into a position where I could get a shot at the suspect, and put a stop to the fight. I didn't say a word while waiting for him to turn a little and give me the angle I needed. But, as he was turning into the position I wanted, he looked up at me, stopped fighting and began laughing. He pulled his hands out and, while still laughing, raised them saying, "Man, you'd just flat kick my ass. I can take these two guys, but I wouldn't fight you on bet. What do you want me to do?"

"Just do what these officers say, and everything's gonna be fine," I said with a shrug, and wondering what had just happened.

He got to his feet, looked at me and just shook his head. A moment later he said, "Man, I could tell just by lookin' at you, that you'd kick my ass."

I admit leaving the cellblock, and scratching my head, but later I recalled what Mr. Miyagi had said in his letter. "There will be times when it will not be necessary to fight." Well, this was the first time I could recall not having to fight, but what surprised me most was the fact that the man was already fighting with two police officers. Usually someone doesn't stop fighting, especially when he has the upper hand. And, this man didn't just stop struggling with them he started laughing.

There were other times when I was certain that it would be necessary to fight, but the situations didn't escalate to physical battles. And in each of those incidences the men said basically the same thing, "He just had a look about him that said it wasn't a good idea to fight with him."

***

Dan Simons, Bruce Charity and Will Adams had reached the rank of black belt, and were a gold mine to me. They were loyal and trusted friends, who stuck it out, and helped form the foundation for our dojo. Each had taken giant strides over the years, and proved their value time and again with their abilities to teach, and keep things on track when my work schedule conflicted with that of the class.

The arrival of the video age opened many new doors and possibilities for us. Mr. Miyagi and I began an exchange of tapes, and suddenly there were new katas to learn, and we were learning katas without weapons as well as weapons katas from the tapes. There were Bo Katas, and Sai Katas to add to our routines, and Mr. Miyagi could watch our progress and make corrections through videotape.

Naturally, Mr. Miyagi wouldn't be Mr. Miyagi without that unannounced surprise that I had come to know so very well as his trademark. With the video exchange came my promotion to Sixth Degree Black Belt, which was completely unexpected. And this time there was no prior warning that a promotion was forthcoming. That certainly eliminated any possibility of protest on my part, and I wondered if that's why it came without warning.

Our class size had dwindled over the years, because so many of our students had graduated from high school and gone off to college. Still, that didn't dampen our spirits, or keep us from finding a place to practice. Danny, Bruce, Will and I worked hard and often together, learning the new katas, and we vowed that nothing would keep us from our desire to learn and improve. From time to time, a new student or two would come along, and find there was an energy among our core group that could only be described as contagious. And, there'd be a few who the bug would bite, and they became our next 20 plus year students, and future teachers.

One of those bitten by the desire to learn was a young lady by the name of Jody Tookey. She was all of 4 feet 11 inches in height, but she'd spent years pursuing her goals in gymnastics and was amazingly strong. Of course, the last thought in my mind when she began class was that nine years down the road we'd be married. In fact, there was never a notion that we'd even go out on a date. When people ask how we eventually got together, I always say that one evening I answered a knock at my door, she walked in and never left.

At about the same time she arrived for class, Jody was also chasing another dream, a dream of becoming a police officer. She began working with the Howard County Police Department, almost immediately after graduating from high school, as a dispatcher in the Communications Division. But, the police bug had bittern her much earlier and, at the "ripe old age" of 14 she became a member of the department's Police Explorer Post.

When she began her quest to become a police officer, she found the road to reach her dream was filled with many obstacles. Although nobody would step up and say it, and even with all of the new laws in place prohibiting discrimination for any reason, Jody's size immediately went against her. It took many rejections before the Howard County Police Department hired her, and then there were those who were certain she was destined to become a failure. But, it didn't take long for her to prove that she had as much, or more brass than many of her male counterparts.

Of course, everyone knows the inevitable tests had to come, and it was a certainty that there wouldn't be many challenges from someone her size.

Her first confrontation came with a night time traffic stop on I-70, when she pulled a car over for a speeding violation. As she approached the car, the driver's door flew open and a man, she'd later discover was 6 feet 4 inches tall and close to 250 pounds, jumped out. He came toward her with the same type of flashlight she was holding in her left hand. She said that what happened next was a blur and she doesn't remember exactly everything she did, but she recalls the man bouncing off the hood of the car. A moment or two later he landed on the roadway, and her knee was in the middle of his back while she handcuffed him. At the end of the evening, she said she knew she was all alone and there was no doubt the man intended to hurt her. "I just reacted. I did what I was trained to do." Then there was a big smile of satisfaction.

Without a doubt, she'd have to have at least one battle that had its comical side. It took place in a convenience store in Savage, Maryland, when she went in to buy her Diet Coke.

The manager told her there'd been an unruly customer in the store minutes earlier and he was about to call the police, when the young man left. At almost that same moment, the young man came back into the store, cursing and swearing. Jody told him to knock off his belligerent behavior, or leave the store. He turned on her with a string of obscenities, and was now told to leave the store or be arrested. Flexing his beer muscles, he unleashed another chain of obscenities and told her he wasn't leaving and that she wasn't going to arrest him. After taking a trip through the Tasty-cakes, Twinkies and potato chips, he found himself in the backseat of a police cruiser and on his way to the police station.

As so often happens in these instances, the arrested party has to save face and will embellish the story of his arrest. It was no different this time, and the young man told his friends how the police brutally beat him and arrested him for no reason. And, the way he spun his yarn, he led his buddies to believe it was several police officers who'd set upon him.

When his trial date arrived, his friends flocked to the county courthouse to support their friend and see the police officers that had beaten him. They stood at the back of the courtroom looking around at the officers assembled for scheduled trials. Finally they asked him to point out the officers and they were more than a little surprised when he pointed to only Jody. "Her!" they exclaimed, and exited the courthouse, leaving him to face his consequences alone.

1989

The letter announcing that Miyagi Sensei was coming to visit was in characteristic Miyagi tradition, a complete surprise. The letter began with his normal greeting. "How are you getting along?" It was the second line that jolted me upright. "I'm coming to the United States in July. Can I stay at your house?" I was positively exhilarated that I was going to see my teacher and good friend again. And, at last, my friends and students were going to meet the man they heard me speak fondly of so often. A moment or so later I was shaking my head and laughing.

Mr. Miyagi had done it again. Without so much as a passing hint, he declared that he was coming to visit. But, there wasn't a lot of time to make preparations.

I called Danny, Bruce, Will and Jody and told them Mr. Miyagi was coming to visit. Danny went into an immediate panic, because Miyagi's visit coincided perfectly with his vacation and he'd be in Hilton Head, South Carolina. Suddenly, his vacation didn't matter. He was going to meet Miyagi Sensei, no matter what.

Miyagi's schedule included a list of places he wanted to visit while in the United States. He said he'd fly into New York, and spend a day or two there before flying on to Maryland. He arrived in New York early on a Friday morning and telephoned late the same day, telling me he didn't like New York and would be coming to Maryland ahead of time. He said he'd make sure I was notified of his departure and arrival location and time. That was simple enough. But, his trip wouldn't have been complete without complications. He asked someone in New York to help him choose his departure and arrival sites, and they agreed.

The party in New York, making the decisions, waited until Miyagi's plane was in the air to call and tell me that he was on the way. That's when they also informed me that they'd sent him to National Airport in Washington, D. C. instead of BWI Airport in Baltimore. As it turned out, this day would become the Saturday from hell traffic wise. I rushed out the door, jumped in the car and sped off, hoping to make it to National not too long after Miyagi's arrival. Traffic on a Saturday morning in July is bad enough, but it was also the weekend of the LPGA Tournament and every roadway leading to D. C. was jammed. At times the traffic speed reached a monumental 15 miles per hour. I suddenly realized that it was going to be a very, very long day.

Somehow I finally made it to National Airport and began my search for Mr. Miyagi. I found him waiting patiently and, after shaking hands and exchanging greetings, I said, "Have you been waiting long?" He nodded. "Yes." His answer was short and to the point, just as I would have expected. It didn't take long to escape the airport, but wouldn't you know it? The traffic was now bumper-to-bumper, stop and go, going in the opposite direction. A round trip that would have taken, at best, only two hours if Miyagi had been sent to BWI, turned into a five and a half-hour adventure.

At last, we arrived at my home in Mt. Airy and I think we were both relieved just to be out of the gigantic traffic jam, which seemed to fill every Maryland roadway. It was time to change into something comfortable and relax. But, as always, Mr. Miyagi didn't waste a lot of time before springing a surprise by saying he had something for me from Mr. Katsuya Miyahira. A moment later he presented me with two certificates.

Mr. Miyahira was now a 10th Dan, and had been President of the Okinawa Shorin-Ryu Karate Do Association for many years. Mr.

Miyagi said that Mr. Miyahira was presenting me with a certificate promoting me to Sixth Degree Black Belt, and the other was my Teacher's License. I learned that henceforth any promotion, I received from Mr. Miyagi, would have to be recognized by the President of the Okinawa Shorin-Ryu Karate Do Association, and the members of the board, at which time another certificate of promotion would be issued.

Later that afternoon when I went to take a shower and dress to go out to dinner, Mr. Miyagi sat and talked with Jody. During their conversation, Jody asked why he didn't like New York. He was quiet for a few seconds and then said, "What son-of-a-bitch mean?" After Jody tried to tactfully explain that it wasn't exactly an endearing term, he said he'd heard it very often in New York.

Jody and I took Mr. Miyagi to the Crab Shanty in Ellicott City for his first dinner in Maryland. He asked me to order for him, and I first asked our waitress to bring him a bottle of ice cold Coors Lite. When it was served, he took a sip, smiled and said, "Ah, decent." Then he asked if I remembered the term, decent. I laughed and soon we began talking about Len, and how he used the word to describe anything good—from food to women. Of course, like anything else in those days back in Okinawa, certain words were part of Marine Corps jargon. And "decent" was one of those words.

When Mr. Miyagi's dinner of steak and lobster was served, I learned for the very first time that he'd never eaten with a knife and fork. The custom in Okinawa was to serve the meats already cut in portions, sized to eat with chopsticks. Like me learning to eat with chopsticks, it didn't take long for Mr. Miyagi to get the hang of the knife and fork. He enjoyed his first taste of Surf and Turf, and soon after that filling meal he was ready for some much needed sleep.

Sunday began with an early breakfast at the Forest Diner, and then a non-stop tour of our Nation's Capital. Jody drove, and as fate would have it, she made a wrong turn at one point in the trip and blurted, "Son-of-a-bitch." This, of course, drew a rather lengthy chuckle from Mr. Miyagi.

He had told us he wanted to see the Washington Monument, the White House, the Lincoln Memorial, the Vietnam Memorial, the Iwo Jima Memorial, and visit Arlington National Cemetery. Our last stop was Arlington, and we made it in time to see the changing of the guard, which Miyagi thought was most impressive.

While at the Vietnam Memorial, Mr. Miyagi told Jody and I about the Peace Memorial in Okinawa. He described, in intricate detail, the construction of the walls and how they were erected in such a way as to represent waves rolling in off the ocean.

By the time we arrived home, the phone was ringing. It was Danny, telling me he'd just gotten back from Hilton Head and was on the way to Mt. Airy. He'd left his wife, Pat, and their family in South Carolina and hurried back to meet Miyagi. Jody, however, wouldn't be able to stay, because she was in the first weeks of the Police Academy and Monday would be a busy day.

Before long, Mr. Miyagi, Danny, and I were seated around the dining room table talking about, what else, karate. We talked about history and tradition, changes that had been made in the katas, a book that had been published on Shorin-Ryu Karate, and the mistakes Danny and I had found in that book. Miyagi looked those pages over, smiled and agreed that the instructional pictures were incorrect.

Soon the topic was weapons katas, and suddenly we were moving furniture around in my living room and dining room. A few minutes later, Mr. Miyagi was demonstrating some of the finer points in a Bo Kata. Thankfully, the house is a log cabin and the ceilings rise to 12 feet at the highest point. Still, there were a few thuds against the lower portions of the ceiling, but no harm done.

Much of Monday morning was spent touring Howard County Office facilities, including the police station. Afterward we took a stroll along Main Street, Ellicott City, browsing in a number of shops and purchasing some gifts to take back to Okinawa. The last stop in the old town was to introduce Mr. Miyagi to my father and brother at their office.

By noon we were back home, and soon Danny arrived along with Will Adams and Sam Chayt, another of my students and a black belt. We ate a leisurely lunch and, although a class was scheduled for that evening, we were too anxious to wait. So, not long after the table was cleared, we were suiting up in our gis.

We went down into the basement and began going through katas, while Sam videotaped the session. After we completed a number of the katas, Mr. Miyagi was asked to demonstrate the bunkai, or self-defense application of the moves in those katas. He smiled and nodded. "Okay, but you must remember I've gotten old and slow."

Danny went through a portion of the kata, Gojushiho, and Miyagi Sensei said the moves involved defending against multiple attackers. Miyagi assumed the position of the defender, while Danny, Will and I acted as the aggressors. We moved to strike, and as sudden as we'd attacked, the assault was repelled even quicker. Sam Chayt blinked and said he'd missed getting the entire sequence on tape. The attack and defensive moves were repeated, and again he said he'd missed them. That's when I found that he was trying to start the tape at the moment of the attack, but by the time the camera was recording, the entire series of moves had been completed. I suggested that he might want to turn the camera on and let it run to capture the event. Obviously his reaction time pressing the start button on the camera was much more sluggish than Mr. Miyagi's "old and slow" response to the attack.

The Monday evening class began promptly at 7:00 PM, and prompt is the key word when Miyagi is involved in any activity. He was, and still is a staunch believer in punctuality. Class attendance was at its peak, with Danny, Will, Bruce, Jody, Sam Hammond, Sam Chayt, Nelson Rebert, Jennifer Knutson, and Greg Cunningham. It was obvious to all, early on, that everything I had told them about Miyagi's Spartan classroom regimen was true.

As for me, it felt great to be a student again. Suddenly it was as if I was back, once again, in Okinawa. Miyagi Sensei was still the man I remembered from those days long ago. The keen-eyed master, who didn't miss even a minor slip up from anyone, no matter how well they thought they were hidden within the ranks. Now, I could only smile inwardly when I recalled how, so many of my former pupils had complained about my classroom discipline. If they could have been a part of this very first class Miyagi was conducting in America, they would have had the opportunity to meet my role model.

Tuesday had no real agenda, but as we were driving to

breakfast, Mr. Miyagi commented on the large number of tractor-trailers on I-70. In Okinawa, there aren't many trucks of that size because of the much narrower roadways. He said he'd like to see where so many trucks could come from. So, after breakfast, Bruce Charity, Nelson Rebert and I drove him to the truck stop in Jessup, Maryland. Needless to say he was amazed to see so many of the big rigs in one location. After our visit to the truck stop, we took him on a tour of the U. S. Route 1 Industrial Corridor, which he also found fascinating.

There was a class again on Tuesday evening, and everyone from the previous night's session attended. Once again, they found Miyagi was watching their every move and searching for even the smallest detail that wasn't to his liking. They also found that if he didn't like something, his way of driving home the correct technique was repetition. I remembered this tactic very well from my awkward days as a beginner, and even later when my footsteps were not so uncertain.

That night, immediately after class we had a social gathering, and my mother had prepared food, which included some of her home baked cakes and cookies. Over a plate of food, a cold beer or soda, everyone had an opportunity to talk with Miyagi Sensei and get to know him. There were a few humorous moments, especially when I told Bruce it was okay to have seconds on the cake because it was diet cake. Suddenly, Mr. Miyagi reminded me that he understood certain parts of the English language better than others. He chuckled and nodded. "Diet cake," he said and continued to chuckle.

Mr. Miyagi was leaving on Wednesday morning to fly to California and visit Hollywood. To everyone and, me especially, his stay in Maryland was too short. But, his first journey to the United States had not been planned as a lengthy stay. Still, we managed to cram a great deal of sightseeing and practice into those few short days.

Mr. Miyagi and I spent the latter part of Tuesday evening discussing my class, its members and their progress as he saw it. The conversation continued on Wednesday morning over a quick breakfast and the drive to BWI. I was flattered and humbled by his observations of my class. But, too soon he was boarding the plane and leaving Maryland behind.

The drive home seemed a little longer, but I had time to think about Mr. Miyagi's first visit to America. Indeed it was great to see my teacher and good friend once again. His visit rekindled that friendship, though it was never far from our hearts when the distance of half a world separated us.

1992 – 1994

The visit from Mr. Miyagi in 1992 was planned in advance. I was retiring from the police department and opening a new dojo and Miyagi Sensei was going to be there for the opening. Of course, it wouldn't be an authentic Miyagi event or visit if he didn't pull a surprise out of his bag. True to his nature, he calmly announced that he would be promoting me to Seventh Degree Black Belt on August 10th, the day of the dojo's Grand Opening.

It was an honor, but a humbling experience to stand in front of my family, my friends, my students, and those who attended the opening, and be promoted. This was my first promotion awarded in front of my family and friends in America. The last time I had stood in front of a class and accepted a promotion certificate was before my fellow students in Okinawa, June 1964.

Moments after receiving the certificate and belt, which was the Red and White Belt worn by those who achieved the rank of 7th and 8th Dan, I was removing a frayed and very much worn Black Belt. I was putting aside a belt I had worn for so many years and, as I folded it and put it down, I felt as though I was stepping away from something that had become a part of me. I wrapped and tied my new belt, stepped out before my family, friends and students and for a fleeting instant I felt like that young Marine from another era, walking out for the first time wearing a brown belt. And, for a few minutes, I felt as out of place as I did as that young Marine from years ago. Why? I can only guess that I was remembering a rainy night in November 1963 when I was told I would never be anything other than a white belt.

There wasn't much time to dwell on my new belt and promotion, because so much was on the day's agenda. I took my place beside Mr. Miyagi in front of the class, called Dan Simons from the ranks and promoted him to Sixth Degree Black Belt. From there it was down to the business of presenting our Grand Opening Karate and Kubo demonstration to those present.

When the demonstration concluded it was time for some very well earned nourishment. There was a buffet with ample food and drinks for everyone. But, after a time, it was obvious that Mr. Miyagi was nowhere within the sea of people who walked about the dojo, talking and eating. After a few minutes of searching, Jody called out that she had located him. I walked from the office to our storeroom where I found Mr. Miyagi, seated on the floor, eating his lunch and surrounded by a mob of children. He was completely encircled by dozens of young children, who seemed very content sitting on the floor and having lunch with Mr. Miyagi. I wasn't surprised. Miyagi cared deeply for children and these youngsters probably sensed that the moment they met him.

During his visit, Mr. Miyagi noticed in the advertisement for my dojo that there was a clause stating "No Contracts. No Testing Fees." He asked what this meant, and Dan Simons and I tried to explain that the majority of dojos in the United States required students to sign a contract and pay a fee to be tested for a belt. He couldn't understand this at all. He said, "Students should not have to sign a contract to come to class. If they want to come, it is okay. If they don't want to come, that is okay too. If they don't want to come to class, they should not have to pay."

The testing fee payments confused him, because he was always of the belief that each and every class was a test. He said he would not judge a student for promotion to a higher rank based on his performance in one class only. Mr. Miyagi believed that a true martial arts student would strive to do his very best in each and every class and not wait for only one night to impress his sensei.

When Danny and I began to tell him that some dojos require their students to purchase gis, books, patches and other equipment from them, he simply laughed.

Early in his visit, Mr. Miyagi also had the opportunity to talk with Len. Although they had corresponded by letter, they had not spoken since 1964. After the conversation Mr. Miyagi turned to me, smiled and said, "Neidert still the same. Still joking like he did in Okinawa."

I had invited Len for a visit during Miyagi's stay, but he was unable to make it. Mr. Miyagi and I had hoped that the three of us could sit down and talk about old times and our lives over a cold beer, but it wasn't meant to be.

***

After Mr. Miyagi's departure, I very quickly began to learn that running a full time dojo was not at all like what I had become accustomed to over the years. The expense alone was an eye opener, and I had to get used to something entirely new—advertising. I had never used outlets of any type to advertise my dojo, and all students came by word of mouth.

There was another headache that became evident early on and, sadly, there was no remedy for this agitation. It was obvious that the parents of many of our younger students had been exposed to the "Martial Arts Belt Factories" that polluted the traditional ideals of the old school masters, and belts were given away like candy at a neighborhood party. I was bombarded weekly with "My neighbor's son got his black belt in a year. Such and Such Dojo promises a black belt within 18 months. My friend's four-year old just got her black belt." Well, as politely as possible, I told them if that's what they expected in my dojo, they were in the wrong place. Some of them left in no time at all, but a few stayed on to see what "tradition" was all about. Still, others would arrive with a child or two and enrol them, expecting to see their children promoted within a week of their arrival. Again, I explained this was not the way my dojo operated. Then there was the mother who demanded that her son be promoted on the spot, because she was of the opinion that he was better than students who had been there for weeks or months. And, this was his very first day in class.

Some parents couldn't believe there were requirements to be met before a promotion was awarded. I explained, time and again, that each student was promoted on his or her individual merit, and then only after they reached an approved standard of proficiency. Additionally, the standards became more stringent for each higher level of belt. No one under the age of 16 would be promoted to black belt and adults would, in most instances require five years (two to three classes weekly) to reach the rank of Shodan or First Degree Black Belt. There were indeed exceptions, but they were few and far between.

There were a few parents (very few actually) who brought a child to class and sat attentively through their first lesson. When they arrived for the second lesson, the parent presented me with a list of things they saw, which they believed needed to be changed in our teaching methods. Of course, they had no knowledge of, or training in the martial arts whatsoever, but based on their observations, our teaching techniques were wrong. It took only a few seconds to lay out the rules of engagement, who was in charge and how things would be done. There were no subsequent lists.

It wasn't long before I faced the first big challenge. A woman stopped by and asked about enrolling her son in class, but said immediately that he had a lot of difficulty with self-confidence and dealing with people. After a few minutes she had related a story of a young boy who seemed to have a deep fear of even being around people, especially strangers. When our conversation ended, she purchased a gi and said she would bring him the next day.

The following afternoon, Susan McMahon looked as though she was completely lost when she came through the door. Sean refused to get out of the car and come in. I walked to the car with her and began talking to a teary eyed boy, who was obviously scared of what was on the other side of the door. It took time and patience, but Sean finally got out of the car, but that didn't mean it was going to be an easy stroll to the classroom. Once out of the car, he froze again and said he didn't want to take karate lessons.

This was going to be a challenge, but somewhere in the back of my mind Mr. Miyagi was whispering to me about patience and understanding. What happened next seemed akin to a hostage negotiation as I talked him, one step at a time, to the dojo door and, at last, inside. Well, a quick turn into the classroom wasn't on Sean's program for the day. He wouldn't go into a room where a dozen other people, most of them children in his age bracket, waited.

A second classroom was not in use at the time, and another step-by-step process began. Slowly we walked, as I continued to talk with Sean, and we made it to the empty room. Again he balked, and the only way he would enter the room was if I allowed his mother to go in with him. With that concession on the table, Sean warily stepped into the room. Patience and understanding I thought while I knelt beside him on one knee and showed him the proper way to make a fist. Then, with his mother on his left side, and I on his right, he took the first step in what was to become a remarkable journey.

There was no magic wand to wave, or mystical fingers to snap and change him overnight, but experience had taught me to help others take the steps at their pace. And, in time, perseverance would prevail and the rewards would come.

After a few classes with just the three of us, Sean agreed to join the others and practice. I think Susan was as surprised as Sean when he walked into the classroom and the other students acted as if he'd been there all along. Still, he wanted his mother to be nearby and she sat just outside the classroom and watched. In a week or so, she was with other parents around the corner, talking or watching television. Soon, she was able to leave Sean there and shop or run other errands.

Sean seldom missed a class and, while he was out of sight of his mother and father, who came by from time to time, something good was happening. But, I didn't want to rush out and tell them that he was doing great. I decided to wait until our open house just before Christmas and let them see for themselves.

The night of the open house, I took Sean's parents aside and told them that I would have him come out and lead the class when things got underway. He father stared at me and said he'd never do it. I just smiled and said, "Wait and see."

While family and friends of the students watched, we lined up and bowed in. After a brief introduction, I called Sean to the front of the room. A moment later, the once scared, blonde haired little boy, took command and led the class (adults included) through a series of punching and blocking exercises. Much to the surprise of his parents and grandparents, he looked as though he'd been taking charge for years.

Later that night his grandparents talked with me about Sean's progress. They were overwhelmed by what he had accomplished in only four months. I told them the strong kid was always there. We simply guided him along until he found the confidence to let the other boy step out.

Months later, Deborah Weiner, who worked at FOX 45 in Baltimore, overheard a conversation I was having about Sean with a Howard County Police Officer. She called me aside and asked for more details about him. When I related the story to her, she said she'd love to do a feature about Sean on FOX News. On May 27, 1993, Sean made his television debut.

There was also a surprise in store for those of us who worked with Sean. In his elementary school class he had taken it upon himself to help those who were having problems with their studies. Without fanfare, he worked with fellow classmates and did so never expecting, or asking for a reward in return. When the strong young boy emerged, the things he did in his everyday life showed the qualities Mr. Miyagi often spoke of. Looking back, I wonder how many people would believe that for the entire first month of classes, Sean never spoke to me.

***

From day one, my students hear my "sermon" about never being the one to start a fight. I reinforced that point many times over, but made certain they also understood it was okay to defend "yourself, your family, or a friend" if necessary.

As fate would have it, the mother of one of our younger students, Brandon Sandosky, came to me and said Brandon had gotten into trouble at school for fighting. She went on to tell that he had rushed to the aid of a friend who was being beaten by another student. He stopped the attack and left the assailant whimpering on the ground. Up to that point he was okay, as a number of teachers had witnessed the incident and said that Brandon did the right thing. However, after he began to walk away, he turned, went back and gave the other boy "a few more punches" for good measure. And, that's when they decided he had crossed the line.

Mrs. Sandosky asked if I would talk to Brandon about what had happened, and I agreed. Brandon's father had perished in a car accident, and his mother said she thought I was a good father figure for him. So, a few moments later I was in the office, on one knee talking with a teary eyed boy about what he had done. I told him I believed he did what was right by defending his friend, and that his actions were commendable in that respect. However, it was a very delicate approach in trying to explain that he should have settled the matter completely during the initial encounter. I told him that once the "battle" had ended, he should have walked away and left any further issues to the principal and teachers. He said he understood and, as far as I was concerned, the matter was settled.

The next matter on the program for the evening was a chat with two of the "bigger kids" from the class. It was a telephone call, which awakened me at 2:30 AM that brought about this scheduled conference.

Sergeant Dan Coon, a member of my former drug unit, called to tell me he had stopped two Jeeps that were in somewhat of a hurry as they travelled east on Old Frederick Road. It seemed they were in so much of a hurry, they were "driving side by side" on the two lane roadway and one of the Jeeps was occupying his (westbound) lane. He told me the vehicles were being driving by two of my students, a Justine Burrows and Matt Corell. He also said that Matt, a former Force Recon Marine, was still standing at attention in front of his car. He said he had informed them he was offering them two options. The first, he would write each of them a citation for negligent and/or reckless driving and send them on their way, or option number two, he would call me and have me deal with it He said they were too eager to have him address the problem, and immediately knew they feared facing me far more than receiving a traffic citation.

I told him, in that case, tell them to be outside my office door at the dojo at 1700 hours. Dan laughed and said they would probably sweat for the next 14 or so hours.

When I opened the door and escorted Brandon out to his mother, Matt and Justine were standing side by side, and looked as if they expected to be shot at any moment. In a matter of seconds they were in front of my desk and Matt was frozen in the position of attention. His eyes stared straight ahead as though he expected to find that familiar set of eyeballs from Parris Island somewhere on the wall behind my desk. It didn't take much time to explain that I hated being jolted out of a sound sleep by a ringing telephone. My dislike for the call grew as the reason behind it was made clear, and the icing on the cake was learning the identity of the knot-heads who were responsible for my rude awakening. My tirade was short and to the point, but probably more effective than paying a fine.

***

Another student would present a new challenge and, as is sometimes the case, would be a test of patience and perseverance. Mark and Cindy McFall brought their son, David, to class and told me he wanted very much to learn karate. David was an eager student and he showed right away that he wanted to excel. But, he was going to have to work so much harder than most, because he had trouble concentrating and retaining what he had learned. He didn't allow that to bother him and he showed an exceptional discipline when he was told to do something. If David were told to repeat a drill, he would continue the repetitions until he was told to stop, and that was a quality I admired about him.

When he began classes, I told Mark and Cindy not to worry, because David would advance at a pace he could manage. And, as far as promotions, he would be awarded his promotions based on his accomplishments and meeting the required standards.

In some ways, David reminded me of Vince from my initial years of teaching. He didn't question why others were promoted or moved on to another kata. He simply put forth his best effort and kept working to improve. Unlike Vince, David had a little mischief in him and after a number of weeks he decided that maybe karate class was a place where he could bring out a bit of his clown. He soon found that jokes and fooling around in class meant the push-up corner when the session was over.

Weeks turned to months, and months to years and David was moving ahead, and getting much stronger from his time spent in the corner doing push-ups. It seemed that as he got older, he searched for newer ways to test my patience. Of course, that meant that I had to find newer and better ways to remind him who was in charge. By now push-ups were no longer an unpleasant style of discipline, but merely another form of exercise for him and it looked to me as if he was beginning to enjoy them.

Our main classroom in the dojo had blue shag carpeting on two of the four walls, from floor to ceiling. The business, which occupied the space before us, must have had a carpet fetish and specifically shag carpet. Various colors of shag carpet covered floors and walls throughout the space. When we worked to remodel the space to suit our needs, we decided to leave the carpet on two walls in the main room. When the work was at last completed, the carpet didn't detract from the room at all.

One day, that magic blue carpet gave me an idea. When David arrived for class, he had "trouble about to happen" written all over him. And, when class began, he wasted no time in trying to be funny. Today, however, I was ready for him. I marched him to a corner, sat him down and told him to start counting the shag threads. He was also told he would have to give me an exact count at the end of class. I told him that in the future this would be his punishment when he acted up in class. He would sit in a corner during class and count threads, instead of participating in the session. To drive home my point, I told David not to make up a number, because I knew exactly how many threads were in each row, and the total number for each segment of the wall. Naturally, he believed this to be the gospel truth, but the other children believed it as well.

True to his work ethic, David sat on the floor and began to count the threads while the rest of the students went through katas, blocking drills and bag work. He remained on the floor in the corner, diligently counting until I told him it was time to line up and bow out. Within a few days I discovered that counting threads wasn't something he liked to do, because he found there were no benefits in the task, such as he found in push-ups. The very thought of having to count threads, while others practiced, seemed to dampen his desire to be the class clown.

It took a lot of hard work, patience and perseverance, but David finally earned his brown belt. In fact, it took several years before he was awarded his brown belt, yet he never complained because of the time. The night I presented him with his certificate and brown belt, I told him that I was very proud of what he had accomplished. He worked harder to earn his brown belt than most people work to reach their Shodan level.

David stayed with the class for more than 8 years but, as happened to so many, school and homework took priority over the karate. That was a standing rule with our dojo. If studies and grades would suffer because of class attendance, preference had to be given to education. Although I admit I missed having David around. He gave me a challenge and surely he tested my patience and willpower, but those weekly sessions helped keep me focused, and reminded me of what Mr. Miyagi wanted me to be as a teacher.

During his years in class David surprised me with two things, his knowledge of Godzilla and the DeLorean Motor Car. I don't believe there was anything he didn't know about either. As I recall, he had collected and watched every Godzilla movie made and the only car he wanted was a DeLorean.

Jody and I had talked with David about Godzilla and the fact that the goal of this monster of the deep was to protect and defend Okinawa. Suddenly, he was extremely anxious to meet Mr. Miyagi. When he had that opportunity in 1996, he spent time talking with Mr. Miyagi about Godzilla.

As far as the car he always wanted, well, he didn't get a DeLorean. However, he and his father located a Black, 1979 Pontiac, Trans AM, called "The Bandit" named for the role played by Burt Reynolds in the movie Smokey and The Bandit. I had the opportunity in June 2010 to see the car and, and as I expected, David had "The Bandit" looking as if it just left the showroom. He's won several awards in car shows, but I'm not surprised.

***

It would be a phenomenal achievement if I could write

nothing but success stories about everyone who walked through the doors into our dojo. Life in the real world is often a very harsh slap across the face for those who believe only in fairy tale endings. As much as I, or anyone else would like to catch the impossible dream and have nothing but success after success, human nature has the final say, and sometimes the message isn't pleasant.

Not long before I retired from the police department, Miss Margaret, a woman who worked on the cleaning crew, and someone I had known for many years, asked if I could help her. She said she had three great grandchildren, Kenny, Kenisha and Devin, and she desperately wanted to have some positive influence in their lives. She said she didn't have a great deal of money, but was hoping I would take them into my karate dojo and work with them. I assured her that I had never turned anyone away because of money issues, and I wouldn't begin now by turning my back on her.

When they arrived at the dojo, I learned that Kenny and Kenisha were brother and sister, and Devin was their cousin. Miss Margaret said she just didn't feel right about bringing them to class and not paying some type of fee. In matter of a few minutes we had negotiated an agreement that her great grandchildren would come in on Friday evenings and help me clean the dojo. At the time, I didn't realize that cleaning the dojo would become such an entertaining event.

The first night they arrived to help with the cleaning, the three of them began a very heated argument over who would clean the bathrooms. I was more than a little surprised to find that they were arguing, because each one wanted the job of cleaning the bathrooms. Now that was a first for me. I've known people who would hide to get out of cleaning a bathroom, but not these kids. I settled the argument by telling them I would keep a written record on the office calendar, to ensure that each one would have their very own Friday evening to clean the bathrooms. We marched to the office, I wrote their names in the Friday slots for the next three months and peace was restored.

Danny, Bruce and Will knew the children were coming to classes and were well aware of the financial situation of their families. Without a moment's hesitation, they opened their wallets and purchased gis for them. The kids were grateful and seemed quite proud of their new, crisp white uniforms the first time they put them on and stepped into the classroom.

Following their first night in class, Jody and I were talking about them and what we saw in their future. Kenny was the quiet one and certainly more of a follower, but seemed to have his act together and did well in school. Kenisha, we thought, would be the one to test the waters and see how far she could push the buttons. True to our belief, in a matter of weeks she began acting up and disrupting classes. Several trips to the corner for push-ups didn't dampen her will to try my patience. The next time she disrupted the class, I sent her out of the classroom and made her sit alone until class concluded. She was warned to change her behavior or the next time she would be suspended from the class for a month. The threat worked for a week, but then she had to push the buttons again to see if I was serious about the suspension. She was sent packing for 30 days and, upon her return, Kenisha arrived with a new outlook and work ethic. She no longer disrupted the class and worked harder than ever to advance.

As Jody and I discussed Devin, we agreed that we could see a hard edge to him. It seemed as if he was already one step in the wrong direction and without close supervision he could easily fall to the wrong side of the law. I made certain that Danny, Bruce and Will were aware of our discussion and they devoted extra time to Devin.

In spite of what I saw, I liked Devin from the very beginning. He had a big smile and that smile often signalled a devilish side of him. He could make anyone laugh and I looked forward to Friday evenings and cleaning the dojo. On those nights the clown in Devin was at its best, and his antics seemed to make the chores easier and the time pass quickly.

The three of them seldom missed a class and their hard work and steady progress was rewarded with the appropriate promotions. But, in time, they stopped coming to class as school and additional homework was the higher priority. Kenny and Kenisha continued with their schooling and found their place in the job market.

Devin, on the other hand, walked the path Jody and I feared

he would. As he grew older, the dark world of drugs beckoned, and he became involved in a shootout at a local barbershop and was wounded in the gun battle. There was no lesson learned from that incident and, once again, he picked up a gun. This time he opened fire spraying a house with bullets where a Christmas party was being held. There was no specific target, but a bullet found an innocent victim in the basement of the home and killed him. Devin is now awaiting trial on charges of murder and weapons violations.

The sad truth is, some people can't be saved and I believe there are some who just don't want to be saved. As I said when I worked with the Howard County Police, "We can't be everywhere at once and, unfortunately, we can't protect everybody all the time."

And, it is also a certainty that, no matter how hard we try, we'll never save everybody. Although I wish it were possible to protect and save everyone, reality is a cold fact of life and, regardless of our successes, we will have our failures.

***

There were some comical moments over the years in our Ellicott City dojo, and one of the first arrived via the U. S. Mail. I opened the envelope from The State of Maryland and was surprised to find a renewal application for an elevator license. I read the document carefully, which stated that I had to call and request an inspection date for my 17 passenger 15,000-pound capacity elevator. There was also a notation that I would have to be present on the day of the inspection. I doubled checked the information to be sure the address was correct and knew immediately someone had made a big mistake. Our dojo was in a one-story building.

I called the telephone number listed on the renewal form and told the woman who answered my call about the error. She was quiet for a moment, stuttered for a few seconds and finally said she couldn't talk to me and hung up.

I certainly wasn't going to call and request an inspection date for an elevator that didn't exist. I put the papers in a desk drawer, thinking they would be good for a few laughs over a beer some day, and promptly forgot about them. About three weeks later another envelope arrived from The State of Maryland. I opened it and read in very bold letters, "Congratulations!" In smaller print, "Your elevator passed inspection and your license has been renewed for another year." Then the notation, "Please display this license in a prominent place." What the hell, I thought. I have a notorious sense of humor. I posted the license in the center of our bulletin board.

Like clockwork, for the next several years, this procedure was repeated. The application for renewal would arrive, I'd stuff it in a desk drawer and, three weeks later our new elevator license arrived and was posted prominently on the bulletin board.

About a week after receiving our elevator license, I found a way to put it to good use. Soon after the dojo opened, calls began coming in from people who said they wanted to become a Ninja. At first, I simply told them we didn't teach Ninjitsu and they would have to call elsewhere. But, the calls persisted and I decided it was time to give a little payback to the annoying callers.

When the next Ninja wannabe call came in, I told the caller he would have to pass a test. I told him there was an elevator hidden within the dojo and he would have to find it in order to be accepted into the Ninja classes. In most instances, there would be a long pause. So, I would continue, telling them that the elevator was so well hidden, we called it "The Invisible Elevator" and so far, no one had managed to find it. Usually, calls ended abruptly after that.

There were other Ninja calls, but one holds the prize as my favorite. First, let me apologize, because writing the accounts of these calls won't bestow upon them the proper "fame" they deserve. Writing cannot duplicate the voices on the other side of the phone. Anyway, I answered another call late in the afternoon and knew immediately I had a live one on the line. He spoke loudly, and spat out his words to emphasize each one. "I want to be a Ninja."

Oh, God, another one, I thought. "Is that right?"

"Yes, it is imperative that I become a Ninja." The tone and emphasis was still there.

"Why?"

"I want to master the art of invisibility."

"You want to master the art of invisibility?"

"Yes," he practically screamed. "I wanna to be able to hide in plain sight." He was getting louder. "I want to be invisible."

Very calmly, I said, "This is what I want you to do. During the next snowstorm, I want you to jump in the shower and make sure you get soaked from head to toe. After you are completely soaked, roll around in some white cooking flour and go outside. If nobody sees you, you've mastered the art of invisibility." Click.

The next caller didn't want to be a Ninja, but wanted to tout himself as the clone of Jean-Claude Van Damme. He spoke in the schoolyard tone of a child who was trying his best to talk down to his classmates. Kind of that aggravating "Nah, nah, nah, I'm better than you are" voice.

I answered his call, and almost he immediately went into his obviously rehearsed speech. "My kicks are just like Jean-Claude Van Damme's. Are your kicks just like Jean-Claude Van Damme's?" I didn't have the opportunity to reply, because he rambled on. "My kicks are so great, my teacher won't even let me use my hands. I use my feet and beat everybody because my kicks are just like Jean-Claude Van Damme's."

Finally he paused and I said, "That's good, but what happens if you're engaged in a street fight and find yourself backed into a spot where you can't use your great kicks? What happens then?"

"Never thought about that." Click.

Many funny moments were unintended, and in a few of those instances I should be very grateful that the parents laughed and saw the humor in the situation. Some things were misunderstood and caused a few chuckles, but others—well, some young children took things I said in jest as an order they should follow.

Earl Wheeler worked for the Howard County Government as an auto mechanic, and, as he worked on my police car often during my career, I got to know him quite well. He had a son, David, and eventually Earl asked if he could bring him to class. At that time there was only a small group of us working out at my house. One warm evening in May, after David had been in class a few months, I decided to have the class outside.

Jody had brought her dog, Mack, with her and didn't want to leave him in the house while we practiced. I was standing beside David when she asked what she should do with Mack. I pointed and said, "There's a chain over there by the tree. Take him up there and chain him to the tree."

Suddenly, there was a look of complete panic in David's eyes and he backed up a few steps toward his father. I realized that he thought I was telling Jody to take him and chain him to the tree. After a hurried explanation that I meant the dog and not him, there was a round of laughter from Earl, Jody and I, and a very big sigh of relief from David.

As time passed, I found that David listened much more carefully to my comments and/or advice than I thought. At the end of one of the classes I casually remarked to him that he should eat more spinach, because it would make him stronger. A day or two later Earl told me that on the way home from the previous class David said they needed to stop at the grocery store. When asked why, David replied, "Mr. Jim said I need to eat spinach to get stronger. We need to stop and get some."

Eating spinach, of course, was a positive, but the next bit of advice, intended only as a joke, proved that sometimes kids did take my spoken words as a must. I had joked with others over the years about how good I thought they would look with a Mohawk haircut. One evening, I commented that he would look good with a Mohawk. David asked what a Mohawk was and, without further thought, I told him about the hairstyle right there in front of his father.

The following week, Earl was laughing when he brought David to class. He called me aside and told that a few nights ago, while they were watching television, David got up and went into the bathroom. He said he thought he was staying there much longer than normal, but let it pass. A few minutes later David came out of the bathroom, wearing a baseball hat that was pulled down rather snuggly around his ears. Earl asked him why he was wearing the hat, but he didn't seem to have an explanation—at least not a good explanation. With a little coaxing, he removed the hat and Earl began laughing.

While watching television, David apparently recalled what I

had said about the Mohawk and decided to give it the old "do it yourself" effort. He went into the bathroom and took his father's razor to give himself the Mohawk haircut. Needless to say, his first effort at becoming his own barber failed miserably, which was also the reason David appeared for his next class with a crew cut.

Jody later suggested I should thank God that Earl had a good sense of humor about the whole incident. She also reminded me that because the kids in the class looked up to me, I should be extremely careful about what I said, even in jest. It might be a joke in my mind, but to them what I was saying was advice to be taken seriously, like the word of the Gospel.

***

I decided that we should have a summer camp for the kids, but I wanted to have something very different for them. Our camp would be one week only, but a week the kids would talk about for the rest of the summer. It would also set the stage for future camps.

The first hour of each morning was devoted to practice of kata, reflex drills, bag work and self-defense. Because our dojo space allowed us to darken certain rooms during daylight hours, I put together a very different game of hide and seek for the students. The senior students, who helped with the camp, would take handheld bags and go into the darkened rooms, where there were dozens of hiding places. One at a time, the younger students would set out to search the rooms, knowing an attacker lay in wait for them. When attacked, they had to fight off their attacker and move on to the next room and repeat the process. During these practice drills they made full contact with punches, kicks, elbows, and knees against the bag held by their adversary. By the end of the first session, those who initially showed a fear of the dark eagerly welcomed the opportunity to go through the drill again.

The next morning the drills were conducted again, but now students in pairs conducted the searches. They were taught the concept of working together as a team and looking out for each other. And, it didn't take them long to adjust to the idea of working as a team. But each time the drills were repeated, the students were paired with a new partner. The more they worked, the better they became, right to the point of planning how the search would be conducted—including who would conduct the initial search and who would act as cover. Jody jokingly told the parents that by the end of the week their children would be SWAT Team certified.

On Wednesday, Thursday and Friday, after the first hour of practice, the students were given a special treat.

On Wednesday, PFC Tommy Harding of the Howard County Police Department brought in his K-9 Dogs. The students were given a lecture on the purpose of the dogs and how they served the police department and the community. Next they were treated to a demonstration of attack training, the tracking of a suspect and finally how the dogs searched for and located drugs and guns.

On Thursday morning, R. C. Bartley and Al Hafner of the Howard County Police Department's Forensic Services Division were the featured guests. Soon, the students were learning the art of processing a crime scene. R. C. and Al demonstrated and explained various items of equipment utilized to process crime scenes. Of course, they couldn't wait to learn the art of recovering fingerprints. Al used his car to teach them how to lift fingerprints and, in turn, each student had the opportunity to test their newly learned skill. At the end of the day they could proudly show their parents what they had accomplished.

By Friday morning the dojo was rocking with anticipation. This was the day all of them had been talking about. The police department's Tactical (SWAT) Unit was coming to visit. But, first to arrive and give them an extra treat was PFC Sam Hammond, who brought the County's Mobile Command Post for the students to see. Sam gave them a tour of the center and explained its function and equipment.

Sergeant Bill McMahon and Officers Tom Marello and Rob Dell Erba arrived with the Tactical Van and would spend the rest of the morning with the students and explain their roll with the police department.

The students then went out to the parking lot and crowded around the van as Officer Marello talked to them about the various equipment carried on the truck. From weapons to gas masks, raid vests and ballistic helmets, the students hung on to his every word.

Certainly there were dozens of questions and each was answered, but that didn't seem to satisfy their curiosity. So, the next thing to do was have them try on some of the equipment, however all weapons were strictly off limits. Soon boys and girls were being helped into raid vests and ballistic helmets, which probably weighed more than the student wearing the equipment. But they didn't seem to care.

The display ended when we took them to the darkest area of the building where Sergeant Bill McMahon set up the night vision equipment. One by one, the boys and girls scanned the darkness for those who went to hide. There were a number of excited "Wows" when they found that they could actually see in the dark.

One particular summer camp's final day even caused some parents to take off from work or and, in some cases, a few may have even made up elaborate excuses for missing a few hours.

I was looking for something to make the final day of the 1996 summer camp very different from the others. I began planning weeks ahead of time by calling long time friend, Dick Schnell who was a Colonel with the Maryland National Guard, and asked if he could help. Within a matter of minutes, Dick had an idea on the table that would surely thrill the students. But, a few things would have to be cleared before the plan was finalized. Dick made the necessary calls and everything fell into place for the camp's final day.

The students and parents were informed of what had been planned for the final day and to be at the Howard County Fair Grounds at 9:00 AM. I arrived early, but Dick was already there directing three Humvees to locations in the large field used for parking. One was the standard U. S. Army Humvee, the second was an ambulance and the third was set up with a TOW Missile launcher atop.

As the students began arriving, the last feature of the display was approaching. A U. S. Army Huey Helicopter flew over, circled back and was directed to a landing site by Colonel Schnell. After the Huey landed, Dick spoke to the students and the parents who had said they were not going to miss out on the fun their children were having.

After Dick talked with them, the children were allowed to get into the helicopter, sit in the seats and feel the movement of the controls. Well, that is after the parents were chased out of the helicopter. The rule for the day—children first, parents second. And, from where I was standing, it looked as if the parents were enjoying the last day of camp as much as their children.

In groups they went to the various Humvees and talked with the soldiers who were manning the vehicles. Rides were given in the standard Humvee, while some climbed atop the second and learned how the TOW Missile functioned. Others were taken aboard the ambulance and given a quick lesson on its equipment and mission.

All in all, this was one of the most eagerly awaited summer camps and it was indeed a big success, as all of the summer camps were. I will always be grateful to Colonel Dick Schnell, the soldiers of the Maryland National Guard and Sergeant Bill McMahon (Now Chief of Police Bill McMahon). My gratitude extends to all of those from the Howard County Police who gave their time and support over the years. Police Officers Sam Hammond, Tommy Harding, Tom Marello, Rob Dell Erba, Gil Feldman, Mark Joyce, Dave Dixon, Mark Thomey, and Mr. R. C. Bartley and Mr. Al Hafner for their help in making those camps what they were. Because of their combined effort and support, the children, teens and pre-teens, had the opportunity to meet and interact in a positive way with members of the United States Military and Law Enforcement Communities.

1995

The year 1995 would be my first trip back to Okinawa in over 31 years. I admit my return was long overdue, but worth the wait. There was a twofold purpose for the visit. The main focus for me was the 40th Anniversary of Miyagi Sensei's dojo and secondary was the Okinawa World Pre-tournament Competition.

A total of 15 of us made the journey to Okinawa in August 1995, flying out from Dulles International Airport.

As Miyagi's inaugural visit to the United States was much like a hurricane blown tour, so were our first days in Okinawa. It began with a press interview during the afternoon of our second day and a welcoming party at the dojo that evening. Then we were taken to meet the Governor of Okinawa, the Mayor of Urasoe City and a visit to the U. S. Consulate. There were sightseeing ventures in the mornings and afternoons, and karate classes every evening.

The night of our welcoming party Mr. Miyagi waited until the customary speeches were given before taking me aside. He asked if I remembered the young boy who seemed to appear from nowhere when I arrived early for class and sit and watch me go through kata. How could I forget? It seemed like he would arrive the very instant I stepped outside in my gi. "Yes, I do remember him."

He introduced me to Yoshiaki Kohagura, telling me he was the boy who came to watch me. Mr. Miyagi told me that after I left Okinawa, Kohagura came to join his class. But I was stunned when he told me that the young boy said I was his inspiration for wanting to join the class. At the same time I felt deeply honored, because I couldn't imagine an American being a role model for an Okinawan boy—especially in an art that belonged to Okinawa.

I also quickly learned that Yoshiaki was now almost totally blind. He began losing his sight sometime ago, yet continued his participation in the class. I was indeed surprised that he continued to practice, but I was in for a much bigger surprise. When it was time to leave the party, he stepped out of the dojo, put on his sandals, turned and walked home. Although he could barely make out images, he learned to walk to and from the dojo by counting the number of steps. And, his home wasn't exactly three doors away. There were several left and right hand turns along the path he travelled.

My first meeting with Yoshiaki Kohagura was merely the beginning of many new lessons I would learn on my return to Okinawa and his courage and determination would be an education for my students.

Charles Jacobs, a brown belt and a member of my former drug enforcement unit, was practicing kata in the dojo prior to an evening class. He was working with a group of students and, a few minutes before Mr. Miyagi called the class to line up, he walked over and told me one of the Okinawan black belts had worked with him and corrected a few mistakes he'd made. Then he and pointed to Kohagura, saying he was the one who had helped him.

I don't know why, but I wasn't at all shocked that Kohagura had corrected a flaw in Chuck's kata. After all, I had learned over the years that people, young and old, who put their body, mind and spirit into a task, were capable of accomplishing what so many deemed impossible.

Chuck was positively astonished when I informed him that Kohagura was almost completely blind. "Blind?" he blurted. "How did he know I made a mistake? How could he correct me?"

"It doesn't matter how he knew, or how he was capable of

correcting you," I said. "Was he right?"

Chuck scratched his head. "Yes, he was."

"Then that's all that really matters. And, today you learned a lesson from a blind man."

Several hours of practice, over a few days, at the dojo and the Urasoe City Hall Auditorium showed how Kohagura's friends and fellow students kept him as a part of the class. When the class began moving into position to perform a kata, Kohagura held the bottom edge at the back of another student's gi jacket. He trotted out behind the student, stopped when told he was in the correct position and turned to his right, facing the front. At the conclusion of the kata, he turned to his left and the student who had been to his immediate right moved behind and a step to his left, clasped Kohagura's left elbow and guided him from the stage. When the class performed a weapons kata, the students followed the same procedure and, as I expected, Kohagura's execution of the kata was flawless.

During the visit, Kohagura asked if I would like to have a videotape of him performing the katas. I thanked him and quickly accepted his offer. In the years that followed, that videotape became a great source of inspiration, especially when I dealt with the "I can't do it" students. I would have them watch the tape and then ask what they saw wrong with the performance of the man going through the katas. When they said "nothing" I would inform them he was blind, and suddenly "I can't do it" was left behind on the dojo floor.

***

Miyagi Sensei had arranged the travel route for our initial sightseeing tour, and ensured that I took a ride along a route I had travelled so many times years ago. It was so different now, with businesses lining the divided highway—a highway that had once been a two-lane road, which Len and I knew as Highway One. I looked for old familiar sights, especially the Oyama Restaurant, but it was no longer there. At first, I thought I had missed it among all the new buildings, but Mr. Miyagi said it had closed, but wasn't sure of the date.

As we neared the location of my old base, Camp Sukiran, I

couldn't hide my smile. The bars still lined the street and I recalled the nights Len and I crossed that road to quench our thirst. We had laughed over how convenient it was to have a bar with a front door, which seemed to line up perfectly with the gate we exited. It was simply a matter of walking a straight line to the door. Whether or not the return trip was made in a perfectly straight line was another matter.

I noticed that the business next to the bar appeared to be the same as it was some 31 years ago. A quaint little building we knew as "Suzie's Tea House" was, shall we say, a house of entertainment for the lonely Marine, Soldier, Sailor, or Airman who sought female companionship.

Before I knew it I was looking across the highway at Camp Foster, which had been Camp Sukiran when I was stationed there. The Marines had shared the base with the 173rd Airborne in those days. The 12th Marine Regiment was now the sole occupant of the base, and the entrance, which had allowed free access back then, was closed and guarded by Marine Sentries.

We were allowed entry to the base and, as we slowly drove along the main road, a flood of memories rushed back. Images of familiar, but much younger faces, flashed by and I wondered how the passing of time changed them. When the bus passed by the location where my old barrack used to be, I remembered the laughter and friendships that were formed behind those walls.

I could still picture Len, with a big grin on his face, as he prepared to rip into someone with a well-placed barb, or smiling over the special liberty pass I had just forged. Of course, the image of the "Mad Bull" jumping up to accept or throw down a challenge was as clear as it had been then.

There were so many other memories from that era and maybe they are just a little too "colorful" to share in this book. Those are tales that should be shared, over a drink, with Len's sons, Joe, Brian and Chris. I would like them to see their father, a man who loved and cherished them, through my eyes.

***

Our initial karate classes were in preparation for the 40th

Anniversary Celebration of Miyagi's Dojo. Although my class had practiced for weeks before our departure, we had to work with Mr. Miyagi's class to fine-tune the demonstration. Then there was a rehearsal at the Urasoe City Hall Auditorium on Saturday evening to be sure everyone was prepared for Sunday's big event.

From city hall, we returned to the dojo, where we were told we would be going to a nearby park to take part in a festival. Jody, Kristen Demastus and Jennifer Harris were taken aside by Mrs. Miyagi and several Okinawan women and dressed in kimonos. As soon as they were dressed, we were ushered to the park and almost immediately I found myself seated at a table as one of the guests of honor. The moment I sat down an ice cold Orion Beer "magically" appeared in front of me.

There was no time for anyone to catch their breath, and Jody, Kristen and Jennifer were hurriedly "coaxed" into a circle with other women, where a traditional Okinawan Dance was being performed. They followed along and it seemed as though the spirit of the dance captivated them in no time at all. But, the evening wouldn't end until I took the class on to a stage in the park and had them perform a kata for the crowd. Naihanchi Shodan brought a rather boisterous round of applause from our audience.

Sunday morning was a blur and before we knew it we were at Urasoe City Hall, preparing for the much anticipated demonstration and celebration. I stepped behind the stage curtains and immediately heard someone call out, "Lilley San." I turned and was greeted by Meiyu Takara. As all of us, Takara had aged, but he still had the broad shoulders of the young man I had met over 31 years ago. He was there with members of his class to honor his teacher.

The first order of the day was a series of speeches. I had been informed about a month prior to our departure for Okinawa that I would be asked to give a speech. I was called to the podium to speak and gave the following address to Miyagi sensei and those gathered in the audience.

"I am happy to once again return to Okinawa and celebrate with you the 40th Anniversary of Miyagi Sensei's Dojo. I consider myself most fortunate to have met Mr. Miyagi on rainy evening in

November 1963. I recall that evening well, as it was truly a night that would help shape my future life.

I sat in Mr. Miyagi's house and drank tea with him and told him that I wished to study karate. He smiled and said, 'No American has ever stayed in my class longer then three months.' He told me his class was strict and there would never be an opportunity for me to be anything other than a white belt. But, he also told me, 'If you really want to learn, and you are sincere, come and I will teach you.' I returned the following evening because I believed Mr. Miyagi to be honest and a man of great integrity. And from our first meeting a friendship was born that has endured for 32 years.

Upon my return to the United States and leaving the U. S. Marine Corps, I began teaching my own karate class. It was a humble beginning with two students and classes were held in the basement of my father's house. As more students joined the class I tried to instill in them the principles of discipline and the value of hard work. I wanted them to learn from me as I had learned from Miyagi Sensei.

In life each of us should have a role model to respect and one we wish most to be like. I have been blessed because I found two such men in my life. The first was my father, and the other, Miyagi Sensei. From them I learned the meaning of courage and honor. I learned to respect others and to grow in body, mind and spirit. And, as they taught me, I have tried to teach others and hope that in my teaching I have brought honor to them.

Many years have passed since I began my karate training with Miyagi Sensei, but I have always remembered the lessons I learned while here in Okinawa. The training I received here has helped me throughout my life in so many ways. I became a better person in my work and in my studies at college, because through my practice of karate I developed a much stronger character.

I offer to Miyagi Sensei my sincere congratulations on the 40th Anniversary of his dojo, not only as a student, but also a friend."

Almost immediately after I walked away from the podium, I asked a young Okinawan man, who had lived in America and acted as a translator, if my speech was acceptable. He smiled and said, "Everyone here loves you. You just put Miyagi Sensei a step above the Emperor."

When the comments concluded, the demonstration began. Senseis from various dojos and styles of karate throughout Okinawa came to honor Miyagi Sensei on the 40th Anniversary of his dojo. Members of my class performed Pinan Kata Yondan and Bunkai, along with other katas with Miyagi's students. There were also exhibitions of traditional Okinawan Dance and music by Taico Drummers.

Dan Simons and I were also asked to perform kata separate from the others. Danny was asked to present the weapons kata Shushi No Kon Sho and I offered the kata Kusanku Sho.

When the demonstration ended around 4:00 PM, we made our way to the cafeteria of city hall. There we found tables with platters of sushi and cold Orion Beer, along with a buffet style dinner waiting for us. Indeed the mood was festive and one of the leaders of the merriment was Mr. Funakoshi. I had met Funakoshi when he joined Miyagi's class in 1964. His height of 4'10" (that's stretching it) did very little to conceal his enthusiasm for leading the way to a good time. The party had barely started when he took Jody by the hand and escorted her to the small stage in the cafeteria. And, she wasted no time in pointing out that she was indeed taller than Funakoshi, even though she barely scratched the height marker at 4'11".

Soon he was rounding up other members of my class and having them join he and Jody on stage. A big round of cheers and laughter filled the room when he had them join him in singing Old McDonald Had a Farm. Funakoshi kept the chorus going over and over, while working feverishly to get the entire gathering to join in with them in the singing.

The food was delicious, but I made certain that I had my fill of sushi, something Mr. Miyagi introduced me to in 1964. Over the course of three or four hours I think I consumed close to four-dozen pieces, along with an ample quantity of Orion.

When the celebration concluded at city hall, it picked up and carried on back at the dojo. The beer was flowing freely when the first bottles of Sake were opened. Jody and I were seated on the floor with Mr. Miyagi, when the first bottle of Sake reached us. When one of his students offered to pour a glass for me, I quickly waved my hand and said, "No. No thanks."

Miyagi pointed a finger at me and laughed. "You still remember. You won't drink Sake."

I politely replied, "Hell no. I still clearly remember my last encounter with Sake."

In spite of my strong warnings, everyone else was going to sample the "Nectar of Hell" as I called it. Raphael Rappo, who had joined our class while working in the United States, reminded me that he was from Switzerland, and could handle alcohol of any type. The following morning, however, he looked more suited to lying in a coffin than attempting to stand upright. When I asked how he felt, he said, "Oh, God, my hair hurts. I swear I can feel my eyebrows growing." A retort of "I told you so" wasn't necessary.

Before those at the party reached the point of no return, Mr. Miyagi told me that he and I would not be meeting in the dojo in the morning at 5:00 AM to work out. Soon after my arrival, he had me join him in the dojo at around that time each morning, where he would take me through the katas again and again. I looked forward to those mornings and the time I could spend under his always stern, watchful eyes. But, I understood why the upcoming Monday session would be called off. It was time to celebrate with his friends and students who came to honor him.

It was also a night he would open another door from long ago and confess the feelings of the class. I had taken Jody back to the apartment where we were staying, kissed her goodnight and returned to the dojo.

I sat down again with Mr. Miyagi and he turned back the hands of time. He said, "When you first came to class, everyone was certain you would quit. Each night after class we sat and drank tea, waiting for you to leave. And, each night it was the same when you left. Everybody would say 'he won't come back again.'"

I smiled and nodded. "I had no intention of quitting."

"Then the next class you were there again. And you kept coming back and soon everyone was gaining great respect for you."

We talked for almost an hour about my awkward beginning and where those early days eventually took me. We agreed that 30 plus years was a long journey, but I believed there was a long road still to be travelled.

***

Shortly after our arrival I learned that Nakanishi (George) had been hospitalized with a stomach ailment, which required surgery. I wanted to see my old friend and mentor, and Mr. Miyagi took me to visit him.

It felt strange seeing him in a hospital bed, because I only remembered the strong, lightening quick young man who stood next to me all of those nights years ago. Still, he flashed a big smile and shook my hand. Then it was my turn to smile, as he held his grip while he checked my knuckles. I'm sure that was his way of making certain that I had continued to practice in the traditional way, which included striking the Makiwara board to condition the knuckles into solid weapons.

Our meeting wasn't long, but it was good to see George again and renew another friendship that was forged on a dojo floor so long ago.

Later that day I spun some tales, for my students, about George from the old days, including our encounter with the men on the motorcycle. I know Danny, Bruce and Will had heard them all before, but they seemed to enjoy them as much as they did when I first spoke of my days in Okinawa.

***

We also travelled to Okinawa to take part in a The World Tournament Competition, commemorating the 50th Anniversary of the end of the Pacific War and the Battle of Okinawa.

For the majority of my students this would be their very first competition and stepping on to a world stage in Okinawa was a good place to begin. There were competitors from Spain, France, Russia,

Australia, New Zealand, South Africa and America, to name just a few countries represented in Okinawa.

The Okinawans are very strict about the rules of competition and those of us who were named as judges would be drilled in what was expected. From kata competition, to weapons and kumite, the rules were laid out and fully explained. And, one of their strict rules was the timing of events. The day's activities would start and end precisely at the times indicated, and this included all preliminary and final events—no exceptions and no excuses. I thought this would be a first. I had never attended a competition in America that had once started or ended on time. In fact, every tournament I had attended in America usually ran hours beyond the advertised ending time. So, maybe I was a little sceptical as to how this would be accomplished in Okinawa.

The competition, which was held at the Okinawa Convention Center, began on Saturday, August 27th at exactly 10:00 AM (on time) and was scheduled to end at 5:00 PM. The day's events did not conclude until 5:05 PM, which I thought was a miracle to run only five minutes over schedule. But a five-minute overrun was totally unacceptable to the Okinawan organizers. Very early the following morning, every member of the officiating crew was standing tall on the carpet and being told that it would not happen again. Sunday's competition ended 15 minutes early, and that included the presentation of awards.

My students opened their kumite team competition facing the best Okinawa had to offer. There's nothing quite like drawing the champions of Okinawa as an opponent the first time you step into the ring to compete. But knowing they would be squaring off against the best didn't seem to intimidate them. In fact, they welcomed the challenge and when they stepped into the ring to face their respective opponents, they indeed surprised everyone.

I was with Mr. Miyagi, standing near the ring and, while watching, he turned to me. "Your students are doing very well."

"They practiced very hard," I said.

He nodded. "Yes. I can see that."

In the end, the Okinawan team prevailed, but I was very

proud of the showing my students made. They didn't go out with a whimper and, in one particular bout, there was a near stunning upset. Although only a brown belt, Chuck Jacobs fought in the black belt division and drew an undefeated champion as his opponent. From the outset, Chuck was the aggressor and grabbed two points before anyone realized what was happening. With time ticking away, the Okinawan rushed in close and Chuck responded instinctively, but with an illegal tactic. He wrapped his adversary in a chokehold and the judges ruled a forfeiture of one point. This, the Okinawan used to his advantage and charged him again, guessing correctly that Chuck would react according to his training. Another chokehold led to the forfeiture of his last point. Chuck's opponent then managed to score a point with only seconds remaining in the bout and won. At the conclusion of the tournament they held a fifth place finish, but who knows where they would have been standing had they pulled off an unimaginable upset.

Nelson Rebert participated in the weapons katas, taking fifth place in the Sai kata competition.

***

The closing of the World Tournament also marked the closing days of our visit to Okinawa. There was a farewell party at the dojo, which was a time to say goodbye to old friends and the many new friends made during our stay. And, once again, I found myself saying goodbye to Miyagi Sensei and so many others I considered my family in Okinawa. Although this time there was no uncertainty as it had been when I left Okinawa so many years ago. It would be only a matter of a few months before we met again, as Mr. Miyagi and many of his students were planning to visit us in the United States the following summer.

There were well wishes of another kind as we prepared to leave—a blessing from Mr. Miyagi and everyone for an upcoming wedding. Jody and I would be married on Saturday, December 2, 1995 and Miyagi Sensei and our many old and newfound friends sent us on our homeward journey with best wishes for our future.

1996 – 2002

In the latter part of 1989 our dojo lost Black Belt, Tom Wiswell, to cancer, but the late 90s would touch our dojo with a number of very tragic losses. On April 15, 1996 a plane crash in Lakeland, Florida would claim the lives of Black Belt, Sam Chayt and former student and Brown Belt, David Libergott. In 1999 we lost Kimberly Barber to Breast Cancer and Susan MacFarland to a Brain Aneurysm. To all of us, those losses were not a mere passing of acquaintances or friends, but members of our family.

***

Jody and I recall the day when Nancy Trimble-Oliver (formerly Miecznikoski) came to us and, before she spoke a word, we knew she was about to empty her soul of her frustrations. She truly looked as though she wanted to scream, and her first words were, "I would like to enrol my son in your class. You're my last hope."

Soon, she was telling us that she had almost lost her son, Andrew, to brain cancer when he was only five years old. Through the grace of God and the skilled, steady hands of Doctor Ben Carson of Johns Hopkins Hospital, Andrew's life was saved.

Andrew was waking in the morning and vomiting clear fluid, but afterward he felt fine. After an initial examination Doctor Allan Leffler felt that something was very wrong and asked that Andrew be brought back in two days. Andrew continued to throw up and was becoming more lethargic. During the next examination Doctor Leffler noticed a slight flutter in his left eye and sent him to an optometrist for further evaluation. There a MRI with contrast was ordered. It was during the MRI, his mother was informed that Andrew had a malignant brain tumor and was in imminent danger of having a stroke. He was rushed to Johns Hopkins Hospital, where Dr. Ben Carson operated immediately to remove the pressure on his brain. Another surgery was performed to remove the tumor, which was the largest ever seen by Doctor Carson. Although Andrew's life was saved, his road back would be long and tedious. From radiation treatments to physical therapy and speech therapy, days soon turned to months.

His mother told us that after his hospitalization, Andrew found life was not always picture perfect. He was ridiculed and the focal point of jokes because of his problems with balance and other issues from his battle with cancer. I assured her that he would not be taunted or the subject of jokes in my class. She informed us he had problems using his left hand and would have difficulties with his right side as well. Then she asked if it would be a problem if Andrews's brother, Michael, took classes with him. Of course, it wouldn't be a problem.

A few minutes later Andrew and Michael began their first class. Jody and I took them to a room where we had several heavy bags and started them exactly the same as we did everyone else. The correct way to make a fist and throw a punch was the initial item on the agenda. Then light contact with punches on the softest of the bags, but never telling Andrew we were aware that he had problems.

We had Michael step to the bag first to lead the way for his younger brother. When Andrew stepped to the front of the bag, he was told to punch with his right hand and then with his left. He didn't turn to either of us and say he couldn't do it. He followed Michael's lead and punched with both hands. Next came a front snap kick, which he did, although awkwardly. Still, he didn't say he couldn't do it. He merely followed Michael's lead again.

I believed then as I believe now, that had we told him that we were aware of his problems, Andrew might have taken it as a sign from us that we didn't think he could be a member of the class, or that we might offer him an easier path.

By the end of his first month in class, Andrew had taken remarkable steps and, as I had told his mother, his fellow students uttered not a word of ridicule. The other students treated him as an equal and I'm sure this helped Andrew.

He worked hard and Jody and I knew we could count on him for a top-notch effort in every class. He and Michael moved ahead at their pace and their efforts and work were rewarded with a yellow stripe placed on their white belts. Their hard work continued without a complaint and, in time, they were promoted to yellow belt.

A big moment for every young student was the day they were told they would be breaking their first board. They looked forward to that day, which was usually the last day of our summer camp. Of course, there were some that would doubt that they could really break a piece of wood, but Jody and I assured them that they had the strength and proper technique to achieve that goal.

When Andrew's turn came, he seemed a little timid when he walked to the center of the room. I stood behind him and told him he could do it and he stepped up to face his biggest challenge to date. He rested the side of his fist on the board and again, I told him he could break it. He raised his hand and when he began his downward strike I let out a Kiai with him. His fist went through the board and he stepped back quickly, staring at the broken piece of wood. There was a momentary expression of disbelief and then the biggest "I did it" smile I had ever seen. Of course, there were photographs of the moment and, as was the practice with everyone when they broke their first board, his name and the date was written on the pieces of wood and given to him.

Andrew never questioned Jody or me when we told him to do something. He just turned and went to work on performing the task and, each time he reached a particular goal, he eagerly awaited the next challenge. There was no "smoke and mirrors" magic to what Andrew accomplished. Certainly he worked much harder to reach a goal, but his rewards were far greater than if we had cheated and rewarded him simply for show, or to make him feel good.

As a very young boy, Andrew had faced almost certain death, but he took the fight right to the Grim Reaper's door and won the battle. There was no reason to expect that he would accomplish anything less in the karate class.

During Mr. Miyagi's 1998 visit we arranged a Martial Arts Demonstration to raise and donate money to The Johns Hopkins Children's Center. Members of Miyagi's Dojo, my dojo, Lee Cunningham's Snow Tiger Dojo, Pat Raphael's Ju-Jitsu Dojo of Columbia, and Frank Faris and members of Chesapeake Aikido Club took part in the combined effort, which was held at Centennial High School in Ellicott City.

Mark Vernarelli of News Channel 2 volunteered his time to act as Emcee for the opening of the event.

Doctor Ben Carson took time out from his hectic schedule to stop and spend time with us and to watch Andrew take part in the demonstration. When I was introduced to him I was very surprised. Because of his reputation I had envisioned a much older man, but from my experiences through the years, and examples set by some of the children, especially Andrew, I should have remembered great things can be, and are accomplished, regardless of age.

***

During the 1996 and 1998 visits from Miyagi Sensei and his students, tours were arranged for them to include historical as well as entertaining excursions. Visits to the Nation's Capital, Baltimore's Harbor Place and Old Town Ellicott City were on the list. During a Sunday trip to the Nation's Capital a guided tour of the United States Supreme Court was arranged.

When their visit was coming to an end, Yoshiaki Kohagura, his wife Shoko, and his brother Yoshinobu decided to remain in the U. S. to continue sightseeing. But, what began as a fun-filled visit, and was to go on for several more days, took a tragic turn with news from Okinawa.

I was awakened by a telephone call shortly after 3:00 AM, telling me that the father of Yoshiaki and Yoshinobu had died as a result of a traffic accident in Okinawa. Mr. Kohagura was riding a bicycle when he was struck and killed.

***

In 1997 another tournament was being held in Okinawa, but this time only seven of us would make the trip. It seemed that this trek was destined to have a black cloud over it from the start. A number of students, who initially signed up for the trip and the competition, decided to cancel at the last minute. Still, others who said they were thinking about making the trip, but not competing, left us hanging until the last minute. Their decision was not to go this time.

When we at last left from Dulles International Airport we learned that a typhoon was rapidly bearing down on Okinawa. By the time we arrived in Tokyo on Saturday afternoon no flights were allowed to leave for, or land in Okinawa. With the help of employees of All Nippon Airways (ANA), we found a hotel where we would stay to wait out the storm. The highlight of that stay was watching an American Western, Five-Card Stud, starring Robert Mitchum, in Japanese without English subtitles. So, we decided to add our own translations to the action on the screen and turned the movie into comedy.

We were allowed to depart for Okinawa on Monday and the flight was a rather bumpy ride all the way into the airport at Naha. By the time we arrived, I was feeling the first indicator that a cold or flu bug was calling. But, I tried to pass it off as being tired from the extended time to reach our destination. I forced myself to step up, bite the bullet and try to keep up with the expected whirlwind of activity.

I made it through the welcome party, a few tours and daily workouts. I made it to the banquet, which was held to greet the competitors who had arrived from various countries. Of course, the crowing moment of the banquet took place for me while Mr. Miyagi was driving Mrs. Miyagi, and Jody and I to the reception hall. We were halfway there when he said, "Oh, by the way, Jimmy, you have to give a speech."

Naturally, I damn near fell out of the car, but managed to say, "What am I supposed to talk about?"

Very unconcerned he replied, "Don't worry, Jimmy, I'm sure you will think of something."

At the reception hall, Danny, Will and the others thought it was rather amusing that Miyagi sprang the surprise speech on me. In spite of being the second speaker called to the microphone after Mr. Katsuya Miyahira, I managed to casually roll off what Jody, Danny and Will called a masterpiece. Even though I had no idea what I would say until I stepped to the microphone, they agreed that everyone in the hall stopped and listened to my speech. But, I never had the opportunity to hear what I had said, because when we were presented with the videotape of the banquet, the speeches had been edited out.

There was another surprise in store on the evening's agenda, but nothing like the one sprung by Mr. Miyagi. Mr. Miyahira presented me with a Certificate of Appreciation for contributions made over the years to the international promotion of Okinawa Shorin Ryu Karate.

The 1997 Tournament would be held at the new Okinawa Prefecture Hall of Martial Arts (Budokan) in Naha. Within the hall was a museum displaying a history of Karate and Kobudo in Okinawa, including a statue of Chojun Miyagi and a gi worn by Choshin Chibana. Mr. Miyagi escorted me through the museum and, along the way, he gave me an on the spot history lesson.

At the very beginning of my guided tour and history lesson, an impatient and not so understanding young man loudly proclaimed to no one in particular, "Why aren't these plaques and papers written in English?"

I turned to him and said, "We're in Okinawa. This isn't our country, and that's why they aren't in English. But, Mr. Miyagi is giving me a tour and translating for me as we go along. I'm sure he wouldn't mind if you joined us."

"This is ridiculous," he snapped. "Everything should be in English." With that he angrily stormed out of the museum and his arrogance caused him to miss a great opportunity to learn.

The time in the museum with Mr. Miyagi was well spent and enlightening. I was especially fascinated with the display of the various weapons, but one particular set of nunchaku captured my attention. They were longer than today's standard nunchaku and on one side ridges had been carved into the wood.

Soon I was learning something new. Mr. Miyagi explained that the nunchaku on display had been used as a horse bridle in ancient times. The sticks were longer, and the ridges in the wood were for placement of the fingers to allow the rider a better grip and control of the horse. The connecting rope for the two sticks was originally made from the hair plucked from the manes and tails of horses, and woven together to make the rope. And now, as I looked at the nunchaku displayed, I could easily understand how they were used.

I held up into the first days of the tournament, but by the last day I had a very ugly cough, along with chest and nasal congestion. I left immediately after judging my last event and returned to the apartment where Jody and I were staying. I drank a very generous shot of 12-year-old Macallan Scotch Whisky and went to sleep. After sleeping for almost 11 hours I was not feeling any better.

That's when Mr. Miyagi decided to take me to one of their hospital emergency rooms. Jody and I were impressed with the efficient check in system and soon we were seated in a waiting room. The room was spotless and, of course, the daily Okinawa Soap Operas were on TV, which Jody swore she understood.

In no time at all I was summoned for my appointment and walked through the drawn curtains. I knew immediately that I had stepped into a time warp and had been transported back to the World War II era. This was not the type of ER I had become accustomed to in America. I was in a large open room, where I was directed to sit in what was obviously a very old dental chair. I sat down and the chair started rocking from side to side. The chair wasn't bolted securely to the floor! I looked around and saw nothing but primitive, old-fashioned instruments from metal tongue depressors on to the instrument sterilization cabinets.

Now, imagine me trying to explain my problem to a doctor who could not speak or understand a word of English. Mr. Miyagi was summoned to the back to try and translate, but I wasn't sure the message was getting through. Eventually, I believe the doctor understood that I was trying to tell him that I was sure I had a Bronchial infection. A few moments later I was seated in front of some type of machine that pumped out steam, which seemed to be scented with menthol. I was directed to inhale the steam by a smiling nurse and did my best to follow her instructions.

When the time came to check out, Jody and I found there was no person to deal with. We had been transported through another time warp to the future. We simply slipped the papers detailing my condition and treatment into a computerized check out station. The papers were processed and we were instructed to make payment by inserting the correct amount of Yen into the appropriate slots. Yen in, release and receipt printed and we were on our way.

There was no improvement in my illness, but that evening Mr. Miyagi offered me a glass of his home remedy. I didn't know what he was offering me, but I did hear Mrs. Miyagi telling him to pour only a small amount. He grinned and continued pouring until he had filled a water glass with what he called "medicine." He handed me the glass and said, "Drink. Everything will come out." Translated that meant I was going to begin to sweat at some later time.

Immediately after my first sip, Miyagi began laughing. I quickly learned that his home remedy was a combination of Sake and apricots. The apricots had been cut from a tree, including a segment of the branch to which they were attached and then placed in a large jar of Sake. The concoction had been fermenting for more than a year, but he quickly assured me it had not yet reached its full potential. He promised that by the time we made our next visit to Okinawa, the mixture would be up to full capacity.

Of course, his big chuckle was over my swearing that never again would I drink Sake. I argued that he tricked me into drinking the home brew, but I had to admit it actually tasted very good. I'm certain the apricots had toned down what I had experienced on a December Saturday evening in 1963.

I drank the entire glass of his home brewed nectar and sat down to share in the feast, which was our farewell party. Jody and I left the party early and went back to our apartment. I fell asleep the moment my head hit the pillow and around 5:00 AM I woke out of a sound sleep, aware that I was soaking wet. I sat up and perspiration ran down my face and dripped over the sheet. A second later I realized that my hair was soaked as well. It was like I had spent two hours in the dojo on a hundred-degree night. Well, Mr. Miyagi was right. His home medicine had done exactly what he said it would, although it didn't completely cure my chest and nasal congestion. That would have to be taken care of on the home front.

***

Again in 2002, I took members of my class to Okinawa for a World Tournament. As always, there seemed to be certain special invitations extended to us, which were the result of Mr. Takehare Higa's connections throughout Okinawa. Mr. Higa was very well known in political and military circles and, at times, it seemed as though there were few people within those circles he didn't know.

Colonel Danny L. Brush, Camp Commander, Marine Corps Base, Camp Kinser extended the first invitation, asking members of Mr. Miyagi's Dojo and my dojo to join him for a luncheon on the base. We joined Colonel Brush and other Marines for lunch and soon found many new friends.

Immediately following lunch, Colonel Brush invited us to tour the Base Museum, which held a history of the brutal Battle of Okinawa. From photographs to flags, rifles, bayonets, canteens, and uniforms of the era, we walked back into another time.

I'm certain that for Mr. Miyagi the tour brought back a flood of memories from his boyhood days. As a young boy, his home had stood on the grounds now occupied by Camp Kinser. He lived there with his father, mother and brothers until the Japanese invaded and destroyed the home and childhood happiness. The Japanese took the land, forcing families from their homes before destroying them and constructing runways for their planes. And now, Miyagi Sensei's current home stands only a five-minute walk from the gates of Camp Kinser.

During the luncheon, Master Sergeant Shane Franklin the Director of the Marine Corps Martial Arts Program, Far East, invited Mr. Miyagi and I, along with members of our dojos to participate in a combined demonstration of skills at Camp Hansen. We accepted, and when the tournament ended and our visit was coming to a close, we spent several hours at Camp Hansen.

Prior to the demonstration, I asked Master Sergeant Franklin about the Marine Corps Martial Arts Program. He told me the Corps' program was designed to train Marines in all facets of hand-to-hand combat. The program incorporated many aspects from various systems in order to give the Marines the best training possible. But, the curriculum was not for infantry units only. The Marine Corps Martial Arts training was mandatory for every Marine, regardless of rank, gender or military occupational specialty (MOS), and there were no exceptions to the order. Surely this had to keep complaining or grumbling to a minimum. It's tough to gripe about being dirty, sweaty and bruised when the man training beside you is a Major General. On the other hand, at least to me, it would be very inspiring to have an opportunity to mix it up with a general on the training ground. But, from the standpoint of leadership by example and morale building, the Marines are standing front and center.

Our dojos performed weapons katas, katas without weapons and the bunkai for each kata executed. The Marines demonstrated their skills in hand-to-hand combat, armed and unarmed. When it was over, everyone joined together, talked about respective training methods and, as always, a few new friendships were found.

***

Mr. Higa also arranged for us to meet and spend time with Okinawa's Chief of Police. During our time with him I mentioned the efforts across America enforcing the traffic laws and specifically the laws prohibiting drunken and impaired driving. He pointed out that Okinawa's laws are very rigid, with a first offense carrying a mandatory sentence of 30 days in jail. A second offense brings a compulsory six-month jail sentence and there are no deviations from the law. The chief was quick to point out that the recidivism rate for drunken and/or impaired drivers is very low. Maybe America should take a page from Okinawa's book.

It was interesting to note that the department's Roll Call, or briefing is held outside (weather permitting) and officers assemble in military formation. After beat assignments and orders of the day are read, all officers take part in a 15-minute session of defensive tactics training. To be more specific, this is a daily refresher of the training they received in the academy. They have baton (nightstick) training, handgun retention tactics, come-along methods and hand-to-hand fighting techniques.

***

The 2002 World Karate and Kobudo Tournament would also mark the first time a woman had been invited to participate as a Judge/Referee. Mr. Miyagi had submitted Jody's name and this, of course, brought a storm of opposition. As was the custom before each tournament, judges and referees were required to take part in practice events for kata and kumite competition.

Jody was to judge kumite competition and when the evening arrived for her to take part in judging practice matches, her eager opposition was drooling with anticipation. The men, competitors and senseis alike, were eagerly waiting to pounce on her at every opportunity, certain they could intimidate her.

She calmly took her chair in one of the judge's corners, flags at the ready to signal points as scored. The instant she raised a flag and indicated a point for one of the fighters they swarmed her corner like vultures attacking a carcass. Yelling, screaming and pointing fingers they tried their best to force her to change her call.   The vultures found themselves in a hornet's nest. Instead of backing down, she very firmly, but politely told them to get the hell out of her corner, she saw the point, called it, and her ruling would stand.

Jody went on to judge kata and kumite in the tournament and did so without a whisper of a compliant about her performance. In fact, when the events concluded, Mr. Katsuya Miyahira immediately went to her and said he liked the way she handled her position as a judge. At one point he smiled and said, "You are very authoritative."

After the tournament, Jody and I accompanied Mr. Miyagi to the site where the farewell banquet was being held. We arrived well ahead of schedule and were escorted to a room off the banquet hall. The three of us were talking when Mr. Miyahira appeared and joined us.

Soon, Jody was asking questions regarding his life, especially in the world of karate. We were quite surprised at his candid and sometimes humorous remarks. I guess no one expects a man who is a revered 10th Dan and President of the Okinawa Shorin Ryu Karate Do Association to confess that he was not at all serious about his study and practice of karate in his early years. In fact, he admitted to being the class clown and very disruptive during training sessions. He said he believed he could get away with his behavior because, at that time, his father was his first teacher. However, when his father sent him to study with Choshin Chibana, his attitude very quickly changed and he became a serious student.

When the banquet room opened, Jody and I began to walk away from Mr. Miyahira and Mr. Miyagi to join our students. A moment later Mr. Miyagi stopped us and said Mr. Miyahira wanted us to join him at his table.

In no time at all we were being seated at the head table with Mr. Miyahira and top members of the Okinawa Shorin Ryu Karate Do Association. It was truly an unexpected honor for Jody and I to be invited to dine in such elite company.

Certainly the evening would not have been complete without an unexpected call to the stage, along with nine other senseis, to receive an award from Miyahira Sensei. Next, of course, was the unprepared turn at the microphone. As was the case in 1997, I gave my hastily devised speech immediately after Mr. Iha and once again managed to say all the right things.

Looking back, I should have suspected that Mr. Miyagi knew well in advance the agenda for the evening, but preferred surprise to preparation. I often wondered if Miyagi Sensei simply wanted to see how well I handled the stress of facing unanticipated problems. If so, I passed the test, because he said nothing afterward. But that was Mr. Miyagi's style. If I had blundered in some fashion, rest assured I would have been told in very straightforward terms. Again, that was Miyagi's way.

The Miyagi bag of surprises wasn't emptied until the evening of our farewell party at the dojo. After a few rounds of sushi and Orion Beer, Mr. Miyagi signalled the room for silence and asked me to stand. A few moments later he was reading the certificate for my promotion to 8th Dan. As he began reading I couldn't help but recall a night so many years gone by when I stood in front of the class to accept my first promotion. Although the current dojo was enclosed, I felt as if I was standing on the exact spot of the rock-hard dirt floor of 1964. Yet, I'm not really certain which was the more humbling experience.

Later that night as I took time to remember my very first awkward, stumbling steps on that dirt floor, I was truly amazed by where those uncertain, timid steps had carried me. I had reached a destination never thought of in my beginning days and had far surpassed a point I was told I would never reach. But, I could smile and think that the journey was ongoing and there was much yet to learn and a long way to travel before it would be over.

Okinawa 2007

I returned, along with my wife, Jody, to Okinawa in July 2007. The primary reason for the visit was to gather information from Mr. Miyagi for this book. The visit proved to be a walk into history, but with a first hand view from a man whom, along with his family, suffered and lived the terror of World War II.

Today, the island of Okinawa exhibits a beauty, which is at times breathtaking. Rolling brilliant blue ocean waters mixed, with shades of shimmering green surrounds the island. The ocean's water tumbles over coral reefs and sand and, in many places, breaks with a resounding crash against the faces of the high cliffs, or surges up over the white sandy beaches. Yet, that majestic beauty holds, and hides within it, a darkness from a time not so long ago. A time when blood covered its glistening sands and the stench of death filled the air. Hillsides of the tiny island were pockmarked with bomb craters, while shredded remnants of trees and smoldering homes told a silent story of the horrors of war.

The bloody Battle of Okinawa is told through the eyes of the Okinawan people who endured its daily nightmares, at The Okinawa Prefectural Peace Memorial. Jody and I visited the Peace Memorial Park with Mr. Miyagi in 2002. It was immediately evident that the park was built with deep respect for those it honored. The museum was a walk back in time to days and nights filled with machinegun and rifle fire, bombs and shells from both sides exploding over the battleground, and screams of the wounded and dying. Outside, the rows of black stone walls display the names of the over 240,000 people who died during the Battle of Okinawa, including soldiers and civilians. Mr. Miyagi pointed out that the walls were set to represent waves rolling in from the ocean. When you look over the vast expanse of those black stones standing solemnly under a hot afternoon sun, they do indeed appear as hundreds of waves flowing over the land. Mr. Miyagi also said that the Peace Memorial Park had not been built only as a monument to those who had died, but as a symbol to encourage peace.

***

Shortly after our arrival in Okinawa, Jody and I sat down with Mr. Miyagi and asked how the war touched his life and that of his family.

"I first realized how much the war would impact my life when I arrived at school on September first and found the classroom filled with Japanese soldiers. I was in the third grade at the time, attending Urasoe Japanese National School. The soldiers looked at me and told me to go home. We went outside and questioned them, but the soldiers told me not to come back to school. They said go home and do housekeeping. The Japanese soldiers stayed at the school and they gave orders to the principal, and he also told us to go home.

When students from the fifth, sixth, seventh, eighth and ninth grades arrived at school they were sent to the airfield. That is where the present Marine Corps base, Camp Kinser, is now located. My older brother, Kenichi, was one of those students sent to the airfield. There, the Japanese soldiers forced them to work—forced labor, carrying buckets of stones, soil and rocks to build runways for their planes."

Years in the future, Kenichi Miyagi would enter the political ring and go on to become the Mayor of Urasoe City.

"Later, students were allowed to attend school at Nakanishi

Middle School. But, for two years they were forced to make clothes, which were National Uniform Clothes.

Okinawan people were not permitted to speak the Okinawan dialect, because Japanese soldiers could not understand the language. Anyone caught speaking the Okinawan dialect would be executed immediately. Within a year I was able to understand the Japanese dialect." (Today, the Okinawan and Japanese dialects still differ.)

"During this time there was also a lack of sufficient food, and someone broke into one of the storage houses and stole food. Even though the lack of food was the same for everyone, the Japanese blamed the Okinawans for the theft. They kept saying the Okinawan people took the food.

In 1944 we were forced to leave Okinawa and go to Japan. The older men, 15 and older, were ordered to stay behind and fight the Americans, even though they did not want to do this. My father, who was the Vice-Principal of a Japanese National School—an elementary school, was one of those forced to stay in Okinawa. Anyone (Male) who was 15, 16, or 17 years old was useful to the Japanese. They would be forced to fight the Americans. They did not want to, but the Japanese forced them.

United States Marines killed my father when they landed. Five years ago (2002), Mr. Kenji Akamine came to me and told me he was with my father and saw him die. My father was 39 years old at the time of his death. Mr. Akamine was 15 years old at the time and was wounded, being shot in both legs. After that, the Americans treated his wounds and Mr. Akamine became a prisoner of war.

Together we travelled to search for the location where my father died. But over the years there had been too many changes and we were unable to locate the spot. So, my father's body has never been recovered.

It was August 1944 when me, and the rest of my family, my brothers and my mother were ordered on to a ship to go to Japan. There was a convoy of three ships, and we were on the middle ship as we headed to Japan. The ships would zigzag to try and avoid the submarines. But, on August 22, 1944 the United States Submarine Bowfin attacked the convoy. The ships we were on had no radar and there was no way to detect the torpedoes. So they would stand watch to look for submarines or torpedoes. My family and I were on the middle ship, which was a military ship. It was the ship in front of us, the Tsushima Maru that was struck by torpedoes and sunk. There were 1,484 Okinawan civilians on the Tsushima Maru, and 826 of those were students. Many, many people died."

***

Historical accounts show that Commander John H. Corbus commanded the USS Bowfin during this period of World War II. Records indicate that the Tsushimi Maru was an unmarked Japanese cargo ship, which was sunk off the Tokara Islands between 10:00 and 10:30 PM on August 22, 1944. Military archives reveal that 59 children survived the attack. The USS Bowfin is now a submarine museum and open to visitors at Pearl Harbor, Hawaii.

***

"The remaining ships continued on to Japan and docked at Kyushu Island. My family and I were taken to Miyazaki Prefecture, which was not very far from Nagasaki. There we found some of the Japanese soldiers were very kind to us, while others were very harsh, and mistreated us.

The remaining ships continued to Japan and docked at Kyushu Island. My family and I were taken to Miyazaki Prefecture, which was not very far from Nagasaki. There we found some of the Japanese soldiers were very kind to us, while others were very harsh, and mistreated us.

We were in a school with three to five teachers from Nakanishi Elementary School. There were 92 of us, who were students grouped in an open room and we made clothes for every day wear. The clothes were like uniforms, so we all looked the same. We stayed in that room, also sleeping in the same room. We were there for almost two years.

The older students, fifth grade and up, which included my older brother, were forced to do military drill every day by the Japanese. The Japanese were very strict. Every day we would see the upper ranks, sergeant or up, kick ones of lower rank.

One Japanese soldier talked to me often, but he had to be careful for fear of getting into trouble. One day he came to me and said, 'this is a secret. Flash. Boom. This World War will be over soon.' He was referring to the Atom Bomb, which had been dropped. If he had been overheard telling me this, he would have been taken away to jail, or killed.

Later I went to visit Hiroshima and Nagasaki when I was a university student and we went there to tour."

***

Kyushu is the third largest of Japan's Islands, and is the most south westerly of its four main islands. It is recognized as the birthplace of Japanese porcelain, and is often called the Island of green gardens, smoking volcanoes and steaming geysers. Nagasaki, Kyushu's largest city is also its Capital. The United States dropped the Atomic Bomb; code-named "Fat Man" on Nagasaki on August 9, 1945. Over 80,000 people died as a result of the bombing, and on August 15, 1945, Japan surrendered. The Instrument of Surrender was signed on September 2, 1945, officially ending the Pacific War.

As a result of the bombings of Hiroshima and Nagasaki, the term Hibakusha is widely used in Japan to refer to the victims of those bombings. Its literal translation means, "explosion affected people." As of March 31, 2008 there were 243,692 living, certified Hibakusha, most of who reside in Japan.

Today, Miyazaki Prefecture is home to the Seagaia Ocean Dome, the world's largest indoor water park, which opened in 1993. The Ocean Dome displays a false flame spitting volcano, artificial sand, and the world's largest retractable roof. The retractable roof gives the appearance of blue skies on rainy days. The Prefecture Capital, Miyazaki City, is an agricultural and trade communications center.

***

"I returned to Okinawa, with my family, in 1946. As we approached the harbor in Naha there seemed to be nothing left. Everything had been burned and everyone was very sad. We were taken by an American truck to an area near White Beach, where we remained for two or three days. Later we were taken to Urasoe City and then on to Gusukuma.

It was a very difficult time for us. There was not much food for us and we had very little clothing. I can remember being very cold and shivering.

In 1947 we built a wooden house in Gusukuma. Times were still difficult for us and my mother, who was a schoolteacher, would plant sweet potatoes after she came home from teaching. Then she would collect wood to make a fire so she could cook."

The home Mr. Miyagi referred to as having been built in 1947, is the very home where Len and I fist met him.

"Americans helped to rebuild our schools. The first was built from a Horse House (barn). Students gathered and helped by making chairs and desks for the classrooms. The classrooms were wide open and if there were very heavy rains or typhoons there would be no school." (Here Mr. Miyagi laughed about returning to school after a typhoon). "After the heavy rains, we would return to school and the classroom floors would be nothing but mud. I also remember there was no electricity, so we had no lights in the homes or schools.

In the classrooms, at first, we had no textbooks for study. We had only notebooks and we could only study from the notes taken in class while the teacher talked. It would take two to three years for textbooks to become available to us.

I attended school at Nakanishi Elementary School, Nakanishi Middle School, Shuri High School and Shuri University. The Shuri University has since become Dere-Kyu University. Everyday I walked from Gusukuma to Shuri to attend school. It was a one-hour walk each way.

After my first two years of college my mother became very ill. So, I stopped attending classes and worked at Camp Kinser Marine Base. I worked there as an inventory clerk and while working I met Atsuko, who would later become my wife. She also worked at Camp Kinser as a typist.

At first I did not ask her for a date. When I returned to college at Shuri University, I finally asked her to attend a festival with me. I never dated anyone afterward and later Atsuko and I were married in 1961. My first son, Takeru, was born in 1962 on April 1st. My second son, Hironagi, was born four years later— 1966. We call him Hiro. My daughter, Kimiko, was born in 1971."

Miyagi's son, Takeru, would grow up to become an architect and would design one of the many shopping centers on Okinawa, and Hironagi would go on to become a top rated chef. But, it was daughter Kimiko and her husband, who would present Mr. and Mrs. Miyagi what they had been dreaming of for a very long time—a grandchild. Their granddaughter, Yuhki, was born on July 26, 2010.

***

"Before I began karate, I was in gymnastics, starting when I was around 13 years old. I was about 17 years old and attending Shuri High School when I started my practice of karate."

I recalled Mr. Miyagi telling Len and I that he had tried to keep his karate practice a secret from his mother. I asked if he remembered that.

"When I was going to my first teacher, Mr. Takara, my mother didn't know that I was in karate class. We practiced at his house and there were no lights. So we practiced outside in the dark. One night while walking to class my mother and I passed each other, but we said nothing. We just continued on our way. My brothers already knew that I was practicing karate, but after that night my mother was also aware. When she became aware she did not try to stop me.

I learned from different teachers. In school I learned from Mr. Ishikawa and then Mr. Takara (Shigeru Takara). Mr. Kensei Kinjo and Mr. Takamine were also my teachers and then Mr. Katsuya Miyahira. I studied kobudo (weapons) with Mr. Hohan Soken and I learned the Sai from Mr. Takara.

In the beginning there were no degrees of black belt. There was just the rank of black belt. I am uncertain of the exact date when degrees of black belt were first issued.

I was already a black belt when Mr. Miyahira and Mr. Chibana awarded me certificates for the rank of San Dan. I continued my practice with Mr. Miyahira and received my other promotions from him. My longest association is with Mr. Miyahira.

Over the years I learned many, many katas because of my practice with other teachers. But now, because I learned so many, I am not certain of the number."

As we talked, we discovered some very striking similarities in the path we took in our early days of karate. Mr. Miyagi began practicing in 1953, and I started with his class in 1963. He began teaching in 1955 and I started teaching in 1965. Each of us began our teaching with two students.

"My very first student, Mekaru, who began class at the age of 16, became ill with cancer. Over time it attacked his eyes and he became blind. He died very young, and I believe he was only 22 or 23 years old. He was a very strong student and no one could win against him. He was also the very first student I promoted to black belt."

As Mr. Miyagi spoke of his first black belt, I recalled my first black belt, Rick Lubinski, who was also very strong and deceptively quick. And, like Mekaru, no one stood as his equal.

Miyagi continued. "Nakanishi was about 14 years old when he started class. His brother brought him to class because he was a troublemaker. He was always starting a fight with somebody. But, day by day and year by year he learned discipline."

Of course, this was not the Nakanishi I remembered. When I first met "George" he was very quiet—very humble. So, it was difficult for me to picture him as a "wild man" and one who set out looking for fights.

Suddenly, I realized that I was no different than Nakanishi when I was 14 and 15 years old. Then I wondered if Mr. Miyagi somehow sensed this and that was the reason for pairing me with Nakanishi.

During my freshman and sophomore years of high school there were probably weeks when I spent as much time fighting as I did in class or studying. In fact, in a single day of my sophomore year I engaged in seven separate fights. I should, however, point out that these seven fights were the result of seven boys huddling together on a second floor landing, calling my name and spitting on me. I chased them down one at a time, knocked them to the ground and proceeded to pound the snot out of them. One thing I will not, and have never tolerated, is someone spitting on me. In looking back, the majority of the fights I engaged in were instigated by the other party or parties. In spite of those fights, I managed to make it through my first two years of high school without being suspended, or worse yet, expelled for my pugilistic endeavors.

I shared another similarity with Nakanishi, that being our stature. Throughout my high school days I never tipped the scale at more than 135 pounds, but that didn't stop me from fighting. I guess I was like a Chihuahua with a junkyard dog's attitude and mentality, size be damned. When the "bell rang" the fight was on and no matter what it took, I was determined to win.

Mr. Miyagi went on and spoke of the Americans that came to his dojo. "I open my dojo to anyone, and welcome those who come to join. Over the years many soldiers came, but soon they all left. Some left after one week of class. When you and Neidert arrived and stayed, I was very pleased. But the most important thing to me is that you never quit. You are the only one (American) who continued on and you always remained in touch with me. My students too are very proud and pleased with this."

***

Mr. Miyagi taught Junior High School (Middle School in the U.S.), for 36 years "I taught about 7,000 students, ages 13 to 15 years old. As a teacher I was responsible for teaching Social Studies, which included Geography, History, Politics, Law, Economics and Sociology. I also taught and coached physical education, track and field, gymnastics, volleyball and basketball.

I taught at six junior high schools during my teaching career. I taught at

Urasoe Junior High School – Seven years

Yasuoka Junior High School – Six yeas

Naha Junior High School – Five years

Johoku Junior High School – Six Years

Nakanishi Junior High School – Five Years

Minatogawa Junior High School – Seven Years

Some of my students also went on to become teachers, but I am not certain of the number."

Mr. Miyagi pointed out that the schools in Okinawa close for only about one month during the summer. They close for "summer vacation" in late July and open again around mid August. Yet, while the schools are closed many students will attend various classes, such as math or science. The school gymnasiums also remain open and students participating in volleyball or basketball will be there during the day working to improve their skills.

In 2002 and again in 2007 Jody and I were invited to visit a mathematics class. Students from the first grade through high school were seated in one room, taking part in a very strict, almost drill like routine. A series of numbers were flashed on the chalkboard and, when the flashing ceased, the students already had the correct answer. This drill went on, with the tempo of the flashing numbers increasing each time it began anew. Still, each time the flashing ceased, students offered the correct answer. As if that wasn't enough of a test of mind and discipline, there was another exercise. In this instance the teacher would read out a series of numbers in what was almost a musical chant. When he stopped, the students provided the answer. This too increased in rhythm, the chant becoming faster each time it was repeated, but as always the students gave the correct answer.

We learned that female students are not permitted to wear long hair while they are attending classes. This is the rule from first grade all the way through high school. The only exception to the rule is that girls participating in the traditional Okinawan Dance routines may have long hair, but it must be worn on top of the head while they are in class.

Students also wear uniforms from first grade through high school. Each school district has its own colors, such as blue pants and white shirts for the boys, while the girls wear blue skirts and white blouses. The summer class sessions are "more relaxed" as uniforms are not required.

***

Miyagi Sensei took Jody and I to several museums and other historical locations during our visit. It was at one of the museum stops that Jody and I viewed photographs of the devastation suffered by Okinawa and its people during World War II. It is impossible for me to put into words the shocking story told in those photographs. The destruction of the Island of Okinawa was almost complete— trees, buildings, homes, historical treasures and even cemeteries were in ruin. There didn't seem to be a single thread left of their lives. Yet, the Okinawan people refused to have their spirit broken by what they came home to. They toiled for years to restore their lives and the island to its proud heritage.

One treasure that was almost completely destroyed during the Battle of Okinawa is Shuri Castle. Although historical documents indicate that the castle had been totally destroyed and rebuilt on four other occasions, the destruction during World War II overshadows previous events.

Little by little, the magnificent castle has been restored, and this too is a sight that can be truly breathtaking. Mere words cannot describe, nor photographs show its majestic craftsmanship and color. Shuri Castle is a monument that has to be visited to be appreciated. Mr. Miyagi has taken Jody and I to Shuri Castle on four occasions and still, we want to visit it again.

Shuri Castle is believed to have been built around the end of the 14th Century by King Satto. During those early days, Shuri was the Capital of Okinawa and remained so until 1879 when the title was relinquished to Naha. Even today, while standing outside of Shuri Castle, there is a feeling of those years so long ago when emperors, feudal warlords and warriors walked about the small island.

After its restoration, Shuri Castle was reopened to the public in November 1992. Mr. Miyagi and members of the Miyagi Karate Dojo took part in the opening ceremony and performed a karate demonstration for dignitaries and other guests.

The restoration of lost arts and treasures cannot bring back the lives of the many Okinawan people killed during the war. Entire families were killed, and in some cases, only a single member of a family survived. One man, the only surviving member of his family, told us of surviving by hiding in caves and stealing food from the Japanese soldiers. He said he was seven years old and had hidden in the hills and caves from the soldiers. He also told us of finding a .45 caliber pistol, which he assumed had belonged to an U. S. Marine or Soldier, and keeping it. "I kept it for a long time, but later I threw it away."

Not only Mr. Miyagi, but also dozens of other Okinawans have told us of the atrocities committed against the people of Okinawa by Japanese soldiers. What they told us did not come from accounts they had read in books or newspapers, but their personal experiences. They told us of the Okinawans who jumped from suicide cliff and the lies told by Japanese soldiers, which caused them to jump. They were told American Marines and Soldiers would butcher them, and how the U. S. Servicemen would rape and torture the women. One account relates that there were 240 high school girls who were forced, by the Japanese, to act as nurses for their wounded. When American forces were closing in, the Japanese sent the girls on their way. The majority of them perished either by suicide, which was encouraged by Japanese soldiers, or when they were caught in the gunfire between U. S. and Japanese forces. Yet, as many in Germany want to deny the Holocaust, the Japanese too want to change historical documents to show certain events never occurred on Okinawa during World War II.

While we were there in 2007, Japanese Prime Minister, Shinzo Abe announced that the history books would be changed to show that these atrocious deeds did not happen. This brought a collective cry of outrage from the Okinawan people, and rightly so. The men and women I have spoken to certainly did not fabricate the circumstances of the suffering and death. It was a horror they and/or their families lived, and that reality still vividly survives in their hearts and minds.

With Prime Minister Abe's announcement, Mr. Miyagi said, "He is not very popular here in Okinawa."

***

Jody and I also had the opportunity to spend several hours touring Okinawa's Aquarium. Again, this is a sensational attraction to local residents as well as tourists, and offers indoor and outdoor venues. To be sure, the aquarium holds a beauty and allure all its own and, it would require much more time than our few hours to truly appreciate each and every exhibit.

It was fascinating to see a Whale Shark swimming lazily among the hundreds of other fish. Yet, what truly captivated me was the shark tank, which could be viewed from above, or on a lower level of the aquarium. Standing on the lower level only the thickness of the glass separates tourists from the man-eaters.

As I stood on the lower level, a Tiger Shark swam directly toward me and turned slowly, giving me the opportunity to look squarely into its black eyes. I can only describe the feeling of looking into the eyes of a Tiger Shark as chilling. Next to swim to the glass and stare coldly at me was a Bull Shark. Regardless of the icy glare, I watched the Tiger and Bull Sharks repeat the routine again and again, realizing all the while that we were only inches apart. Being face to face with these creatures, so deadly and so close could also be described as seductive, but I have still no desire to dive into the water and swim with them.

***

The parties celebrating our arrival and departure were much different from those parties held when we arrived with a large group. Mr. Miyagi told us, not long after we arrived, that the welcoming party would not be held the following night as was customary. In addition, the party would not be held at the dojo, but at a restaurant. The party took place on Saturday evening and was indeed a pleasant surprise for me.

Miyagi Sensei had contacted many of the students who were members of the class when I first began in 1963. What a thrill it was to see the friends I had made so many years ago. Of course, seeing Gibo brought back the memory of the very first party Len and I had attended at the dojo. The night the Jim Beam ran out and I was introduced to Sake, and the worst hangover of my life. But, it was also the evening when Gibo said, like Mas Oyama, he too could kill a bull and wanted Len and I to accompany him while he proved it.

When I introduced Gibo to Jody she asked him if he wanted to go out later and search for a bull. With a somewhat sheepish smile he said, "Not tonight."

Sitting around the table with my many long time friends, drinking beer and eating sushi certainly opened the door to life's long held memories. In spite of clumsy first steps on my part and cynical attitudes on theirs, time had not eroded the eventual bonds of friendship that were formed with hard work, determination and many nights of pain, sweat and a few drops of blood. I was deeply honored that those I had not seen for over 40 years would come to talk of days gone by and drink a toast to friendship renewed.

At the farewell get together, Mr. Miyagi opened another door to the past and the days and months I had spent in class. For the very first time he began to tell the stories of the goings on in class as they related to me. I was truly surprised that he could recall so much, especially since, back then, I thought he was unaware of some of the things I did. So, while I ate sushi and drank Orion Beer, Mr. Miyagi took everyone on a journey back to my beginning.

Those gathered for the farewell party that evening had not been a part of Miyagi's class back in my days of 1963-1964, but soon they were all laughing. Mr. Miyagi was telling tales of my teaching lessons in humility to new American students that came by when Len and I were part of the class. I was not aware that he knew how Len would sic me on any American who arrived at the dojo with a "smart ass" or "know it all" attitude.

After our first few months in class, Len said, "Those damn wrists of yours are like getting hit with a steel bar." I'm certain that night after night, the constant pounding my wrists and forearms took from Nakanishi produced the desired effect and they developed into rock solid blocks. So, when a "wise ass" would appear, Len would pull me aside and say, "That son-of-a-bitch needs a few minutes with those arms of yours," or "He needs a lesson from the Bone Man." So, after class I would casually suggest that the "attitude" step out for some extra conditioning drills. And, they always accepted.

Mr. Miyagi began telling them of one particular night when I invited a student who stood just over 6'5" out for a bit of additional "conditioning." The laughter grew as he told them that after just a few strikes the guy tried to walk away. I grabbed him by the arm and told him to get the hell back out there, because we were just getting started. He lasted about a minute, but he approached the next class with an entirely new outlook.

Then there was one who showed up with an attitude that he was already better than everyone was, and it seemed that included the Okinawans too. By the time class ended, Len was that now very familiar stampeding, raging bull I had come to know so well. He was on the verge of breathing fire when he grabbed me by the arm. "Jimmy, get that son-of-a-bitch out of here."

I invited Mr. Bad Ass out to the center of the "floor" for a few minutes of "after hours" training. The arrogant smirk on his face disappeared with the first crack across the top of his wrist. He too wanted to walk away quickly, but I would have none of that. I didn't like his attitude any more than the others did and I wanted to be certain he got the message. A few minutes later he bowed, picked up his clothes and disappeared into the night, never to be seen again.

By the time Mr. Miyagi finished his library of stories, I had probably consumed an entire octopus and an assortment of very tasty vegetables. That's when someone in the group suggested we go to his favorite club for some entertainment and a few more beers.

Soon, Jody and I were seated in Dante's Inferno waiting for a beer and listening to the band. We were truly amazed by this talented group. They were so close to a carbon copy of Carlos Santana and his band that they seemed to have been cloned directly from Carlos and his group. The lead singer was an Okinawan Carlos in every sense—voice and attire and right down to the hat he was wearing. Later, Jody and I said that if we hadn't known we were in Okinawa, we would have sworn we were at a Santana concert somewhere in America. Yes, they were that good. But, Santana numbers wasn't the only music they played. They were just as adept with music from the Eagles.

During one of the breaks, Jody spoke with the drummer from the group, a young woman who said she had also played with a band in New York. All in all, it was a most enjoyable and entertaining evening.

As always, it seemed the time to part came much too quickly and soon we were standing in line at the Naha Airport waiting to board a flight to Tokyo.

***

The year 2007 also marked a bump in the road in my life. Only five weeks before our departure date, I was told that I had cancer.

During my annual physical in February, my doctor and long time friend, Larry Silverberg, noted my PSA level had increased. It had risen from a two to a three, which under normal circumstances wouldn't be cause for alarm. However, because of a family history of cancer he believed every precaution should be taken. Doctor Silberberg suggested contacting my urologist and having a follow up exam. Still, he felt there was nothing to worry about, because I was in good health and excellent physical condition.

I scheduled an appointment with Doctor Kenneth Langer of Chesapeake Urology and met with him in April. He too believed that the numbers were nothing to be worried over, but said he would rather err on the side of caution and ordered an Ultra Sound and a biopsy. The Ultra Sound was clear and the biopsy was performed in May.

On the evening of June 5th, Jody and I walked into his office and sat down across the desk from Doctor Langer. Somehow I knew what he was about to say. Maybe it was the fact that we were the only two people that remained in the waiting room at the end of the evening. Then again, it could have been that sense I often seemed to have when something was amiss.

Doctor Langer looked across the desk and said something along the lines of, "I didn't think you had cancer, but the biopsy shows that you do have cancer."

Later, Jody would tell me that from that point on she didn't really hear a word he said. On the other hand, I very clearly heard and understood everything he told me. I was lucky because the cancer had been caught in its early stages, and that was due to my stubborn belief in the annual physical. Having been detected in the very early stages, it also gave me several options of treatment. He explained each of them and said I would have to talk with other doctors who would fully explain them again, and tell me what role they would play in my choice of treatment.

After we left his office, I began to call family members and tell them what the results of the tests had been. Oddly, when we arrived home our two German Shepherds and two cats immediately sensed that something was wrong. It was as though someone was able to communicate to them what my diagnosis had been.

Stranger still was the behavior of the older cat, Pudgy. He had been born on our front steps, part of a litter of five. As it turned out he was also the docile one in the litter and was eventually chased away by the others. I saw him almost every day and he would meow as I went by, as though saying he wasn't enjoying his lifestyle. A year passed and I found him injured and bleeding on the sidewalk. I took him to the vet and, after he was treated and released, he became an indoor cat and my almost constant shadow.

When Jody and I finally went to bed, Pudgy came in and jumped up between us, something he had never done before. He meowed and sat there looking from Jody to me, before he stretched out and continued looking at us. Once again he meowed, as if he was trying to tell us that he understood there was a problem. Jody turned out the light and Pudgy rested against me and began to purr. For the very first time he stayed with us and slept so he was touching me in some way all night long.

Early the following morning, when I awoke, I looked at my diagnosis from a positive side and knew I would beat cancer's curse. I had a strong faith in God and looked at it as just one more street fight. I went to Mass at Saint Michael's Church that morning and told Father Mike of my prognosis, but we decided not to announce it.

Doctor Langer had told us not to cancel our trip to Okinawa, but to go and enjoy it. We took his advice, but found that the next few days and weeks would be a whirlwind of activity. Although I had already decided to select radiation therapy as my method of treatment, I would still have to listen to each doctor's explanation of the other treatment methods. Of course, Jody refused to wait home while I travelled from doctor to doctor. She said she wanted to be there so she too would understand exactly what I would be facing.

First, Doctor Brian Levin told us about the surgical procedure that he could perform using the DaVinci Robot. Next came Doctor Richard Hudes, who explained the radiation treatment options to me. After talking with him, I opted to undergo twenty-five radiation treatments and the seed implants. Of course, that also meant other procedures would have to be completed before we left for Okinawa. But, this visit brought a little comical relief into the picture.

Doctor Hudes said I would have to have hormone shots before leaving on our trip. I said that Doctor Langer informed me that I would not have to undergo hormone shots. With that he left the office to call Doctor Langer. When he returned he had a rather blank expression on his face. A moment later he said, "Doctor Langer said both of you carry guns and not to get anywhere near you with a hormone shot."

I went for a CT scan and then a visit with Doctor Sanford Siegel for marker implants, which was followed by another CT scan. Immediately upon our return from Okinawa there was a telephone message telling me I had an appointment the following morning with Doctor Levin for a bladder scan.

The first Monday of August marked the beginning of my radiation treatments. I met Jeff Zemencik and Shawn Campbell, Radiation Therapists, who would become my daily companions in the weeks ahead.

Although Jody was working the night shift out of Howard County's Southern District, she insisted on making the trip with me every morning. I tried to talk her into staying home and getting her sleep, but she refused, saying she loved me and wanted to be there with me. She missed only three days of the drive from Mt. Airy to Owings Mills, and that was due only to scheduled court cases.

Jody asked Jeff if she could see how the treatments were administered and, with my blessing, she saw the entire process from beginning to end. When it was over, she said she felt much more at ease about my treatments, because she had a better understanding of the procedure. She said she was amazed over the precautions that were taken by Jeff and Shawn to ensure the radiation treatment was properly administered.

On October 3, 2007, I underwent the seed implant procedure. Follow up visits showed successful results for my treatments and I continue to have favorable reports.

I was certainly blessed along the way, because I had very little in the way of side effects from the radiation. I was able to continue with my normal workout routine, which Doctors Langer and Hudes insisted upon. I taught my weekly karate classes and kept up with my typical weight lifting routine. I'm certain that keeping a determined mindset helped as well.

My greatest blessings, however, were the love, care and support from Jody, my family and friends and my faith in God. And, I never forgot my sense of humor. Jody and I kept the doctors on their toes during the pre-treatment visits, and I'm sure they might have been somewhat surprised at times by our comments. But, maintaining my sense of humor kept me focused on the positive rather than the negative.

2011 - Miyagi Visits America Again

In early March of 2011 I wrote to Mr. Miyagi and reminded him that he had not visited America since 1998. At the same time, I extended an invitation to visit during the summer. I was surprised that, in almost no time at all, I received a reply saying he would return to America on August 1st, but could stay for only a week. Of course, when I made the announcement that Miyagi Sensei would be visiting in August, it sent a wave of excitement and anticipation through the three dojos.

Shortly after he had accepted my invitation, Jody decided to write to Miyagi and ask if he would be promoting me during his visit. Again, his response was prompt and he told her the reason for his visit was to promote me. She waited several weeks to tell me, but confessed that she knew preparations would have to be made and she couldn't do so without my knowledge.

With her "confession" behind her, Jody set about arranging for invitations and an after promotion celebration. Then too, there would also have to be a welcome and goodbye get together for Mr. Miyagi, but with such a short itinerary, she thought that a combined "hello/goodbye" gathering would be more appropriate and, indeed, less hectic.

Mr. Miyagi sent a list of things he wanted to do while here

and asked what we had planned for his stay. And, it was at that time I noticed what seemed like a different tone in his letters. It was one of those things that you just can't say for sure what it is, but you know something is out of the norm. Still, I didn't pursue it.

August 1st arrived and Jody and I drove to the BWI-Thurgood Marshall Airport expecting to meet Miyagi Sensei at 5:15 PM. I checked with the airline to be sure the flight was on time and the young lady said she would look to be sure Miyagi was on the plane. I was shocked when she said he was not on the flight, which was scheduled to land in about 15 minutes. After a few telephone calls, I found that he would be on a flight arriving from Atlanta at 8:00 PM. The wait began and soon the delay notices were popping up and his arrival time changed again and again, until the flight was finally cancelled. Planned outings and events were suddenly thrown off course.

Early Tuesday morning I received a call from Mr. Miyagi telling me he would arrive at BWI shortly after noon. He explained that weather had delayed his flight out of Okinawa and one of his students was to notify us by e-mail of the change in plans. But, as fate would have it, the e-mail never arrived.

His flight touched down on time and some minutes later I saw him walking out to greet us. At first glance I knew something was wrong, but then I thought that it might have been the long flight and endless delays and changes that took a toll on him. Maybe he was just tired.

We stopped for a late lunch at Shannon's in Ellicott City and, although he ate, he just didn't seem like himself. When we arrived home, Mr. Miyagi said he wanted to rest and slept for over four hours.

Our original plan for Tuesday's dinner was to take Miyagi to Annapolis to dine at Lewnes Steak House. But, the arrival delay caused a change in schedule and we had to cancel the outing and eat at home. After dinner, Mr. Miyagi and I sat outside and talked for almost two hours. During our conversation he sipped a cold beer, but turned down offers of a second. This too was unusual, as I knew how much he enjoyed a cold beer, especially on a hot summer's evening. Shortly after nine, he excused himself and went to bed.

Wednesday's schedule included a stop by the Howard County Police Academy in the morning, followed by a visit to Circuit Court Judge Tim McCrone's office and karate class that evening. Mr. Miyagi slept for over 13 hours and the visit to the Police Academy was scratched from the list. After a stop at Judge McCrone's office, we ate lunch and, again, he wanted to rest.

Later that evening, when class began, Miyagi seemed to have a renewed energy. He was moving around the room, correcting stances, watching with his always-keen eyes for anything even remotely out of place. The class ran beyond the two-hour limit, but nobody seemed to care about the time. After all, for most of them it was the very first time they had attended a class conducted by Mr. Miyagi. After class he drank a beer and ate pizza and acted more like the man I knew.

Early Thursday morning after breakfast, we were off to Washington, D.C., which Mr. Miyagi always included on his itinerary. We went to the Lincoln Memorial and then on to the Capitol Building, where we also ate lunch. Immediately after eating, he informed us that he had had enough sightseeing for the day and was ready to return home. Almost immediately after arriving home, he said he wanted to rest as we were going out to dinner later that evening with our senior black belts.

We drove to the Crab Shanty (now the Shanty Grille) in Ellicott City, for dinner, which is also the first restaurant where Mr. Miyagi dined on his initial visit to the United States. The mood over dinner was light and he seemed to enjoy his meal and the company, joking with Danny, Bruce and Will. They too would later say that he just didn't seem like himself—the man they had come to know over the years.

Friday morning Mr. Miyagi and I spent almost two hours with Angie Cochrun of The Gazette, talking about those early days in Okinawa and the beginning of my journey with him. It was good to share a few laughs over the awkward, but certainly humble first days of my introduction to Miyagi's class.

It was seven o'clock Friday evening when everyone lined up and bowed to Mr. Miyagi, which signalled the beginning of an event, I had never anticipated in 1963. Only moments later I stepped in front of Miyagi Sensei, bowed and listened to him begin to read a promotion certificate.

For a fleeting instant, time carried me back to another time and place. It was a night during the summer of 1964, when a 22-year-old Marine stood humbly at attention, listening to Miyagi read a certificate promoting him to brown belt. That was a history-making evening in the Miyagi Karate Dojo because he was promoting an American. Now, some 47 years later, Miyagi Sensei was marking another historical first in his dojo with my promotion to 9th Degree Black Belt.

This was indeed a special moment because, unlike my first promotion, members of my family and many long time friends were there as witnesses and to help celebrate. My son, John, daughter-in-law, Laura, granddaughter, Sarah, grandson, Ryan, my brother, Ed, my niece, Terry and her husband, Tim joined other guests in the audience. Of course, Jody was there, but she had been present for my promotions to 7th and 8th Degree Black Belt. Friends from the law enforcement community, Howard County Police Department and the Maryland State Police, along with members from Saint Michael's Church took part in the celebration. Rick Lubinski, my first black belt and, without question, the first rock solid building block for my dojo, drove from Ohio to help share in and celebrate my accomplishment.

After the reading of the promotion certificate and awarding of my new belt, members of our dojos gave a short demonstration for those in attendance. When I asked Mr. Miyagi if he would demonstrate a kata, he politely refused and, at that time, I knew something was definitely wrong. Still, it wasn't until late the following day that I learned that he had confided in Jody he was experiencing troubling abdominal pain. He believed this was after affects from a hernia surgery he had undergone some months ago and did not want it to be a burden to anyone. So, rather than say something to me, he decided to keep it to himself.

Saturday he seemed upbeat and back in his element while overseeing and teaching a weapons class. He demonstrated Sai and Bo katas to ensure we were conforming to his way—the Okinawan way. The class lasted for over two hours and, of course, our film master, Bruce Charity, recorded the entire workout.

Sunday afternoon, Sonny and Betsy Richardson hosted the welcome/goodbye party and, as always, they seemed to make the most of meeting new friends and making them feel right at home.

During the party I noticed that Mr. Miyagi found a chair and, as he did on Friday evening, he remained in one location. This too was out of character for him. I had always known him to move freely about among guests at every gathering during his previous visits. Now, he confined himself to his chair, leaving only to get a plate of food or a drink, which he did not have to do, because someone was always offering to make sure his plate or glass was filled.

Students, and guests alike, took the opportunity to sit and talk with him, which is something he always enjoyed. This day was no different in that respect. He entertained the dozens and dozens of questions and it was obvious that he was thrilled to answer questions about karate or offer historical facts about Okinawa.

Indeed, all visits seem to end too quickly, but this stay felt so much like it ended before it had time to begin. Jody and I shared breakfast with Mr. Miyagi at the airport and then he was on a plane bound for home.

But I wasn't going to allow him to escape completely without my asking about his health issues. I reminded him that we shared a bond of friendship that spanned 48 years and there should be no problems that we could not discuss. He then confessed that he had also had a recurrence of his intestinal cancer (which seems to translate to colon cancer) and he was battling that along with the difficulties from the hernia surgery. Yet, almost in the same instant he expressed confidence that within a year or so, he would win out and be healed.

At that very moment I knew I should not have expected any other answer. Not from a man I grew to admire as a teacher, respect as I would a father, and love as a brother.

2012

Mr. Miyagi was well into his recovery, which was obvious from the tone of his letters. It was easy to read and understand he was more upbeat and happy to be getting back to his teaching and work out schedule. He was back to being the Miyagi Sensei of old, looking forward to his next challenge.

Then came a letter announcing that Mr. Miyagi was President of the Okinawa Shorin Ryu Karate Do Association. That news sent a surge of exhilaration and pride through the ranks of my students here in the U.S. and I could only imagine what Miyagi Sensei's students were feeling in Okinawa.

Throughout the years I had known Mr. Miyagi he had never expressed a desire to hold that position. Though I had no doubt he would fill the office of president with a new pride and energy. Yet, there was no boasting of his accomplishment. He was still the same humble man I had come to know and admire. And, I believe it was more than appropriate that he ascend to the position once held by his teacher and life long friend, Katsuya Miyahira.

It was Mr. Miyahira who promoted him to rank of Judan (10th Degree Black Belt) on June 28, 2004, which is also the date

Mr. Katsuya Miyahira retired from his position as President of The Okinawa Shorin-ryu Karate Do Association.

When Mr. Miyagi studied under Miyahira Sensei he learned Kihon No Kata 1-2-3, and Naihanchi 1-2-3, Pinan 1-2-3-4-5, Pasai Sho and Dai, Kusanku Sho and Dai, Chinto, Gojushiho, Jion and Koryu Pasai.

2013

With the dawn of a new year, the realization was sinking in that I was headed for a milestone I had never dreamed of, or even imagined possible. With each day ahead of me I was moving closer to 50 years in karate. As a young Marine, standing on the dirt floor of the Miyagi Dojo, I didn't think about my future in karate. There was only the present and learning to absorb everything possible to satisfy my hunger. And, of course, I had to prove to Mr. Miyagi that I was not a quitter and nothing he or anyone else did or said was going to make me give up and walk away.

Here it was almost 50 years later and suddenly I was recalling so much from my younger years. As I took the time to reflect on those days of my youth, I wondered why so many people told me "You can't do it" when I said I wanted to achieve a certain goal.

When I announced that I wanted to play football, I was told I was too small and couldn't play. Well, I did play football at Leonard Hall Junior Naval Academy and Mount Saint Joseph High School. Maybe I was the smallest guy on the teams (my top weight in high school was130 pounds at best), but what I lacked in size I made up for in determination and a streak of downright nastiness. I didn't give a rat's ass about the size of the other guy and I certainly had my bell rung a few times. On one occasion I took a knee to the helmet when I was tackling a guy and was pulled from the game. When I asked to go back in, Brother De Porres said, "Do you know where you are?" I answered, "Yeah, where?" He smiled and said, "Go sit down."

A few games later one bigger s.o.b. had been getting away with cheap shots the entire game and I'd had enough. I grabbed his facemask (the old single bar), pulled down and began bashing him in the nose with my fist. I was tossed out of the game, but what the hell, there were only about two minutes left.

Yet, my favorite recollection of playing football at Mt. St. Joe occurred in my freshman year on the Mount's Cub Football Team. I recall it was an away game and raining and it sure as hell looked like somebody had hosed down the other team with Miracle-gro. Every player had to be a head taller and packed the pounds to match. It wasn't long before we were getting our asses kicked and our opponents seemed to have found a special joy in stomping the snot out of us. Well, I was pissed and pacing the sideline, praying for an opportunity to get in the game. Finally, the coach called me and told me to go in. That was it. I was going to flatten somebody's ass no matter how big they were. I lined up, but not in my usual defensive back position. I moved up closer to the line of scrimmage more suited to a line backer. I was snarling mad and just waiting for the ball to be snapped. The instant I saw the center's hands move I ran straight at a gap in the line. The quarterback turned, tossed the ball to the halfback and I was already bearing down on him. At that time I didn't realize how facial expressions could scare the life out of someone and I don't know what my face was showing, but I clearly remember the look of sheer terror on the face of the guy in front of me. His mouth was hanging open and his eyes looked as if they were about to pop out of his head. He stopped his forward progress and started running for the sideline. At that point I didn't give a damn if he ran all the way to the locker room, I was going to flatten his ass. I lowered my head and stuck a shoulder into him just below the groin area and drove him into the ground. I jumped up and looked around for somebody else to hit and then noticed him struggling to a sitting position and staring blankly up into the rain. Talk about satisfaction. I had rung his bell and he was damn near twice my size. Now where were those people who told me I couldn't play football?

Still, the pattern never changed. Everything I marked as a future goal, I was told I couldn't do. "You can't be a Marine. You don't have what it takes." Well, I became a Marine. "You'll never get hired as a police officer." They were wrong again. "You'll never get a book published." Hey, I did that too.

I'm certain that the majority of my tenacity came from my father. He too was so often told he couldn't do certain things. He had polio at a very young age and lost most of the muscle strength in his right leg. Afterward, when he showed up wearing a leg brace to play baseball, he was told he couldn't play. When they found how far he could hit the ball an exception was made. As long as he could make it to first base on his own, he could be a part of the team. If he made it that far, the opposing teams agreed to a pinch runner in his place. He played for a number of years before he had to give up the leg brace and walk with crutches.

He was also told he would never drive a car. Yet, he did and he learned to drive a standard shift, which I'm certain wasn't an easy task. The introduction of the automatic transmission was indeed a blessing and he bought one of the first to be delivered to Parlett Ford of Ellicott City.

He also talked so often about never surrendering, never giving up. His attitude was always "A game is never over until the final out, or final gun sounds." With that was the belief that you should play every game with all your heart and soul and never stop playing until the final out or gun sounds. God knows that sure rubbed off on me.

I hated seeing people give up and playing a game with little effort. At times I was berated by teammates because I kept playing even when there was no hope of winning. I didn't care and it didn't matter that they wouldn't speak to me after the game. I wasn't going to give up until the umpire or referee signalled that it was over. I played like there was a miracle coming with the next pitch or snap of the ball. When the miracle didn't happen, sure I was disappointed, but I just waited for the next game.

Our lives should be lived by the philosophy of the big game. Regardless of the hand we are dealt, we should strive to achieve our goals. Granted, many are deemed to have been born with the "silver spoon" and need not work to achieve much in their lives. I doubt that they will ever appreciate all they have, as much as the man or woman who fought the odds with hard work, oftentimes with more than a few heartaches and setbacks and still found success. There is, and always will be, a deep felt pride and sense of accomplishment when reaching your goal against all odds.

As days passed and that 50th year drew nearer, Jody was completing the final plans for a commemorative celebration. The event would be held on November 26th at the Brick Ridge Inn in Mount Airy and invitations were in the mail. She enlisted the aid of Bruce Charity to put together a photo array and video to be shown at the dinner. Most of the planning was as Top Secret as they could make it and I had little to say or do except provide names of those I wanted on the guest list.

Finally November 26th arrived and the moment I awoke a flood of memories from those long ago first days in Miyagi's dojo were calling. I smiled, thinking no matter how much time had passed I could still clearly see and feel those events as if they were only yesterday. God, how well I remember the humiliation and the physical pain from my arms and legs being pounded and sometimes that pain was almost unbearable. Yet, I kept going back as if I were begging for more. At the time though, I never asked myself why I continued going back. I already knew the answer. I wouldn't quit. But more than that I think it was the determination that I was not going to allow anyone to claim victory by saying they made me give up.

I recalled the friends from those early days and the many new friends found with visits to Okinawa and the trips Mr. Miyagi and his students made to America. From Nakanishi to Takara to Higa, Fujii, Matsujo and Aguni and so many others, a bond forged that would never be broken.

When Jody said it was time to leave for the Brick Ridge Inn, I laughed. I laughed because it was pouring rain—pouring as hard as it had on the night I first met Mr. Miyagi 50 years prior. In reality it seemed most appropriate that the celebration be held on a rainy night and that was the first thing I mentioned when I spoke to those in attendance.

As I walked into the restaurant I saw Rick Lubinski, my first black belt, and obviously the first to arrive. In spite of the rainy drive to Maryland from Ohio, I would have expected nothing less from Rick. Soon, others began arriving and, suddenly, there was another flood of memories from past to present.

Archie Galloway, the fourth student to become a part of the humble beginnings of the Lilley Dojo. Howard Zachmann, Charlie Murray, Bob Lucido, and Tom Guercio, good friends and all black belts from days gone by. State Senator Jim Robey, although not a student, a good friend and former partner from the early days of the Howard County Police Department's first drug unit. Circuit Court Judge Tim McCrone, a more recent black belt and good friend dating back to his days as a State's Attorney. My three senior black belts, Dan Simons, Bruce Charity and Will Adams, who were especially instrumental, from the early days to the present, in building and maintaining the integrity of the Lilley Dojo and the true spirit of Okinawa Shorin-Ryu Karate Do. And many other students and friends from the old days to present came to help celebrate my 50 years in karate.

The buffet dinner was nothing less than outstanding in taste from the salmon all the way to the dessert platter. Jody and I had often dined at the Brick Ridge Inn, enjoying food from the Sunday Brunch to dinner and we had never been disappointed. This too would be remembered as a meal pleasing to the palate and indeed suited to the occasion.

When the dinner concluded, the first thing Jody wanted was the presentation of the array prepared by Bruce. It rolled with photos from my beginning days in the Marine Corps at Camp Lejune, to my humble beginning in Mr. Miyagi's Dojo, on to those early days of teaching and finally to the most recent events. Yet, the big surprise came when a video appeared on the screen of Miyagi Sensei and his students offering congratulations on my 50th Anniversary in Karate. Bruce worked that surprise into the evening by contacting one of Mr. Miyagi's students via Facebook, who then relayed the request to Mr. Miyagi. The students of the Miyagi Dojo gathered and Mr. Miyagi offered his words of recognition for those 50 years.

After that most pleasant surprise I stood to speak to my many friends. I was quick to point out that the skinny young Marine in those pictures from so long ago had no thought of his future path in karate. But I followed Mr. Miyagi's example and also kept my promise to him that I would continue to practice and teach. It was only then that I realized that I had made a life long commitment to karate. I didn't quit, as so many others before me, and I followed in his footsteps without so much as a second thought. I could only smile, thinking once again the wisdom of Mr. Miyagi had proven true—I learned from teaching as he said I would and I also learned from those I taught. Many doors opened as time passed and, without thinking about where they were leading, I stepped through and continued my journey. And, today as I glanced over my shoulder, 50 years were behind me.

My wife, karate family and friends offered many kind words that night, and I was certainly blessed to have them as a part of my life. But, it was Jody who quietly revealed something that made me stop and think. She said, "I don't believe you really know how many lives you've touched, those you've changed and all of those you've influenced over the years. You've inspired people to go on when they wanted to quit and you've helped so many more believe in themselves."

It took time for what she said to sink in and that required a long look back into my life. I had never taken the time to stop and think that something I said or did would have a great impact on someone's life. Somewhere back in time I had come to believe that things I said or did were only those that I was supposed to say or do—as if they were things that I had been trained to do, as though a duty or obligation. I admit that being singled out in a group for praise often made me feel uneasy, but I did my best not to let it show. So often in those situations I tried to pass it off with a quick smile, a nod of the head and wave of the hand, or throwing in a little humor to deflect the compliment. Yet, when all was said and done, Jody was right.

As the evening progressed I knew it was time to spring a few surprises on those who had gathered to honor me. First, I had always believed that had Rick remained here in Maryland and continued his karate training, he would be right behind me rising through the ranks. So, I thought it only fitting to present Rick with an Honorary 9th Degree Black Belt. Indeed, he was surprised by the presentation, but as humble as I'd always known him to be.

My second surprise was announcing that Dan Simons, Bruce Charity and Will Adams would be promoted to the rank of Hachidan (8th Degree Black Belt). Again, as I had hoped, they were caught completely off guard.

Finally, it was time to offer my sincere thanks to everyone and bid them good night and safe travel. It had been a good evening, sharing smiles, laughs and so many fond memories with friends old and new.

2014

It was early January when the call came from Mr. Miyagi asking if I could attend the planned Celebration of Life Memorial and Demonstration honoring Grandmasters Katsuya Miyahira and Seitoku Ishikawa. Without hesitation I said, "Yes." After all, I had known Grandmaster Miyahira since 1964 and it was he who had issued my teacher's certification/license. However, I did not meet Grandmaster Ishikawa until the mid 1990s, but he was a man I deeply respected. Mr. Miyagi also informed me there would be a seminar on Saturday, August 2nd.

Mr. Miyagi said the Celebration of Life Memorial would be held during the 3rd International Friendship Demonstration on Sunday, August 3, 2014 at the Tedako Hall Auditorium, Urasoe City, Okinawa. A letter would follow within a few days informing me of my individual part in the ceremony as well as what would be expected of my dojo's students who attended.

Certainly I always looked forward to those times when I returned to Okinawa or Mr. Miyagi visited here because, once again, I could be a student under his watchful eyes.

I immediately informed my students of the event but unlike

previous years when the announcement was made, only two of my students, David Rees and Joe Pepper, said they would be able to make the trip and take part in the celebration. In the end, a total of four from my dojo in the United States and one long time student currently living and working in Japan, Nelson Rebert, would travel to Okinawa.

About a week later Mr. Miyagi's letter arrived informing me that I would be expected to perform the Kata Unshu. Members of the class would perform the Kata Pinan Yondan (4), and demonstrate the bunkai (application of the moves as they pertain to self-defense). As a group, we would participate in the Kata Gojushiho and I would take part with senior belts in the performance of Naihanchi Shodan.

Of course, my students knew immediately that we would be practicing our parts at every class until we departed for Okinawa. And, as always, I informed them that our departure date would arrive much quicker than anticipated.

I worked daily on the Unshu Kata, vowing to present it as close to perfection as possible. I wouldn't embarrass Mr. Miyagi with a poor showing. After all, he was now not only my sensei, but also the Grandmaster and President of the Okinawa Shorin-Ryu Karate Do Association. Also fresh in the back of my mind was Mr. Miyagi telling me that when he was asked to perform a kata during demonstrations or other events, he now chose the kata Unshu. Being asked to present his kata was an honor and certainly I could not fail my teacher with a poor display.

Indeed, before we realized it, it was Wednesday, July 23rd and our departure date.

We were at BWI Airport by 4:00 AM waiting for our 6:00 AM Flight to Houston. We had time to enjoy a good breakfast in Houston, even though Jody managed to steal my syrup without being caught. She has always liked lots of syrup for her pancakes, waffles or French Toast, but instead of asking for extra, she very deftly lifted mine, leaving me to ask for another serving. But, her syrup theft did provide a rather comical measure of amusement over breakfast for everyone, including our waitress.

We left Houston and, after crossing the International Date

Line and spending hours in the air, we finally landed in Tokyo. We waited through a four-hour layover in Tokyo before flying on to Naha, Okinawa, arriving shortly before 9:00 PM on Thursday, July 24th. But, Nelson and his wife, Debbie, would not arrive from Japan until Saturday afternoon.

Mr. Miyagi and a small group from the dojo met us at the airport and, after collecting our luggage we were on our way to eat. We dined on Sushi and drank cold Orion Beer. While eating, we learned that for the first 10 days of our visit we would be staying at the Governor's house. Mr. Higa, a man well connected in political circles and one of Mr. Miyagi's long time students, had been talking with the governor and told him of our coming visit. The governor, who was going out of town with his family, insisted that we stay at his residence instead of a hotel. This also meant we could cook some of our meals, instead of going out to a restaurant three times a day.

So, after our late dinner, we went downstairs to the grocery store to shop. Jody and I took one cart and began filling it with bread, bacon, eggs, fresh fruit and butter. Joe and David, on the other hand, were filling their cart with Orion Beer and, to balance the cart, they added a watermelon. This even brought a chuckle from Mr. Miyagi.

A short time later we were entering our residence for the next 10 days. Although it was dark, it was still an impressive sight as we passed through the gates. We could see very well kept grounds and gardens and could only imagine the sight we'd see in the morning. Inside was spacious, more so than many of the homes on the Island. Then again, the governor's house was, at times, also a place of business with a large formal dining room, which could be separated into two smaller dining areas. There was also a large sitting room with plush chairs surrounding a table, television and stereo, and a large bookcase.

The kitchen was much larger than I expected, but then I thought that when the governor conducted business or entertained here, it would require a more spacious area to prepare and cook meals. In the cooking area there was ample room for several people to easily work together. A kitchen table, which could comfortably seat eight, was separated from the cooking area by a wall about four feet high. Behind the table was a large cabinet filled with stacks of plates, cups, saucers and dozens of drinking glasses.

We soon found the kitchen table would become a nightly meeting area where we talked about my early days in Mr. Miyagi's class. The talks with David and Joe were much the same as I had with Rick, Danny, Bruce, Will, Jody and other students years ago. And, even now, it was easy to talk of those first days and weeks because they were so much a part of me I could never forget them.

David and Joe looked forward to those nightly sessions and hearing of those days in the beginning and the journey to the present. It was a time to answer questions and also talk of their futures and where their voyage might take them.

When I awoke the next morning I stepped outside on the very roomy deck area, which was accessed through a sliding glass door on the second floor. My reaction to seeing the lawn and gardens by daylight was "wow." Everything from the grass to the trees and shrubs were neatly manicured. The surroundings looked very suited to be on the front of a postcard or an advertising poster for Okinawa. At the very back of the property was a rock formation with three naturally formed caves going left to right from large to small. A later walk revealed that the gardener used those caves to store his garden tools, carts, buckets, and one was used to stow compost.

While walking around the deck I saw the gardener carefully pruning a tree. He was dressed in light color pants and shirt and wore a straw hat to protect his head from the heat and hot sun. The instant he saw me, he stopped and bowed. I returned his gesture of respect and added a wave. And that marked the beginning of what became our daily ritual of greeting each other with a bow and wave. During our stay I never saw him standing idle. He was always hard at work, pruning the many trees and carrying the trimmings to the compost cave, watering the shrubs or raking around the trees and flowers.

Later, as I went downstairs, I found an Okinawan woman who arrived early each morning and began her chores. She was obviously responsible for the appearance of the area at the front of the house. Her daily ritual began with sweeping the walkway from the front door to the entrance at the gate. After sweeping, she took a garden hose and meticulously rinsed the walk, making certain it was clear of everything down to the last grain of sand. And as it was with the gardener, a customary bow was exchanged daily.

Our first full day in Okinawa would also be our first practice with everyone in preparation for the memorial celebration. Well, that session had more than its share of bumps in the road, one of which was learning that we had been practicing a bunkai move incorrectly because it was wrong on the demo tape. The evening felt as if it was dragging and we were repeating katas and bunkai over and over. Finally, it came time for individual kata and I was called to step up in front of Mr. Miyagi to perform Unshu. I went through the kata as I had practiced it countless times before leaving America. When I completed the kata I remained in place, certain that I would have to do it again. Mr. Miyagi simply nodded and said, "Jimmy, your kata is okay." I admit I was stunned but pleased that Mr. Miyagi was satisfied with my performance.

Nelson and Debbie Rebert arrived from Japan on Saturday afternoon and just in time for the welcome party that evening.

Earlier in the day I had given Mr. Miyagi a shirt I had bought while on a cruise in the Caribbean. Needless to say it was very, very colorful and when I presented it to him I told him it was a party shirt. I wore a most colorful shirt, also purchased in the Caribbean, to the party and found that Mr. Miyagi and I were certainly the flashiest dressers at the gathering.

The Orion Beer was cold and the sushi, as always, was outstanding. And, when in Okinawa, I always try to treat myself to sushi every day. Mr. Miyagi and his students find this amusing, but I'd hate to miss out on eating something I acquired a taste for in my early days in karate. After all, it was Miyagi Sensei who introduced me to sushi.

As always, it wouldn't be a real visit to Okinawa without Miyagi Sensei springing at least one surprise. Early in the evening he told me that Jody would be receiving her teacher's license and certificate for Sixth Degree Black Belt from the Okinawa Shorin-ryu Karate-Do Association on Saturday, August 2nd at the conclusion of the seminar. Nelson would also be receiving the same recognition. After announcing his surprise to me, he told me to inform them.

When I told Jody the news she, at first, seemed stunned and then overwhelmed by what I'd said. It took a minute or two for it to sink in and then she just shook her head and said, "I never expected this." She said she felt humbled and deeply honored to receive such recognition from Mr. Miyagi and the association and felt that, more than ever, she had to work harder to prove she was deserving of the recognition. Later she would say, "There are two people I can't disappoint, Mr. Miyagi and you."

I informed Nelson of Miyagi's Sensei's announcement and he too felt deeply honored and humbled. Later, after speaking with me, he said that he did not believe he was ready to receive such high recognition and asked for my permission to approach Mr. Miyagi with his decision. I consented and he spoke with Miyagi Sensei regarding his feelings. After they spoke, Mr. Miyagi's original decision would stand.

It was becoming "tradition" for typhoons to pound the island while we were there. This visit we would have two and the second provided its own brand of "humor." It was the Friday morning before the seminar and Jody and I were going to walk to the main highway to our favorite coffee shop. When we left the house there was little rain, but the wind was swirling with a mixture of heavy gusts.

We walked down the street, made a quick right and began walking up the rather steep hill. The hill and buildings provided us with a readymade shield from the wind and rain. When we reached the top of the hill and took our first step away from our shelter, we were hit by a tremendous wind gust. Jody was lifted off her feet and tossed about three feet into a chain-link fence and my tee shirt was almost ripped completely off. We somehow managed to regain our balance and continue on to the coffee shop, where we would laugh about our bout with the typhoon over hot coffee and breakfast.

As always, it seemed that our days in Okinawa were passing faster than possible. There were daily classes and practices for the demonstration, tours of the island, including Shuri Castle and nightly social outings with Mr. Miyagi and his students. Old friendships grew stronger and, for Joe, doors opened to friendships that he knew immediately would last a lifetime.

Saturday, August 2nd dawned with a bright sunshine and before we knew it we were preparing for the seminar. There were approximately 500 students from various countries including, Germany, Canada, Australia, Japan, the United States, Croatia, Switzerland, Brazil, Argentina, and France.

It wasn't long before I was reunited with my long time friends, Yutaka Nakanishi and Meiyu Takara. Time and distance had not taken away from our bond formed many years ago. And, before this day was over, I would enjoy a very pleasant trip down memory lane.

Jody, David, Joe, Nelson and I gathered with Miyagi's students and talked as others began arriving. Soon the topic turned to the number of persons stepping on to the floor who were wearing red or red and white belts. All of his students quickly voiced their displeasure and obvious objection, saying far too many were wearing belts they did not deserve. They believed that over the years far too many had achieved rank because of standards lowered or ignored by those who were promoting. I agreed wholeheartedly with their assessment.

Of course, if they wanted to see a real bastardization of the promotion process they need look no further than the United States. There are those who have promoted themselves to 10th Degree Black Belt, those who have lied about their promotional history, and those who have received black belts simply because they signed a contract guaranteeing them a black belt within a specified time. And, nowhere in the contract did it mention attending classes and actually learning something before receiving their black belt. Then there is the money making process and so many, especially parents eager to boast of their child's accomplishments, are sucked into what is no more than a farce. Promotional tests for white belts? Really? All students are supposed to begin classes wearing a white belt, but many schools (much different than a dojo) require them to test for the privilege of wearing a white belt. And, they have to pay a fee to take the test. The more belt colors and stripes in the system, means more required tests and more money in the school's bank account. And, each test for a higher ranked belt or stripe costs more. And then there is a question of what are students being taught?

I have had students from the money factories say they don't know the first thing about defending themselves in a street fight. And, one of those said he had been promoted all the way to Sandan (third degree black belt) and didn't know how to defend himself.

The seminar was to begin at 9:00 AM, but one entire group failed to arrive by the designated hour and the starting time was delayed until 9:30. We bowed in and the seminar got underway.

I was immediately impressed and very pleased with the way this seminar would be conducted. In the past, we had broken down into small groups with a higher-ranking sensei who presided over the practice session and ran it at his pace. Not this time.

Miyagi Sensei would be presiding over this seminar from start to finish. He announced that we would be practicing katas favored by the legendary Grandmaster, and one of Mr. Miyagi's teachers, Choshin Chibana. We would begin with Naihanchi Shodan and proceed to the Pasai, Kusanku, Chinto and Gojushiho Katas. Miyagi Sensei would first demonstrate the kata as it should be and afterward all in attendance would perform the kata.

As soon as we began it was obvious that some needed much more than a refresher course and their kata performance more than solidified the position of Mr. Miyagi's students. It was also very evident that some were more than a little overweight and out of shape and were dropping out as we moved on. The brutal Okinawan heat could very quickly take a toll on the less than physically fit.

Then there were those who wanted to argue when they were told their kata was incorrect and, in all cases, the errors were not trivial mistakes. They were easily noticeable. Miyagi Sensei has quickly discovered that some students attending the seminars are adamant in their belief that their way is the right way. Well, my message to them is simple. When the Grandmaster says your kata is incorrect, it's wrong. Don't argue. Thank him for correcting your mistake, bow and move on. The present Grandmaster did not arrive at his current position by being wrong all these years.

Progress was slow because of the pauses for corrections, but my small group had not been corrected. As we moved forward, they were gaining the attention of the others and I noticed some observers beginning to film them.

When we reached Pinan Shodan Mr. Miyagi called a student, who was wearing a red and white belt, to the front of the assembly and told him to perform the kata. His execution of the kata was poor at best and required a great deal of correction. Miyagi Sensei then turned and called Jody to the front of the group and had her perform the kata. To say she nailed it would be understated. It was close to perfect. At the next break, David sent a text to Dan Simons, "Jody did us proud."

During the breaks, Nakanishi spent his time working with David and Joe on kata and bunkai. And, they knew this was an opportunity that few would have and they took advantage of every moment.

While the entire assembly performed kata, I chose to stand behind the student body rather than in front and go through the kata. To my surprise, Nakanishi chose to do the same. There we were, standing side by side, and suddenly it was another time and place. When we ended our first kata together, we looked at each other and smiled. I said, "Just like 1963 and 1964." He nodded and we turned to repeat the kata. And for a time it was as if we were back on the hard dirt floor of Miyagi's dojo, side by side, waiting for the kata's first count. But today I wasn't a student competing with, and trying to impress my mentor. Today we were long time friends, recalling and sharing a journey through the days of our past. Indeed, this would be something I would add to my list of treasured memories.

We went through our katas together and enjoyed the trip down memory lane, but we stepped out after each kata to observe and assist in correcting those who were having problems.

Over the years I had learned Mr. Miyagi's subtle and his sometimes not so subtle way of showing his displeasure with overall performance. If he said, "Your kata needs work," that was his subtle approach. If he called for the kata to be repeated over and over, that was his not so subtle way of saying, "your kata is terrible." On this day, when we reached Pinan Yondan, there would be no subtle hint. I lost track of the number of times we repeated the kata, but I knew Miyagi Sensei was not happy with what he was watching. At one point, he called for a break, which I thought was probably out of frustration. A drink of water, a deep breath or two and it was time to repeat Pinan Yondan until he was satisfied. Eventually we moved on, but because of the slow progression we only reached Pasai Dai before the lunch hour, which also marked the conclusion of the seminar.

Next up, after lunch, would be promotional testing for a number of students. Mr. Miyagi, as president of the association, was trying to establish a more stringent policy for promotions. In order to receive recognition for a specified rank, a student would be required to travel to Okinawa and appear before the board and earn their seal of approval. He would later tell me that because of my rank and tenure within the Okinawa Shorin-ryu System, my students would not have to appear before the board for approval. He said he believed I would not discredit or lower the standards, nor would I do anything that would bring disgrace to the art of Okinawa Shorin-ryu by recommending someone for promotion who did not deserve it. Therefore, he would accept my promotional recommendations.

I obtained a copy of the promotional test requirements, which indicated that testing before the board would begin with the rank of Yondan (4th Degree Black Belt). Additionally, it listed what the students would be required to perform for each rank from Yondan to Hachidan (8th Degree Black Belt).

I have always set the highest possible standards for students to advance and now I would add another step to their requirements for promotion. I would establish a board of review and require them to test the same as all other students appearing before the board in Okinawa. But, I would have them begin the testing process for the rank of Sandan (3rd Degree Black Belt) and I would also include the performance of weapons katas.

The testing process ended with the awarding of certificates and Jody and Nelson accepted their certificates from Miyagi Sensei. Upon receiving her teacher's certification, Jody became the first American woman to be awarded that honor by the Okinawa Shorin-ryu Karate Do Association. Unfortunately, there would be no time for celebration that evening, as the next day was the Celebration of Life Memorial Demonstration.

By 8:00 AM on Sunday morning we were already lining up outside Tedako Hall to prepare for the demonstration, which would not begin until 1:00 PM. The morning would be set aside for a walk through or Dress Rehearsal. Surprisingly, the rehearsal went rather smoothly and before we knew it was lunchtime. We ate lunch with Mr. Miyagi and his students and began our final preparations.

After the customary welcome and introduction speeches, the demonstration began. As always, the event was well planned and many of Mr. Miyagi's students had taken part in the organizational process. Soon, we were lined up and preparing to take our place on stage to perform Pinan Yondan and its bunkai and there, seated in the very front row was Mr. Miyagi. He would have a very clear view of everything we did. Moments later, we stepped into the spotlight and as I stood to the side, first counting the kata and then giving commands for the bunkai, I saw a near flawless performance by my students and those of the Miyagi Dojo who joined us.

There was no time for me to pause and bask in the glow of their accomplishment, as I had to immediately follow, performing the Unshu Kata. I walked briskly to the center of the stage and bowed to the audience. That's when I noticed Mr. Miyagi was no longer seated in the front row and I wondered where he had gone.

I began Unshu, carefully working to demonstrate both the speed and grace of the kata. I completely blocked out the audience, seeing nothing and hearing no sounds, as I stepped through the flow of the kata with the cadence I had practiced week after week.

I bowed to the audience at the conclusion of the kata and left the stage. As I exited the stage, Jody told me Miyagi Sensei had appeared back stage, watched me through an opening in the curtains and departed the moment I ended my kata.

I left the stage area and walked to the room where we had eaten lunch to get a fresh bottle of water. When I opened the door I saw Mr. Miyagi changing out of his suit and tie into his gi. He looked over at me, smiled and said, "Very good kata." Those three words alone made my journey to Okinawa worthwhile and that moment was the highlight of my visit. "Very good kata," said I had excelled in my performance and my teacher was pleased.

A quick drink and I was in line again with students from my dojo, the Miyagi and Nakanishi dojos, preparing to return to the stage to perform the Gojushiho Kata. And, as we had been doing, the kata presentation was near perfect.

As the demonstration and celebration was nearing its end, all senior black belts were called to the stage to perform a Naihanchi Kata. With Miyagi Sensei counting, I found myself executing the moves with Nakanishi to my right and Takara in front of me. I smiled and thought *it's good to be home.*

Immediately following the Celebration of Life Memorial Demonstration for Mr. Miyahira and Mr. Ishikawa there was a banquet held in a large dining area of Tedako Hall. Jody and I gathered with Mr. Miyagi's students and were about to pour our first beer when we were told Mr. Miyagi requested our presence at the head table. Soon we were seated and enjoying the excellent food and good fellowship.

As the evening progressed, it was time to introduce all the Senseis and their students who participated in the day's events. One by one teachers and students from all the countries were introduced and the top-ranking belt spoke briefly to the audience. When it was our time to step on to the stage, it was announced that we were the Miyagi Dojo of Maryland and Mr. Miyagi joined us on stage. For my part, I reminded everyone that it was our responsibility to carry on the tradition of Okinawa Shorin Ryu and pass on to our students, without change, what had been taught to us.

Too soon, it seemed, the time to end the festivities was at hand. Some of those who had flown in to take part in the events would be departing for home on Monday, which included Nelson and Debbie Rebert. For those who remained there would be a "final hurrah" at a beach party and cookout.

The following afternoon Mr. Miyagi and Mr. Higa picked up Jody and I and we drove out to the beach, which was some distance from our hotel. Almost immediately there was food and beer on the table as if by some magician's trick. And, certainly there would be no complaints about the food and there was more time to talk with other teachers and students who had travelled to Okinawa.

One sensei from Canada, Margaret Paul, approached Jody and asked, "Who is your teacher?"

Jody responded, "My husband is my teacher and his teacher is Mr. Miyagi."

She said, "Well, that explains why you and your students are so good."

What a great compliment! Within that praise I saw all the small pieces that combine to make teachers and students good. There was that very strict adherence to the traditions and values of Okinawa Shorin-ryu and the willingness to stand firm and never change what had been taught. Certainly there was also a degree of humility in all that we'd done. Like Mr. Miyagi, I've always worked hard to stay away from the "stand up in front of the crowd and boast of your accomplishments" attitude. It is better to show your best when asked to do so in a public demonstration and then quietly accept those accolades that come your way. Save the "chest pounding" for the times you are together with your students and friends. In those circles it will be accepted and appreciated more than public displays of arrogance.

As the evening began to draw to a close Mr. Miyagi took center stage again to offer his farewell and thanks to all who came to Okinawa to participate in the seminar and the Celebration of Life Memorial for Mr. Miyahira and Mr. Ishikawa.

When he walked to the front of the group he asked Joe to accompany him. Of course, Joe wore a smile from head to toe. While Mr. Miyagi spoke, Joe stood quietly behind him, holding his beer and smiling. Later it was joked that he had been asked to escort Mr. Miyagi to act as his bodyguard.

Tuesday, August 5th was the last day of our visit. David, Jody and I took off for one last shopping run, while Joe stayed back to grab a few extra hours of rest. We found Harley Davidson of Okinawa and purchased a few gifts for our friends in America who were hard-core Harley fanatics. A Harley Davidson – Okinawa Tee Shirt would surely give their friends something to look at with a bit of envy.

While we were walking toward a bus stop I glanced up and saw a sign, which read, Oyama. I paused and glanced across the street and instantly realized that I was looking at what had once been the Oyama Restaurant where Len and I had spent so many hours. It was no longer a restaurant, but there was no mistaking the three-story structure. It still resembled the building from all those years ago, with the very familiar outside, concrete stairway that led to the restaurants on the second and third floors. I wanted to cross the street and look closer at the building, but time said it wasn't possible.

While we boarded a bus to travel to Naha, Mr. Miyagi had stopped by the hotel looking for us. Joe told him that we'd gone shopping and before he knew it, he was in the car with Mr. Miyagi trying to find us. Not knowing where we'd gone, they headed to Naha. Well, at some point Miyagi Sensei took a turn and, after a minute or two, he and Joe discovered that they were in the "Red Light" district. Of course, Mr. Miyagi laughed and said, "Oh, make wrong turn."

Although regular classes were not normally held on Tuesday evenings, Mr. Miyagi made an exception because it was our last night in Okinawa. We bowed in and the pace of the workout was full speed ahead from the beginning. We performed 21 katas in 15 minutes and that included two water breaks.

A quick breather and we were out on the floor once again for weapons katas. We had just begun when Jody said, "Did you see the size of that Okinawan?" When I looked to the door there was no one there. She insisted, "He was the biggest Okinawan I've ever seen." A moment later he appeared at the side door and, yes, sir, he was a mountain of man and it looked as if the mountain was made of solid muscle. He spoke to Mr. Miyagi and suddenly class was stopped.

The Okinawan gentleman was the island's arm wrestling champion and he'd heard about Joe and wanted to challenge him to an arm wrestling contest. Mr. Miyagi told Joe that he was being challenged to a match and wanted to know if he would accept. Joe had the size to back him, but I wasn't sure of his arm wrestling prowess. Joe nodded and said he'd accept the challenge.

Soon, all of us were witnessing a first in the Miyagi Dojo. Class was temporarily halted and students were carrying a desk to the center of the dojo floor. A few of the students had enough knowledge of arm wrestling to insure that Joe and his challenger were in the proper position.

The call to battle was sounded and the war of the mountain men was on and it looked as if Joe was going fall to the champion rather quickly. But, just inches short of having his arm taken to the desktop, he pushed back and steadily moved the Okinawan's arm up and past the center mark. Now, it was a contest of sheer strength, endurance and willpower. Back and forth just beyond the center line their arms moved and it soon became very clear that neither was going to drag the other's arm down to the desktop, at least not in the immediate future. Mr. Miyagi allowed the battle to go on for what he deemed a reasonable time and called an end to the struggle. He declared the match a draw. The clash of the titans ended with smiles, a handshake and a respectful bow to each other. The Okinawan champion exited the dojo, the desk was returned to the corner and class continued for another twenty minutes.

After class we were off to a restaurant for a late dinner, some ice-cold beer and to say our goodbyes to our very good friends and brothers in karate. The food, as always, was outstanding, which seemed to be the case no matter where we dined. Tonight we were in for a special treat when we were introduced to "Okinawan Pizza." The round paper-thin discs were melt in your mouth delicious. Then came the platters of fried chicken and, my favorite, sushi, along with continued refills of Orion Beer.

There were stories, laughs, smiles and toasts to health, karate and friendship, but by the end of the evening it was obvious some of those smiles were forced. It was only a matter of hours until we would, once again, part ways and have only treasured memories to share with friends and family. Yet, I am certain all of us knew the bond of friendship between Okinawan and American was stronger than ever and we would find time in the future to come together and celebrate our alliance.

Before we knew it, we were walking into the Naha Airport and waiting for our flight number to be called. We shared a quick breakfast with Mr. Miyagi and some of his students while waiting for our departure time. There was a round of handshakes, a few hugs and a number of misty eyes as we gave one last goodbye and boarded our plane. As the plane began its take-off, there was a final glance through the window and, like the times before, our Okinawan home became a tiny speck and then vanished.

Commentary

Senseis – Parents – Students

A Dream Come True

I was a sophomore at Catonsville Community College in the spring of 1971 and I needed to take an elective in physical education. I chose a self-defense class, because I thought it might be interesting. I really enjoyed the self-defense class and I had a feeling that I had just experienced the tip of the iceberg—that there was a lot more where that came from.

During the summer of 1971, I worked at a local swimming pool. One night, one of the snack bar staff members, Wayne, was off on the side of the building performing some martial arts moves known as kata. I watched him intently, and when he was through, I asked him where he learned it. He told me about a Howard County Police Officer who taught karate at Mt. Hebron High School. Wayne said the next class was that coming Sunday at 10:00 AM and told me to stop by. The rest, as they say, is history. In August 1971, I met Sensei James Lilley and my journey began, and continues to this day.

Through the years I heard the stories of how Jim met Miyagi

Sensei, his training with George (Mr. Nakanishi) and how Jim and Len would quit, because Miyagi's class was too hard. Jim and Len must have felt that same, deep-down pull that I felt. The kind that draws you in and crawls under skin, making it impossible to ignore. It has you anxiously anticipating your next class with a bit of dread mixed with an unrivalled thirst for more. I often dreamt of one day meeting Miyagi Sensei, maybe traveling to Okinawa and observing him in his home surroundings, but I never actually believed that it would happen.

The years went by and, fortunately for all of us, Jim had continued to write to Miyagi and kept the lines of communication open. At the conclusion of our workouts, the fearless four, me, Bruce and Will (The senior members of the class), would sit down with Jim and talk for hours over pizza and beer. At some point, I don't really remember when, we asked Jim to write Miyagi Sensei and ask him to send us videotape of all the katas. After all, Jim had been back in the Unites States for 25 years without Mr. Miyagi's wise counsel and keen eye. In addition, with the death of Choshin Chibana, the head of the Ryu in 1969, it was rumored that his successor, Mr. Katsuya Miyahira had made some changes to the katas, and we were curious to see what those changes were.

In late December the tape arrived from Miyagi Sensei, and we couldn't wait to sit down and digest it. Surprisingly, there were a few minor differences in the katas, but nothing that stuck out like a sore thumb. This, in and of itself, was a phenomenal feat for Jim to have kept them so close after all those years. We followed the delivery with a tape of Jim performing each of the katas and sent it to Miyagi Sensei. The following month another videotape arrived, providing us further opportunity to hone and perfect our katas. We dedicated the next year to fine-tuning our katas and, when we were satisfied that we had come as close as possible to the recorded version, we sent another tape of Jim to Mr. Miyagi.

Not long after we sent that tape, Jim received a surprise telephone call from Miyagi Sensei. "Jimmy, I come to see you." We couldn't believe it. Miyagi Sensei was coming to the United States during the last week of July 1989. The only trouble—I wasn't going to be here. That time frame was one of the two weeks my family took each year and travelled to Hilton Head, South Carolina to vacation with my in-laws.

Miyagi Sensei was supposed to fly in to New York on Friday morning and spend a few days prior to coming to Baltimore. So, on Saturday morning the family and I departed for Hilton Head. I called Jim that evening to get Mr. Miyagi's itinerary, only to find that he didn't like New York and was sitting in Jim's living room at that very moment. Needless to say my frustration and excitement levels were duelling for first place.

Well, I couldn't believe my luck. I learned that my sister and brother-in-law were driving back to Baltimore on Sunday morning. By early evening I was sitting with Jim in his dining room across the table from Mr. Miyagi. It didn't get much better than that. And, for as far as he travelled to pay us a visit, he was flattered and surprised that I interrupted my family vacation and drove 600 miles to see him. Talk about being humble—didn't he realize what a Super Star we thought he was? We talked for a good part of the night, visited in the mornings, and worked out in the afternoons and evenings for the next several days. It was the greatest karate marathon ever, and I found myself shaking my head a few times in utter disbelief over my good fortune. Although I returned to South Carolina on Wednesday to finish the vacation, my experience was unbelievable. But, as it turned out, it was only another beginning.

In the summer of 1995 we got our big break. Miyagi Sensei invited us to be a part of a demonstration commemorating the 40th Anniversary of his dojo. What an honor! At the same time, there was to be a pre-world tournament to commemorate the Battle of Okinawa. We arrived at the airport amid waves and hugs from Miyagi's students, some bearing gifts. The next day we went to the dojo and worked out with Miyagi Sensei and his students. Needless to say that those two weeks spent in Okinawa were nothing short of unbelievable and life changing. Observing Okinawan traditions first-hand, and being taught the art I had been so passionate about for so long, directly from the source opened up new avenues of not only knowledge, but also new ways of looking at everything I had already learned.

We returned to Okinawa for the world tournament in 1997. I competed in the Bo competition as I had during our first visit, and trained pretty much day and night. It was awesome, tiring and inspiring. We returned to Okinawa again in 2002. During that visit I was asked to be a referee for the world tournament—certainly another honor. Of course, I was required to attend two training seminars before receiving my referee's certification.

Tournaments in Okinawa differ quite drastically from those held in the U. S. Only white gis were allowed to be worn, with pant legs cuffed at the ankles, sleeves to just above the wrist, and one patch representing a particular school or style. Referees were strictly forbidden to have any contact whatsoever with competitors during the tournament.

During my last visit to Okinawa, Miyagi Sensei told me it was time for me to open my own dojo. I was reluctant at first, but he told me I needed to have at least one or two students at a minimum. When I returned home I opened the St. Brigid's Dojo, which is now in its 7th year. Soon I discovered that, as always, Miyagi Sensei was right. I've learned much more than I could've possibly imagined by teaching students from the very beginning. And, as I teach them, they teach me.

I've been practicing and teaching for over 45 years and the journey and the dream goes on.

Daniel Simons

Kyoshi, Eighth Degree Black Belt

Okinawa Shorin Ryu Karate Do

***

Pursuing A Childhood Dream

As a young child, I always wanted to know how to perform karate, as I enjoyed watching Karate on TV and had read about the various styles. Based on what I thought the cost was to take lessons, I never thought I would have an opportunity to learn.

Upon completing my senior year of college, my brother, Herman, a Howard County Police Officer, asked if I was interested in playing Flag Football for the Howard County Police Department's team. I accepted his offer and joined the team.

We practiced at Mount Hebron High School and toward the

end of the season I noticed a Karate class practicing in the auxiliary gym. I asked my brother if he knew anything about the class. He said, "That's Jim Lilley and he's a Howard County Police Officer." I was a physically strong football player, lifted weights and could hit very hard. But, I felt that I wasn't totally confident with my ability to defend my loved ones or myself if needed. Since I always wanted to study Karate, I asked Herman to introduce me.

Jim accepted me in his class in January 1973, and my dream began to come true. The Karate style was Shorin Ryu, Okinawan Karate that Jim learned while stationed in Okinawa with the U.S. Marines. Now I was happy that I was finally able to study and practice Karate, but little did I know what would come about years later. Oh, and Jim's class was never about money--$10.00 a month until you reached Black Belt and then lessons were free. It was all about teaching those who really wanted to learn a true style of Karate, Okinawa Shorin Ryu.

Jim was, and still is, a great teacher, who is very strict and follows the leadership direction from Mr. Miyagi. And speaking of strict – One day after we bowed in for class, my friend, Will Adams, and I decided to punch and kick at each other. We didn't think Jim would see us, but he did. The rule was "no playing around" once you bowed in for class. Will and I found out that day exactly what Jim meant by this rule. I don't remember who started the punching and kicking, but we never did it again.

Jim told us to go to the corner and perform push-ups and sit-ups. I asked, "How many?"

"Until I tell you to stop or switch," he replied.

Well, needless to say, after about 45 minutes of sit-ups and push-ups, my muscles were so tight I couldn't stand up straight or keep my arms straight. But, we had to continue with class and do the katas correctly.

Jim's Karate class brought people together from various backgrounds, professions and many different locations, including a few foreign countries. We came to class with a common goal—to learn Karate. Along the way we became great friends, both inside and outside of the class.

I received my First-Degree Black Belt (Shodan) in the summer of 1975, after a very strenuous test of kata, self-defense and free sparring with two against one. But, as Jim had said, every day was a test and he would watch very closely and make corrections as needed. Getting my Black Belt was the greatest day of my life, but Jim quickly reminded me, as Mr. Miyagi had told him, "This is just the beginning." For the novices who don't understand the true traditions of Karate, this sounds unbelievable, since you are a Black Belt. Well, after studying and teaching Karate for over 37 years, it's clear to me that Jim and Mr. Miyagi were right. There is so much more to learn and perfect after you reach your Shodan level.

Thanks to Jim Lilley's Karate class, I had become a very good student, with discipline and the ability, both mentally and physically, to defend myself. During the early to late 70's Karate had become extremely popular and a "household" word thanks to the "Kung Fu" TV series. At the same time, a lot of tournaments and professional competitions were popping up in the Baltimore/DC area.

Suddenly the question became, "Did I learn well enough from Jim Lilley and his instructors?" and "how well would I do against other Karate styles in Tournaments?" So, I ventured into the tournament circuit and eventually the professional circuit, east of the Mississippi River, to test my ability. Well, I can assure you I was taught and trained very well by Jim Lilley with the Shorin Ryu Karate system. Additionally, Jim's police training and his street fighting tactics provided another level of defensive techniques as well.

I competed against many different styles from Korean to Chinese to American made-up systems, as well as other Japanese Karate systems. One of the most promoted groups around the DC Area was the Jhoon Rhee Tae Kwon Do Pro Fighters. But, they hated to see me show up for competition. My number of kata and sparring wins within this circuit proved that Jim Lilley and the Shorin Ryu Karate system had very well trained me. Although this was quite an accomplishment, the best experience was still to come.

All of us knew that Jim's instructor was Mr. Miyagi from Okinawa, and we had heard many stories about him over the years.

Jim received a videotape from Mr. Miyagi and it was great to see Mr. Miyagi and his class performing the same katas we had been practicing for years. More importantly, it showed the solid bond between Jim and Mr. Miyagi that had existed through the years. For us, as Jim's students, this was extremely important, because we had a direct link to Jim's Sensei (teacher) and his class members. We were part of the Okinawa Shorin Ryu Karate System, with a lineage and history that could be traced back for centuries. This was not a made up Karate system with no history and no roots. This was a real system and a dream come true. I was blessed to have studied with Jim's Shorin Ryu Class and become a part of the link to Okinawan history.

Meeting Mr. Miyagi and His Students

We finally got to meet and workout with Mr. Miyagi in the late 80s (1989) and throughout the 90s, when he visited the U. S. several times with members of his class. Working out with Mr. Miyagi was a mark in our history that will never be forgotten. We were able to experience firsthand the leadership as Jim had in Okinawa many years ago.

The experience became better when we travelled to Okinawa in 1995 to workout with Mr. Miyagi's Dojo and take part in the 1995 Okinawa Karate and Kobudo World Pre-Tournament. Mr. and Mrs. Miyagi, all the students of Miyagi Sensei's dojo and their fellow Okinawans treated us like "Royalty." Their hospitality and support was almost overwhelming. Yet, it seemed to grow with every visit.

The World Pre-Tournament and the Okinawa International Tournaments were held very much like the Olympics, with a host of countries (at least 25) represented. Although we participated in the Okinawa International Karate and Kobudo competition on three separate occasions, working out with Mr. Miyagi and his students was the highlight of these trips.

Mr. Miyagi's Dojo

The very first night we worked out as a combined class let us know just how well we had been taught by Jim. After the first kata, the combined Miyagi and Lilley classes were completely together on every move, and our timing was perfect. Miyagi's students turned to us smiling and applauding to show us their acceptance and utmost respect for our abilities. As a combined class, and never having worked out together before, we were in tune as a single class. This was a great feeling and an excellent compliment to both Jim Lilley and Mr. Miyagi as true leaders. That night alone made us feel like "one class," trained to perfection, but in two separate countries.

Currently, I am an 8th Degree Black Belt (Hachidan) with my own class, but I continue to workout with Jim. My philosophy and goals are to teach as I was taught, and continue to pass on the traditions of Shorin Ryu Karate as handed down by Jim Lilley and Mr. Miyagi.

When I first began, I never thought, even in my wildest dreams and imagination that I would have travelled to such a magnitude and depth in Shorin Ryu. Yet, as I continue to practice and teach, I go on learning from Jim Lilley and Mr. Miyagi.

Bruce Charity

Kyoshi, Eighth Degree Black Belt

Okinawa Shorin Ryu Karate Do

***

Impressions of Mr. Miyagi

I remember my first impressions of Miyagi Sensei were drawn while sitting down and sharing a few beers with Jim, Danny and Bruce. From the stories related by Jim about Mr. Miyagi's belief that no American would stay in his class, and the pictures of Jim and Len sweeping pebbles off a hard dirt area in a back yard, my initial vision of Mr. Miyagi appeared. I envisioned him as being a rock-hard individual who would demand no less than perfection from his students.

My first meeting with Miyagi Sensei proved my impression to be far from the truth. On Mr. Miyagi's first visit to America, Danny, Bruce and I were invited to Jim's house for an afternoon workout. I was quite surprised to be introduced to a quiet, calm, and unassuming man with a big smile. As our workout progressed I also learned what a serious person he could be. We began our katas as usual and we thought we were doing a good job, however, after just a few minutes he stopped us and we started over. We had to work on our stances. The most memorable phrase that day and ever since is, "Well, again."

As we continued our workouts during the week, we realized that we had gained a new friend—a new friend who was pleased with the progress Jim had made with us. It's funny, but he corrected us on the same things Jim had previously corrected. And, I guess we heard him more clearly, because he didn't sound like that broken record that screamed at us so often. Anyway, by the end of the week we finally understood what Jim meant when he told us "now that you are black belts, your education begins." We understood that we still had a lot to learn. Of course, after working with Mr. Miyagi's class during visits to Okinawa, I realized that I still have a lot to learn, but it's comforting to know that they are willing to teach me.

After several trips to Okinawa, I realized that, just like Miyagi Sensei, the people of Okinawa are some of the most pleasant and hospitable I have ever met. During those visits I found many new friends and, as Jim had said so many times, I'm also a member of a family thousands of miles from my home in America.

Since my first meeting Miyagi Sensei over 27 years ago, I have learned many things of great value. First, to continue to stay lower in my stances, second, and the lesson I learned the hard way, kumite is for younger people. Third, and most important, I have been encouraged to continue practicing karate as long as possible, and to pass along the knowledge I have gained to others. Fourth, but on the lighter side, I discovered that, although Miyagi Sensei is a great karate teacher, he should never be asked to join in Karaoke.

William J. Adams

Kyoshi, Eighth Degree Black Belt

Okinawa Shorin Ryu Karate Do

***

My Journey in the Martial Arts

I began my martial arts training somewhat late in life, being 32 years old at the time. I was attending community college in 1978 and there were several karate classes offered. I chose Shotokan mainly because it fit my schedule. At first, I had only a mild interest in karate, but soon found that I was really enjoying it.

After a couple of semesters I moved to another county and, not wanting to make the long trip, I began looking for a Shotokan school closer to home. However, there was only a Tae Kwon Do School nearby. I enrolled in Kane Karate, a Tae Kwon Do school, which turned out to be very good. Even though it was a Korean art, it was obviously a system based on Okinawan/Japanese karate, as the katas were virtually the same, but with Korean names. During my 13 years of training in this style I did a lot of reading about the history of karate and its origin in Okinawa, reading everything I could find on the subject. I earned my First Degree black Belt in 1985.

While continuing my practice of Tae Kwon Do, I began studying the art of Aikido and continued for 20 years. In 1992 my Tae Kwon Do instructor retired from teaching and I began looking for a new school. I dabbled in American Kenpo for a short time, which I liked, but what I really wanted was a traditional Okinawan or Japanese school.

While shopping in a martial arts store in Baltimore, I found a business card for Jim Lilley's Okinawan Karate Dojo. Although it was about a 35-minute drive from home, I decided to give it a try.

After contacting Jim, I went out and watched a class and then went back for a trial lesson. It was exactly what I was looking for. Jim and the others training there were good people and extremely dedicated to their karate training. Many of them had been studying with Mr. Lilley since the 70s and I think that says a lot about Jim.

In 1995 we had the opportunity to make a trip to Okinawa for the celebration of the 40th Anniversary of Mr. Miyagi's dojo. This was a dream come true. Not only were we able to participate in the demonstrations for the anniversary celebration, but also the World Pre-tournament. The tournament also included seminars by the most senior karate instructors in Okinawa. I could hardly believe I was in the company of some of the masters I had read about in the karate history books, people like Katsuya Miyahira and Shoshin Nagamine.

The karate experience in Okinawa was everything I hoped

for. The unexpected part was the hospitality of Mr. Miyagi and his students. We were provided with a place to stay during our two-week visit, taken on many sightseeing tours and various restaurants. And, they wouldn't allow us to pay for a thing.

Although they are very serious about their karate training, they also enjoy the fellowship afterwards. We were treated to several dojo parties during our stay and, in spite of the language difference, we were able to talk and have a great time.

I was unable to go back with the class in 1997, but I did make another trip to Okinawa in 2002. I participated in the world tournament and, of course, found that very same hospitality I had discovered during my first visit.

Even though some may consider karate to be violent, the people who devised the art to defend themselves are far from it. In fact, I'll never forget something that one of Mr. Miyagi's senior students (Mr. Higa) said in comparing the Okinawan people to the Japanese. "If you visit a home in Japan, you are likely to find a sword above the fireplace, while in Okinawa, you are more likely to find a musical instrument."

Richard Kelley

Renshi, Sixth Degree Black Belt

Okinawa Shorin Ryu Karate Do

Catching My Dream

I wanted to study the art of karate shortly after entering the 10th grade. A teacher from one of the local schools performed a demonstration for my high school history class and I was a little impressed. However, my parents told me since I was already involved with gymnastics, they would not pay for karate lessons and I would have to pay out of my pocket. Well, I didn't have a job at the time, so I decided to wait until I was "too old" for gymnastics.

After enrolling in college, I contacted the dojo that performed the demonstration for my high school class and asked about lessons. The call was going very well until the person told me that I had to buy their uniform, pay for and pass a test for white belt, pay testing fees for other belts and several additional charges. I said, "No thank you" and hung up.

I began working for the Howard County Police Department as a dispatcher in 1983. At the same time I heard that a sergeant in the department taught martial arts, but at that point I was too busy with other things to pursue lessons. In October 1986 I finally worked up the nerve to ask Sergeant Lilley about his karate class. He told me that he taught classes, but only in the Okinawan tradition, and said I should come watch a class to see if I was really interested. I asked why he didn't advertise his classes and he said he saw no reason to, and word of mouth was the best advertisement anyway.

I went to watch a class and when I saw the kata Seisan I was hooked. I have been practicing for over 30 years now and I'm still learning. During breaks in the class Jim would talk about his teacher, Mr. Miyagi, and his time spent in Okinawa. The core-group, Danny, Bruce and Will would often talk about traveling to Okinawa to practice and see the birthplace of karate. At the time it was just a dream, but dreams do come true.

During the summer of 1989, Jim received a letter from Mr. Miyagi saying that he was coming to the United States to visit and asking to stay with Jim. Of course, Jim said yes. Certainly all of the students were very excited to hear that Jim's teacher was coming to visit. At last, we would meet his teacher and mentor and have the opportunity to be taught by Mr. Miyagi. The next letter said he would be arriving around the end of July.

By now I was in the police academy and Jim and I had been dating for 18 months. Mr. Miyagi wrote to let Jim know he would visit New York for a few days before coming to Maryland. But, only hours after his arrival, he called Jim and informed him that he was not thrilled with New York and would be coming to Maryland the following day. Of course, the man in New York who "helped" Mr. Miyagi put him on a flight to National Airport in D.C. instead of BWI in Baltimore. To make matters worse, he didn't call Jim until after the flight was in the air. Jim rushed out of the house to go get Mr. Miyagi, but with all the activity in and around the Washington, D.C. area that day, it was a very long trip. It was about six hours later when he finally made it home with Mr. Miyagi.

I admit I was very excited about meeting Mr. Miyagi, but also very nervous because I was going to be the first to meet Jim's teacher. In spite of being nervous, I somehow managed to keep my composure when introduced. Although I was in complete awe, and still am when I am around him, I soon felt comfortable being in his company.

While Jim was showering and getting ready to take us to dinner, Mr. Miyagi told me about his wife and children and the house where they lived. After a while he said he wanted to ask me a question, but wasn't sure how to ask. I told him to take his time and just ask the question. He started by saying he didn't like New York. Then he asked, "What son-of-a-bitch mean? I hear it a lot in New York." I laughed and told him it was not good, but was often said when someone is upset or something goes wrong.

Well, the very next day, Sunday, we travelled to Washington, D. C. and I drove. I made a wrong turn and ended up on a dead end street. Without thinking I blurted, "Son-of-a-bitch," which brought a round of laughter. Even now, when I see Mr. Miyagi, we still laugh over "son-of-a-bitch."

I have learned so much over the past 30 years and I know I'm continuing to learn. At times I look back and think that what I have learned is unbelievable. Then there are the newfound friends from my first and continued visits to Okinawa. We truly are a family—a family of many and still growing.

I have reached the level of 6th Degree Black Belt and hope that some day I will be good enough to earn my 7th Dan. That would be something special, but certainly not as special as receiving my Shodan. After receiving my Shodan, everyone told me that I was just beginning. At first, I had no idea what they meant. As time went on, I found that everyday as you practice and teach, you learn.

I have met two very important and very special people in my life—my husband, Jim, and Mr. Miyagi. Surely, without them and the influence they have had on my life, I don't think I would be as strong as I am today. I have learned so much from them and I look forward to learning new katas and techniques. But, I realize I have a lifetime to learn. And, as Mr. Miyagi said to me during our last visit, "Haste makes waste. Take your time and do not rush. It will all come in time."

Jody Lilley

Renshi, Sixth Degree Black Belt

Okinawa Shorin Ryu Karate Do

***

My Reflections of Mr. Miyagi

During the period 1994 and later, my dear friend and fellow Martial Arts Practitioner, Master Jim Lilley (Shorin Ryu Karate) introduced me to his instructor, Grandmaster Takeshi Miyagi. Jim's dojo and my dojo shared a studio so that we had many opportunities to partake in the cultures and histories of the arts that each of us practices.

Upon meeting Mr. Miyagi for the first time, I was struck by his presence. He was tranquil, yet deliberate in demeanor. His attitude was thoughtful, respectful and quietly powerful. In his stature, one could see the fitness and total control of self that typically results from a lifetime of study and practice of the Martial Arts. He is a very gentle, caring and unassuming man with the capacity to interact comfortably in any environment. These traits are all well suited for a man of his culture. Another observation that I made regarded Mr. Miyagi's ability to speak clear, lucid English. This is the mark of a person who appreciates, is open to and is diligent about learning respective cultures other than his. After a brief exchange of pleasantries, Mr. Miyagi created an atmosphere where I knew that I was welcome to approach him and that he was accessible. This is the mark of a great teacher.

In observing Mr. Miyagi teach the Martial Art, I noted that he was an exacting but patient instructor with a keen attention to detail, while at the same time allowing the student the freedom of self-expression and to maintain healthy self-esteem. In my years of instructing, I have come to appreciate the difficulty of this task and that one who has accomplished it has truly mastered the art of teaching. Mr. Miyagi shared that he emphasizes quality in the students he teaches over quantity. I've taken this advice since our discussion and it has helped maintain my Martial Art club. I was fortunate to have observed Mr. Miyagi at practice. The Shorin Ryu Art emphasizes fluid movements and flexible positions so that the practitioner can be capable of most correctly addressing an attack. Mr. Miyagi's movements, balance, and flexibility, along with his emphasis on the hard and soft power, represent the complete embodiment of Shorin Ryu principles. I observed true mastery of the philosophy and technique of the system. Mr. Miyagi is the perfect example to any practitioner of the system. As a matter of warm up, he performed feats of flexibility that I could not do at over twenty years his junior.

Our discussion about life, Martial Arts and his culture were very insightful. During these discussions, Mr. Miyagi further revealed the "gentleman, scholar and learned thinker" that he is. In his understanding and dignified manner, he taught that religion and Martial Art are similar in many ways and that both or either, if practiced correctly, will result in self-improvement. Mr. Miyagi believes in forging physical, mental and spiritual strength through diligent practice. Forgiveness, in turn, is personally uplifting. He recommends it as something that helped him to meet and overcome his personal challenges.

At some point, Mr. Miyagi paid me one of the highest compliments that I have ever received, when he observed that my students and me are "gentlemen." The compliment was truly high praise coming from Mr. Miyagi.

I consider myself fortunate to know Grandmaster Miyagi and look forward to future meetings. I can't think of a better tribute than this treatise of Mr. Miyagi's life story and I'm happy to make this contribution.

Lee Cunningham

Snow Tiger Combat Systems

***

Dear Mr. Lilley,

This is a brief history on the lives of my sons, Andrew and

Michael, and why meeting you and learning karate played an important role in their lives. Andrew Paul Miecznikoski came into the world premature on July 10, 1989. His delivery was complicated by the fact that the umbilical cord was wrapped around his neck. He was placed in neonatal intensive care for further observation. There, the nursing staff found it quite rare that Andrew was born with four teeth. Unfortunately, he developed pneumonia and his condition was considered critical. Due to the severity of his condition, we were told to expect the worst, and that he would not make it through the night. This was the first time Andrew's will to live surfaced. The next morning the entire staff was amazed at the turn around in his condition, and he was sent home the following week. Andrew was a gifted child—Mensa tested with an IQ of 157. He scored in the 98th percentile for height, had thick blond hair, and the most beautiful blue eyes. He was perfect in every way, was treated as such by everyone, and had a very high self-esteem. Andrew was reading fluently before he started pre-school.

On July 3, 1994, while attending a pool party, Andrew was demonstrating his newly acquired swimming skills when he sank to the bottom of the pool. He went unnoticed for several minutes before his blue, unresponsive body was found at the bottom of the pool. Fortunately, the host's daughter was a doctor and worked feverishly on Andrew for some time before he was sent to St. Joseph's Hospital by ambulance for further observation and testing.

God works in mysterious ways. Unknown to us at that time was this would be a pivotal point in Andrew's life. He turned five on July 10th, and several weeks later in the beginning of August Andrew awoke each morning and ran to the bathroom to throw up clear fluid. Although he looked perfectly healthy in every way, we took him to our family paediatrician, Doctor Allan Leffler, for an evaluation. We suspected that this was a complication from his near death experience in the pool.

Although he passed the neurological exam, Doctor Leffler intuitively felt something was grossly wrong, and asked us to bring him back in two days. Andrew continued to throw up clear fluid each morning, and was becoming increasingly more lethargic. At our next visit, the doctor noticed a slight flit in Andrew's eye.

We were promptly sent to an optometrist for further testing and evaluation. Noting something suspicious, we were immediately sent for a MRI with contrast. The MRI was conducted on August 19, 1994. During the contrast portion of the test we were alerted that Andrew had a malignant brain tumor in the cerebellum, and due to the amount of CFS fluid build-up, Andrew was in imminent danger of having a stroke.

He was rushed directly to Johns Hopkins Hospital, where Doctor Ben Carson performed immediate surgery to release the pressure on Andrew's brain. Once again, Andrew was placed in a life/death situation that would forever change his life and how others would perceive him.

On August 22, 1994 Doctor Ben Carson performed a gross total resection of the medulloblastoma from Andrew's brain. The tumor had tentacles pushing on the brain stem and it was one of the largest tumors Doctor Carson had ever seen. Had those tentacles penetrated the brain stem, he would have been considered a high-risk medull-oblastoma, with metastisis throughout his body. Andrew's life was spared by about one week from this fast growing tumor.

After the second surgery many life-altering challenges faced Andrew. The most obvious change was that he was paralysed on his right side and had cerebellar mutism, making him unable to speak for many months. Other complications arose including double vision, ventriculitis, and spinal meningitis, which exacerbated the recent onset of paralysis.

Andrew went on to receive six weeks of the maximum amount of daily craniospinal radiotherapy, with a dose to the posterior fossa of 5,580 cGy, whole brain, 3,600 cGy, and spine 3,040 cGy. Radiotherapy was completed on November 4, 1994. It is interesting to note that if Andrew had not been advanced in tooth development, the portals of the radiation would have killed his forming second teeth. Secondly, the excessive radiation to his spine stunted his growth. Today, his spine is only 15 inches long, however, because of his projected height, he has an inseam of 34 inches, giving him a normal height.

In a matter of weeks, Andrew went from a very advanced, self-sufficient five-year old pre-schooler to a non-responsive, and profoundly handicapped child. Therefore, the doctors suggested that we place Andrew at Kennedy-Krieger Institute where he would receive PT, OT, speech therapy, recreational therapy, and a multitude of other services to treat this traumatic brain injury. After many months of rigorous therapies, Andrew was sent home.

It was recommended that we continue with PT, OT and speech therapy to further improve his balance, coordination and visual motor processing. It was at this time that we found Jim and Jody Lilley and their karate school. The repetition and discipline of karate helped Andrew's mental attitude toward his recovery. The physical routine of karate helped him develop muscle mass in his atrophied right leg, as well as build up strength in his upper body.

One of the most challenging obstacles of Andrew's recovery was to learn how to become left-handed after growing up as a naturally right-handed person. The karate routines, including standing on one foot, gave Andrew an increased sense of balance. The several years of karate training helped his overall recovery.

Andrew will be celebrating fifteen years of being cancer free on August 19, 2010. Although Andrew looks and acts completely normal, he suffers from short-term memory issues, which make his academic achievements more remarkable. Although he has studied and knows the material, at times, it is difficult for him to recall information for tests. It is also challenging for him to keep up with note taking, and trying to type. Andrew must work three times harder to achieve his goals. Yet, he has made the Dean's List and is an honor student, pursuing a degree in Recreational Therapy. It is his goal to help others who have suffered as he has.

Andrew's older brother, Michael, went along to karate simply to be with his younger brother. However, Michael reaped many unexpected benefits from the karate lessons. Having been diagnosed as ADHD, he was in need of a focus in his life. Karate gave Michael the tools to better manage his impulsive behavior and take control of his life. Michael feels that Mr. Lilley's instruction in karate classes taught him the strategies to cope with his disabilities, and how to think through issues. The discipline of the exercises helped Michael maintain a focus and concentrate on a task until completion. He has made the Dean's List several times and is also an honor student, pursuing a degree in Graphic Arts. He attributes his success to Mr. Lilley's guidance and the karate lessons that helped him find the way to help himself.

Although both boys had very different issues, karate has had a definite, positive impact in both of their lives.

Nancy Trimble-Oliver

Benjamin S. Carson, Sr., M.D.
Professor and Director of Pediatric
Neurosurgery

Department of Neurosurgery
600 North Wolfe Street I Harvey 811
Baltimore, Maryland 21287-8811

JOHNS HOPKINS
Medicine

Dear Mr. Lilley:

The following is the statement regarding Andrew Miecanikosi:

I first met Andrew and his family when he was five years old and presented to the emergency room with signs of increased intracranial pressure, He had a scan that revealed a large tumor of the posterior fossa and hydrocephalus. We treated the hydrocephalus first with a drain and then a few days later resected the tumor. The tumor was extremely large, and we were fortunate to be able to completely resect it. He was left initially with something called cerebellar mutism which means he was unable to speak and had some mild weakness, and it required rehabilitative therapy at the Kennedy Krieger Institute as well as outpatient therapy to overcome these problems. He also had to have radiation therapy because the tumor was highly malignant.

Through all of this, Andrew persisted and worked extremely hard both physically and mentally. He became an excellent student academically and also got involved in martial arts which dramatically accelerated his physical recovery. I believe this was also helpful for his mental attitude and he developed a "can do" attitude, which has persisted until the present time. Additionally, probably because of his own medical problems, he has focused a great deal of attention on helping others. He has done volunteer work in hospitals as well as held jobs in hospitals and is working toward certification in' therapeutic recreation in which he has already had significant experience.

It is very encouraging to see people like Andrew, who were afflicted with often fatal conditions, be able to completely overcome the physical challenge and go on to become outstanding citizens dedicated to uplifting their fellow human beings. I am certain that Andrew will go on to accomplish significant things throughout life, and I am very privileged to have played a role in his health.

Benjamin S. Carson, Sr., M.D.
The Benjamin S. Carson, Sr., M.D. and
Dr. Evelyn Spiro, R.N. Professor of Pediatric Neurosurgery
Director of Pediatric Neurosurgery
Professor of Neurological Surgery,
Oncology, Plastic Surgery, and Pediatrics

Moody D. Wharam, M.D., F.A.C.R.
Willard and Lillian Hackerman
Professor of Radiation Oncology

Radiation Oncology & Molecular
Radiation Sciences
401 North Broadway / Suite 1440
Baltimore, Maryland 2123

JOHNS HOPKINS
Medicine
Comprehensive Cancer Center

Andrew was born in July 1989 and was a very bright little boy. He was using full sentences by age one and could read when he was two years old, In the months leading up to his fifth birthday, he began to have frequent headaches and intolerance of bright lights. He had several episodes of nausea and vomiting and eventually noticed weakness of his hands. This constellation of findings led his pediatrician to obtain an MRI (magnetic resonance imaging) scan of his head which disclosed two things. First, a large tumor in the lower back part of the brain called the posterior fossa. This large tumor was obstructing the normal fluid flow in the brain and therefore, the second finding was markedly enlarged fluid cavities within the brain. Andrew was brought to Johns Hopkins Hospital the day of his MRI scan and very promptly had an operation to place a sterile tube within the brain cavity to relieve fluid pressure inside the brain. This operation was performed by Dr. Benjamin Carson who then, three days later, did a major operation on the back part of the brain to remove the tumor. Dr. Carson successfully removed all the visible tumor which was, on pathologic examination, a malignant tumor called medulloblastoma.

Andrew appeared to be doing well after surgery but only a day later he developed weakness of his right arm and leg, with reduced coordination of his right hand, and had difficulty speaking. This condition known as cerebellar mutism is a not uncommon event after the major operation that Andrew required.

While he was recovering, Andrew had several tests to see if there was obvious spread of his tumor and they were all negative. A medulloblastoma tumor is one that is always associated with spread into the fluid that everyone has within their head. The fluid also descends along the outside of the spinal cord and within the spinal bone cavity. The negative tests that Andrew had simply meant that his spread of tumor was too subtle to be detected by the various examinations he had.

I was Andrew's Radiation Oncologist and first met Andrew and his mother and father a week after his second operation. He was an understandably unhappy little boy. His right arm and leg were weak, he could not talk, and he had two large surgical dressings on his head from his two operations. By this time, Andrew had to be discharged from Hopkins Hospital and transferred to the Kennedy Krieger Institute where he began speech therapy, physical therapy, and occupational therapy. At about that time, he developed a brain infection called meningitis and required weeks of intravenous antibiotics.

Medulloblastoma is not cured with surgery alone but always requires aggressive radiation therapy after the surgery. Currently, all children receive chemotherapy, but that was not being done when Andrew was diagnosed and so he had just radiotherapy. The radiation treatment is amongst the most complex treatments performed by Radiation Oncologists. It entails treating not only the operative bed (the place in the back of the brain where the tumor began), but the entire cerebrospinal fluid space which means the entire brain and the entire spinal column all the way down to the beginning of the coccyx. The treatment requires the patient to be perfectly still for 30 to 45 minutes, an impossible task for any little child. That meant that in addition to his radiation treatment five days a week, Andrew also had to have general anesthesia in order to gain his cooperation for the radiation treatment. That meant anesthesia every weekday for just over six weeks. The treatment is very difficult for a child even without anesthesia. It causes fatigue, upset stomach, a major drop in the blood counts, and hair loss. It continues to have side effects years later, which can include impaired eyesight, below average school performance, some hearing loss, and hormone deficits. The emotional burden of the diagnosis and the physical cost of the treatment is also an enormous emotional burden for parents. However, Andrew and his parents were remarkably upbeat and resilient and Andrew tolerated his treatment well. During his therapy, his right-sided weakness and clumsiness improved and his speech made marked improvement. He and his mom had to come back to Hopkins on a regular basis for follow up examinations and MRI scans. Fortunately, these never demonstrated evidence of recurrence and Andrew, despite what he had been through, did very well in school and went on to complete his bachelor's degree at Frostburg State University. He turned out to be a very determined young man either in spite of, or perhaps in some measure, because of his bout with cancer. Andrew also developed a deep understanding of the toll that a malignant disease can take on one's growth, development, and happiness. Perhaps because of that, he has devoted much of his teenage and young adult life to helping other children and adults deal with serious illnesses and handicaps. Andrew and his Mom are models of how to confront and overcome adversity.

(I am unable to comment on the impact of karate training on Andrew's development).

Yours very truly,

Moody D. Wharam, Jr., M.D., FASTRO, FACR
Professor of Radiation Oncology

MDW/yg

How Jim Lilley and Karate Changed My Life

Little did I realize how the karate class I took in order to confront the other pursuers of my then high school sweetheart, would change my life, make me a better athlete and gain long, true friendships that mean a great deal to me, even today, 39 years later.

At Age 14 I entered Jim Lilley's karate class in order to learn how to scare off any parties potentially interested in my girlfriend. Soon after I joined the class I realized how confident I had become and how little I actually wanted to fight.

Jim Lilley is not only a true karate expert, who lives and breathes this art, but is a true disciplinarian and leader. I was impressed with Jim when I first heard him say that I wouldn't get my black belt in 90 days or less, and that we should avoid a fight if at all possible. Of course, if provoked, we would be fully prepared to defend ourselves.

Looking back at the over seven years that I took lessons from Jim, I realized it had been a total life changing process.

I had less of a desire to fight and was more confident and prepared. Jim taught me discipline and focus. I became much more flexible and my strength and quickness improved greatly. Today, in business I think karate helps me with focus and patience.

In summary, karate lessons and being around Jim Lilley was a life changer. I am very fortunate to have met Jim and his karate students. They not only live and breathe karate, but also are avid about doing it right. Being introduced to karate was one of the best things in my life and meeting and knowing Jim Lilley has been even better. Jim is a true friend, remarkable teacher, but more importantly a real man.

Whoever can call Jim Lilley their friend and instructor is a very fortunate person. I consider myself lucky to be one of these people.

Bob Lucido

Black Belt Certificate June 23, 1977

Epilogue

I have no regrets that the passage of time did not weaken, or change my stubborn adherence to traditions passed on to me by Mr. Miyagi. He gave something to me, which was a part of his heritage, and that was the gift of knowledge of an ancient art. With the passing of time I grew to cherish the gift he passed on to me, but more importantly I learned that his offering to me was something that should remain unspoiled. For that reason I have never had a desire to change the katas and I teach them as they were taught to me.

When an original is altered, it becomes a counterfeit and, over time even the counterfeit will begin to falter and fade to an unrecognizable mixture. And those who rush to embrace the forgery will succeed only in allowing the true beauty and strength of an ancient art to slip away into extinction.

Miyagi Sensei was unbending in his ways as a teacher. He was very strict and demanding of his students, expecting nothing less than 100 percent effort in each and every class. But it was his uncompromising principles, which drove them to excel, and I would not have wanted him to be anything less than the iron-fisted task-master. The harder he made me work the better person I became.

I vowed that I would not let him down by bending or changing his standards when I began to teach. In fact, I'm almost certain that, at times, my students viewed me as a tyrant. I believed (and still do) in discipline, respect and hard work and, those who dared to cross the boundaries paid for straying off course with push-ups. Discipline and a strong work ethic go hand in hand for anyone striving to be successful in business, in sports, or their studies. Success, in pursuit of life's endeavors, is not served up on a platter simply because someone says, "I want to be successful." Success has to be earned. So it was, and still is in my class. No belt was gift wrapped and placed under the Christmas tree.

Those who did not like my strict standards usually quit after only a few lessons. Still, one particular group of potential students set a record with their departure. I know this was said before, but it deserves repeating. A group of eight young men arrived one evening and their spokesman told me they were from a dojo in Columbia. He said they had heard about my dojo and its reputation, and wanted to join. I told them to get dressed and prepare for class.

When the students lined up to bow in and begin class, the new arrivals quickly discovered this would be a no nonsense experience. I assigned one of my senior students to take the young men aside, explain the class rules and procedures and begin teaching them. At the end of the first hour I called a break to allow the students to get a drink of water. Seven of the newly arrived did not return from the break. They simply went into the locker room, changed clothes and took their leave through another door. The young man who remained behind told me the others said the class was far too disciplined for their liking. He completed the entire class but, like the others, vanished into the night, never to be seen again.

In my teaching, I made it a point never to treat those who had problems learning, because of ADD or some type of physical issue, differently from the other students. Beginning with Vince in the 60s and continuing with Andrew, Sean and David in the 90s, I made certain that they were not given special treatment. I believed that treating them with special care would teach them to look for an easy way through life. Treating them with "kid gloves" would have done them more harm than good and, unfortunately, in today's society, far too many of our young children have been taught that rewards also come with failure. In all likelihood, the "every loser gets a trophy too" mentality was born with the dawn of political correctness. As for me, I am anything but politically correct.

Sadly, children, who have been taught that losers receive the same reward as winners, grow up and step out into the work place to earn a living, where they will quickly learn that failure is "rewarded" with nothing—no job, no salary and no future. Or, at best, they will find a job performing menial tasks for low wages.

My "special students" had to meet the same requirements as everyone else for advancement. No belt was a gift to give them and their families to enhance a "warm and fuzzy feeling" about life. It didn't matter if it took longer and harder work to earn their belt. In the end it was the pride they, their families and friends took in their accomplishments that mattered most. The smiles, hugs and the tears said they made it on their own merit and somewhere, deep down inside, their pride was more meaningful.

***

Mr. Miyagi firmly believed in the practice of kata, and he expected them to be performed as close to perfection as possible. After a time, I swore that if my stance in a kata was off by so much as one inch or one degree, he would see it.

I am well aware that there are many that vehemently oppose the practice of kata, saying that kata repetition is a waste of time. Practice of kata is only a waste of time for those who have never learned the Bunkai, or practical application of the moves as they pertain to self-defense. The steps, blocks, kicks and punches, from the very basic to the complex katas, hold a meaning relating to defensive tactics. And, in some cases, the simplest movements of a kata conceal a very deadly application. Thus, when kata is performed with the proper mindset, the practitioner is honing his or her self-defense skills.

Through the years, I have learned the bunkai and have worked to pass this on to my students. But to ensure that nothing has, or will be lost in translation or application, Mr. Miyagi has provided me with videotape and DVD of the kata bunkai. In fact, in addition to the kata bunkai, I have a videotape and DVD library of our katas, including weapons katas.

Kata teaches balance and speed, and improves strength if practiced correctly. But, beyond those concepts are the building of self-discipline and the joining of mind and body as one. All of these are important pieces, which must come together in order for a person to become a true martial artist. Mr. Miyagi pointed out that some people approach and practice karate only with their bodies. He said they have the strength, but lack the spirit or heart, of a true martial artist. He can quickly see anyone who has failed to work with body and spirit and has even pointed them out to me. In time, I too learned to see those who practiced without heart.

In my earliest days with Miyagi Sensei, he spoke of the karate family. He talked of the tie that bound people from many different backgrounds together in search of a common purpose. In his class there were school teachers, bakers, government workers, car salesmen, insurance salesmen, postal employees, construction workers and school teachers and school students who came weekly to learn the art of karate.

Yet, even in my early days, I could see there was a special bond that held them together as a family. There was a friendship that grew stronger with time and as they practiced in class, the senior students helping the juniors learn. With Mr. Miyagi leading the way and setting the example, his students grew into a family with the art of karate as the tie, which bound them as one.

Still, in the beginning, I didn't fully realize how far the bonds of friendship could reach, or how long they would last. What began as a conversation between two young Marines and a karate master opened a door that has remained open for more then 50 years. Over the years, and through that door, many new men and women have passed, and strong friendships, that span thousands of miles, have formed and grown. And, bonds of friendship that were born many years ago have been renewed and continue to flourish.

In my very early years of teaching, I met Bob Moore (1967) a Judo Black Belt and fellow police officer. I met Howard "Z" Zachmann (1968), Dan Simons, Bruce Charity and Will Adams in 1971 and 1973 when they joined the class. Our bond of friendship began its formation when we met, and continued to grow over the years. But, that bond extended beyond our classes and, as a group, we have been through good times and some of the worst times of our lives together. Yet, nothing has broken our ties.

***

Over the years there is something that has come to bother me a great deal. That being the untold story of the Okinawan people and what they suffered at the hands of the Japanese during World War II. The world has heard of the horror and tragedies endured by the Jews at the hands of the Germans. People the world over have seen the faces of suffering, hardship and death from Vietnam to Iraq and Afghanistan.

What happened in Okinawa during the era of World War II is an intricate part of its history. Yet, the story of the Okinawan people and their tragedies remains almost as a forbidden secret, except to those families who lived the nightmare and survived. Why? Is it because many from around the world view them as Japanese and willing participants in the war? If so, this is a monumental mistake that requires correction.

As I pointed out earlier in this book, the bloodlines of the Okinawan people were born of the union of the Polynesians and Chinese who met while traveling the trade routes of the Pacific Ocean and South China Sea. Not only Mr. Miyagi, but also many of the older generation Okinawans pointed out, "We are not Japanese. We are Okinawan."

So, Mr. Speilberg and Mr. Hanks, maybe it is time for you to take up the task and right a misinterpreted course of history.

***

My journey, which began over 50 years ago, goes on and I will pursue whatever lies ahead on its path. However, I remember many bumps in the road and I couldn't see the glass as half empty or half full, only continually filling with things that were not always positive and perfect. There were dark days of unhappiness, sadness and failures. Yet, I am certain that without those things coming into my life to challenge me, I would not have succeeded.

Those days of darkness were, in a sense, a call to battle, asking if I had the courage to stand up and fight back. Well, I did, and along the way I found that each time I was knocked down, I could get up and fight. After a time, the odds didn't matter. It was the satisfaction of saying, "I won't let you beat me" that mattered. Not every battle was easy, but then I wouldn't expect, nor want them to be. That's why I chose the Marine Corps for my military service and law enforcement as my profession. To serve God, Country and Community is an honor, and quite often that service will test and tax a man's will to go on. Yet, the tougher the challenge the stronger the person who emerges from the conflict.

I look back now at my longest running battle and realize it was that fight that changed the course of my life. The struggle began when I was very young, a conflict between good and evil, or maybe it was right and wrong. I learned to hate a man because I saw him as the catalyst that shoved my life into that dark hole of ugliness—the sadness, unhappiness and failures. More than that, I wanted to kill him—not just pick up a gun and shoot him, but to physically destroy him in the most painful way possible.

The years passed and my hate and anger grew—grew into the driving forces of my life. I graduated from high school and enlisted in the Marine Corps, but my goal of destroying this man had not diminished. It was as strong, or stronger than ever. Parris Island might have been hell to many, but to me it was a training ground for what was to come.

Then came the driving desire to learn a martial art, something I could use to break this man into nothing but a pile worthless flesh. My transfer to Okinawa was the door opening on the road to my future. Beginning Miyagi Sensei's class wasn't easy, but I vowed from the very first punch that I would not be driven from his class. After all, he had said that if I wanted to learn and learn the right way, to come back and he would teach me. Well, I was there for as long as it took.

He didn't know my real reason for being there. It was a secret I vowed to carry. Over time I confided in Len and he seemed to understand my drive, but through the years few would ever learn of my quest for retribution. Day after day, week after week, anger and hate carried me through the classes. I was getting faster and stronger and I was learning how to hurt, even kill. Still, that wasn't satisfaction for me. Satisfaction would only be found when the last punch or kick was delivered to the object of my hate.

The night I received my promotion to brown belt something happened and I wasn't sure what it was. I continued to practice with a burning fury, but I felt different. I left Okinawa, years passed, and I had graduated from the police academy. Yet, even as a policeman, that driving itch still waited to be scratched. Then, as though fate had decided it was time for me to face the ultimate test, I was dispatched to a call. Before I arrived at the given address, I knew who would answer my knock at the door. Destiny beckoned and it was time for overdue debts to be paid.

I calmly knocked at the door and when it opened, I stood just more than an arm's length from the man I swore I'd kill. Yet, the moment I looked at him I knew the battle was over. I won. And there behind me was Mr Miyagi's voice, "If you can beat yourself, there's no need to worry about beating someone else." While standing there I realized what a pathetic excuse for a man he really was, and certainly destroying my life for the likes of him wasn't worth it. I helped resolve his problem and assured him he could call me again if he needed assistance.

In one instant, life's glass could have been shattered and the constant flow of the future's offerings lost forever. Life can never promise us only good, but it's how we learn to deal with the bad that dictates the path we will follow. Giving up is easy. It takes no effort whatsoever to quit. Falling down to the gates of hell, but standing and fighting your way out of hell's fire and back to the top takes courage. But, the next time you fall, you might find it a little easier to get up.

I challenge those around me and myself to strive to do better each day. As a teacher I push my students to work toward perfection in their practice of karate, but I demand the same of myself. If I expect the best from those I teach it is my responsibility to lead them by example, not by words alone.

***

The most difficult part in writing this story is that Len wasn't here to share his thoughts about a journey we began together. We opened a door and paved a path that no other American before us had the courage to travel. We took away Mr. Miyagi's doubts about us and won his friendship and respect along with that of his students. We became the first Americans he promoted to brown belt and then black belt, but only one other American would step up and follow in our footsteps and receive his black belt rank from Miyagi Sensei.

Len was, and always will remain an important part in my life. We endured the lumps, bruises and pain of those early days long ago, becoming best friends along the way. Even if we were out of touch for a time, when we spoke again, it was as though we had just had a coffee together the day before. Yet, in his absence I have found that his spirit and heart live on in his sons, Joe, Brian and Chris. They are truly a credit to their father and in them his candle continues to burn brightly—mischief and all.

Katas and Lineage

Kihon Kata 1-2-3 -- Choshin Chibana (We perform as warm up exercises)

Kihon Kata 1-2 -- Shinpan Shiruma

Kihon Kata 3 -- Takeshi Miyagi

Kihon Kata 4 -- Takeshi Miyagi and Yutaka Nakanishi

Fukyu 1 -- Shoshin Nagamine

Fukyu 2 -- Chojun Miyagi

Naihanchi 1-2-3 -- Matsumura—Itosu—Chibana—Miyahira

Seisan -- Chotoku Cyan

Pinan 1-2-3-4-5 -- Itosu—Chibana—Miyahira—Miyagi

Pasai Sho -- Itosu

Pasai Dai -- Matsumura

Kusanku Sho -- Matsumura—Itosu—Chibana—Miyahira

Chinto -- Matsumura—Itosu—Chibana—Miyahira

Gojushiho -- Anshu Tokuda

Jion -- Matsumura—Itosu—?—Miyahira

Unshu -- Takamine—Motobu—Miyahira

Ko Pasai Sho -- Matsumura—Itosu

Chatanyara No Kusanku -- Cyan—Takara—Miyagi

Tetsho -- Miyahira—Miyagi

Tensho -- Higaonna (Goju Ryu Kata)

The katas listed are those practiced in our dojo, and Miyagi Sensei passed the lineage of these katas on to me.

Weapons Katas Sai

Sai Ichi No Kata

Sai Ni No Kata

Chatanyara No Sai

Hamahiga No Sai

Yakah No Sai

Kogusuku No Sai

Tawata No Sai

Bo

Gyosho No Kon -- Miyagi Sensei's Kata—Translation
– Strong General

Shushi No Kon Sho

Shushi No Kon Dai

Sakagawa No Kon Sho

Soeishi No Kon Sho

Tsuken No Kon

Nunchaku

Miyazato

Aguni No Nunchaku

Aguni Ni No Nunchaku (Two Nunchaku)

Tonfa

Hamahiga No Tonfa

Belts and Ranking System

Black Belt Ranks

Judan	10th Degree Black Belt - Title: Hanshi
Kudan	9th Degree Black Belt - Title: Hanshi
Hachidan	8th Degree Black Belt - Title: Kyoshi
Shichidan	7th Degree Black Belt - Title: Kyoshi
Rokudan	6th Degree Black Belt - Title: Renshi
Godan	5th Degree Black Belt - Title: Renshi
Yondan	4th Degree Black Belt - No formal title
Sandan	3rd Degree Black Belt - No formal title
Nidan	2nd Degree Black Belt -No formal title
Shodan	1st Degree Black Belt - No formal title

Brown Belt Ranks

Ikkyu	1st Degree Brown Belt
Nikyu	2nd Degree Brown Belt
Sankyu	3rd Degree Brown Belt

Kobayashi Ryu Lineage Chart

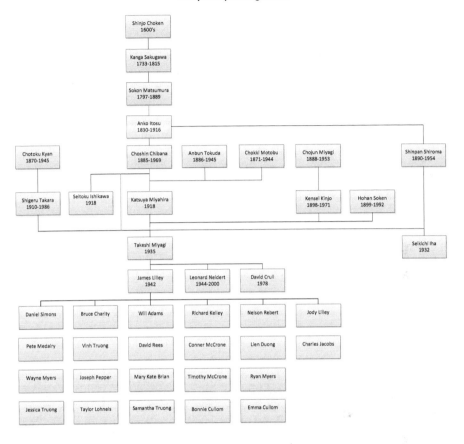

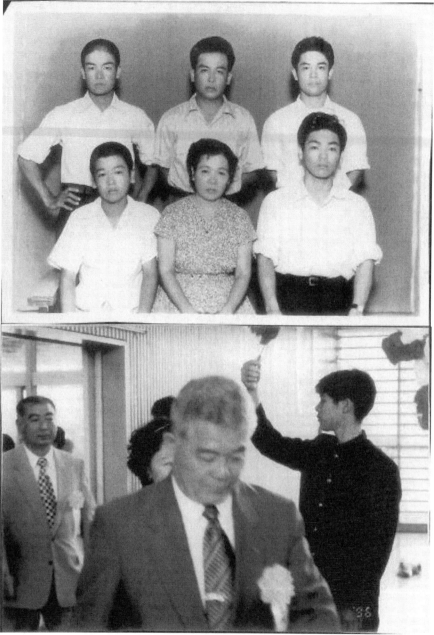

Miyagi Family Top Photo (left to right) Hiyashi, Kenichi and Takeshi
Front row (left to right) Toreo, Mrs. Haru Miyagi and Ketsusaburo.
Bottom photo, Mr. Miyagi's Retirement Celebration after 36 years in the
Okinawa School System.

Miyagi's beginning years in karate.

Mr. Miyagi at Age 28.

Takeshi and Atsuko Miyagi on their Wedding Day, April 1961.

Miyagi the college student (top left) and college graduate (top right).

Teaching Kata to middle school students (bottom).

Miyagi Karate Dojo gathering, December 1963 (top).

Jim Lilley performing a conditioning drill, July 1964 (bottom).

Yutaka Nakanishi, Summer 1964 (top).

Jim Lilley, Yutaka Nakanishi and Len Neidert

(left to right), July 1964 (bottom).

Miyagi Dojo Party, July 1964.

Charlie Murray delivers a kick to Sam Chayt, 1970.

Richard Lubinski's (top) loyalty and determnation made him an excaptional student and teacher. Rick was the first rock solid building block of the Lilley Dojo. Howard Zachmann (below) former Mr. Maryland Title Hold and Black Belt taught special needs children in the Maryland School System for over 32 years.

Jody Lilley (above, second from left) and Jennifer Harris take part in a
traditional Okinawan Dance, August 1995.
Yutaka Nakanishi, Meiyu Takara, Takeshi Miyagi and Jim Lilley (left to
right), August 2002.

Dan Simons and Jody Lilley (above left) perform a Sai Kata, while Takeshi
Miyagi (above right) demonstrates a Bo Kata. Jim Lilley (below) begins a
Nunchaku Kata.

Tori Harper (top left) and Sean McMahon (top left) try on Howard County Police SWAT Gear. Parents and Students (below) look over a Maryland National Guard Helicopter during the Lilley Dojo Summer Camp.

Dan Simons, Bruce Charity and Will Adams (top, left to right) have been Members of the Lilley Dojo since the early 70s. Their unquestionable loyalty, friendship and work ethic have set an example for others to follow and they are a credit to the true spirit and tradition of Okinawa Shorin RyKarate Do. Picutred below is a view of the grounds and garden of the Okinawa Governor's House, July 2014.

Another view of the gardens and grounds (above) of the governor's house, July 2014.

Takeshi Miyagi and Jim Lilley (below) show off their colorful party attire, July 2014.

Jody Lilley (above) receives her 6th Degree Black Belt Certificate and Teachers License from Sensei Takeshi Miyagi, August 2, 2014.

Below, she proudly displays her certificates while husband, Jim, looks on.

Meeting of old friends, Jim Lilley and Meiyu Takara, August 2, 2014.

Jim and Jody Lilley at the farewell banquet following the Celebration of Life Memorial Demonstration August 3, 2014.

Joe Pepper and Okinawa's Arm Wrestling Champion flex their muscles (above) following the "Clash of the Titans" August 5, 2014.
Takehare Higa and David Rees (bottom) on the grounds of the Governor's House, July 2014.

Memories from our last party, August 5, 2014.

32211908R00134

Printed in Great Britain
by Amazon